I0795930

The Campus History Series

Saint Mary's College

Her Memories Beyond The Avenue

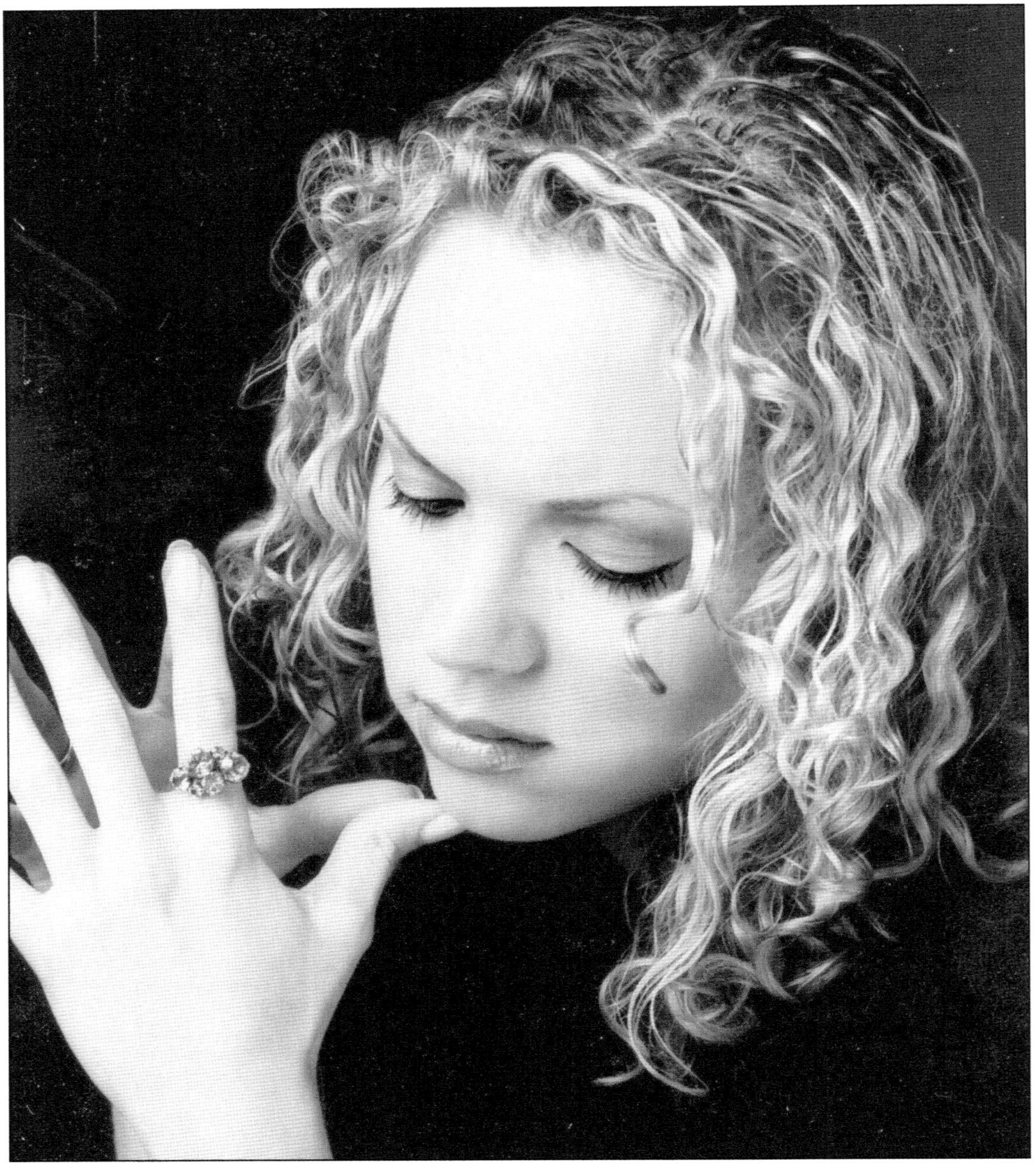

After completing *Saint Mary's College: Her Memories Beyond The Avenue*, I realized there are many more alumnae stories waiting to be documented before they are forever lost. Each one of our stories about Saint Mary's is priceless. I eagerly await to record your stories in a second version. Please contact me through the Saint Mary's College Office of Alumnae Relations. A portion of the proceeds from the sale of this book will be given directly back to Saint Mary's College to preserve our past. (Photograph by Jocelyn M. Artistic Photography; makeup by Nancy Paterra, Todd's Room.)

The Campus History Series

SAINT MARY'S COLLEGE

HER MEMORIES BEYOND THE AVENUE

KYMBERLY A. DUNLAP

ARCADIA
PUBLISHING

ISBN 978-0-7385-3443-5

Published by Arcadia Publishing
Charleston, South Carolina

Printed in the United States of America

Library of Congress Control Number: 2005924978

For all general information, please contact Arcadia Publishing:
Telephone 843-853-2070
Fax 843-853-0044
E-mail sales@arcadiapublishing.com
For customer service and orders:
Toll-Free 1-888-313-2665

Visit us on the Internet at www.arcadiapublishing.com

CONTENTS

ACKNOWLEDGMENTS

I would like to sincerely thank my parents for their unconditional love, continuous support, and for accompanying me on overnight trips to the Bend. There are not enough words in the world to express my gratitude for supporting my dreams, especially this childhood dream of writing my book.

Thanks go to John Kovach, Saint Mary's archivist, for his guidance, patience, and knowledge throughout this process. Without you, this book would not have been submitted on time.

Thank you to Saint Mary's College, Office of Alumnae Relations, and Saint Mary's College *Courier* for spreading the word to thousands of alumnae. You will always be a part of my extended family.

I would also like to give a special thank you to the women of Saint Mary's College who contributed to this book, especially Carrie Powers Powell, class of 1948, and Sheila Kelly Ames, class of 1965. I sincerely appreciate the opportunity for the glimpse into your lives as Saint Mary's students. Without each one of you, this book would be incomplete. It has been an honor to work with you.

INTRODUCTION

Saint Mary's College holds a special place in my heart and will always be a part of me wherever I go, whatever I do, and whomever I become. Every morning as I put on my Saint Mary's ring before I head off to my job, I am reminded of this magical place among the corn fields that I continue to call my home away from home. There are too many memories to count, but not enough to keep me away for very long. Whether it was sleeping in an air-conditioned Stapleton Lounge on a scorching August night senior year with my closest friends only to get kicked out by security or reciting generations of ghost stories on the island late at night, these remembrances are worth retelling a million times over. These experiences have brought me the opportunity to compile this manuscript filled with alumnae's personal reflections and photographs.

I was back visiting Saint Mary's the first weekend in October 2004 as a recent alumna when I came to a poignant realization. It occurred to me that these intriguing stories would be lost forever if they were not documented by the women who experienced them. A prime example was the unfortunate loss of a distinguished alumna, a student during the early 1940s. She and I were corresponding about her contribution to this book. A few days later I received an e-mail that informed me she had passed away on April 3, 2005.

The common bond throughout the women telling these stories is that Saint Mary's College became a part of each one of us. Now it is my wish and a reality that our memories live on so that we may share them wherever we go, whatever we do, and whomever we become.

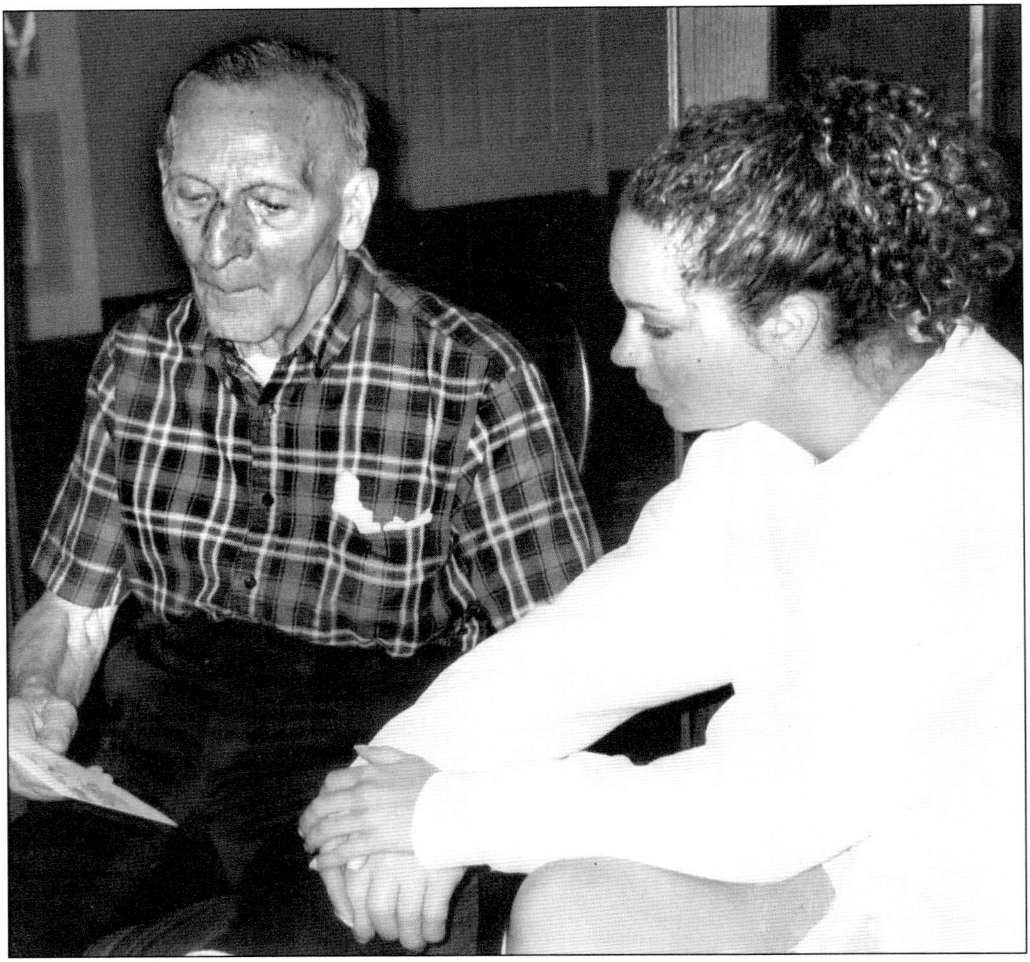

This book is dedicated to my Grandpa, my hero, who battled Alzheimer's disease for years until his death. I hope this book rekindles those decades of memories of younger years lost but never forgotten.

One

A New Place Called Home

She is welcoming you to a new place called home. She embraces you and eases the adjustment of moving. She is the unbearable humidity that masks your skin, testing your concentration. She is the pencil that serves to introduce yourself as well as weave through your hair to hold that bun in place. She is the presentation that proves your skills and enhances communication. She is the exam that questions not only your knowledge, but also your beliefs. She is the fountain that flows even in winter, just when you think she has nothing more to give. She is the mass that brings you together, the music that makes you unique. She is the practice that makes you better and time that makes you the best. She is the spotlight you long for, the luck of the Irish, and the spirit of gold. She is the art of expression and one of revelation. She is about reflecting on your past and challenging your future. She is the bridge that guides you to womanhood. She is why you are intellectually prideful. She is a walk through the crisp air on the tree-lined path to academe. She is Saint Mary's, Notre Dame.

—Jennifer Paluszak Hadden '96

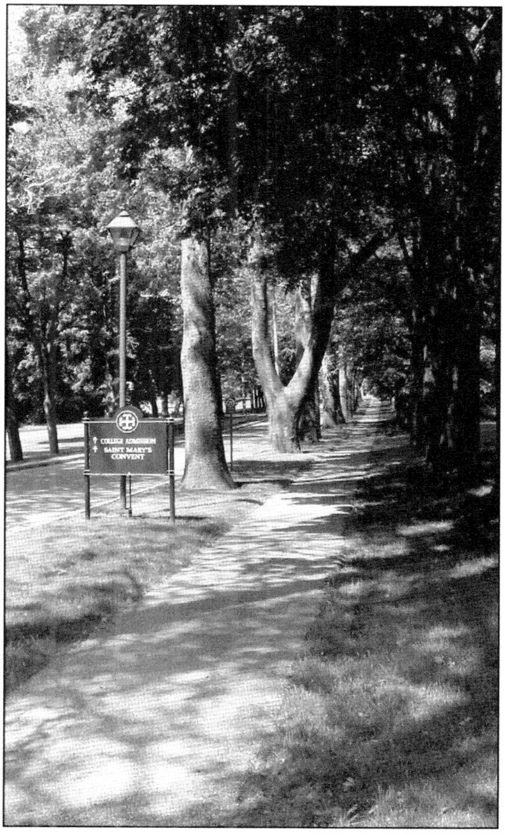

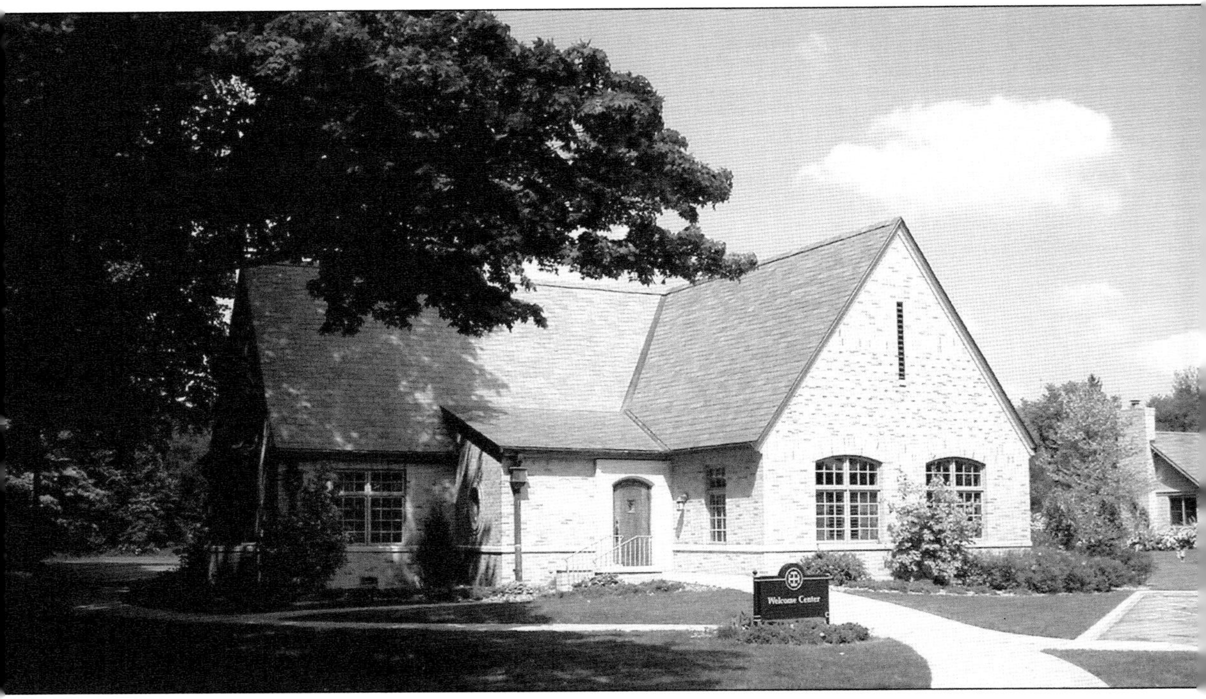

I have so many wonderful memories of Saint Mary's, it's hard to know where to start. I was a senior at a local high school. Mom and I went to Le Mans, where I met my tour guide. She showed me the dorms. I liked how everyone's dorm had a different style that reflected their personalities.

I met my host for the rest of the evening. Her name was Susan Fishesser, and she'd gone to another local Catholic high school.

Some of the girls decided to get out the "dog book" and make prank phone calls to guys at Notre Dame. Even though I never would have done this myself, I couldn't stop laughing. Sleeping on Susan's floor that night, I contemplated how cool it was going to be to live in this community of caring, diverse, funny and sometimes loud-mouthed women.

Although I'd dreamed of Saint Mary's since I was a little girl, swimming in the pool with the nuns while my best friend's mom was working, this was my first real taste. In August of 1995, that dream became reality.

—Erin E. Schmidt Smith '99

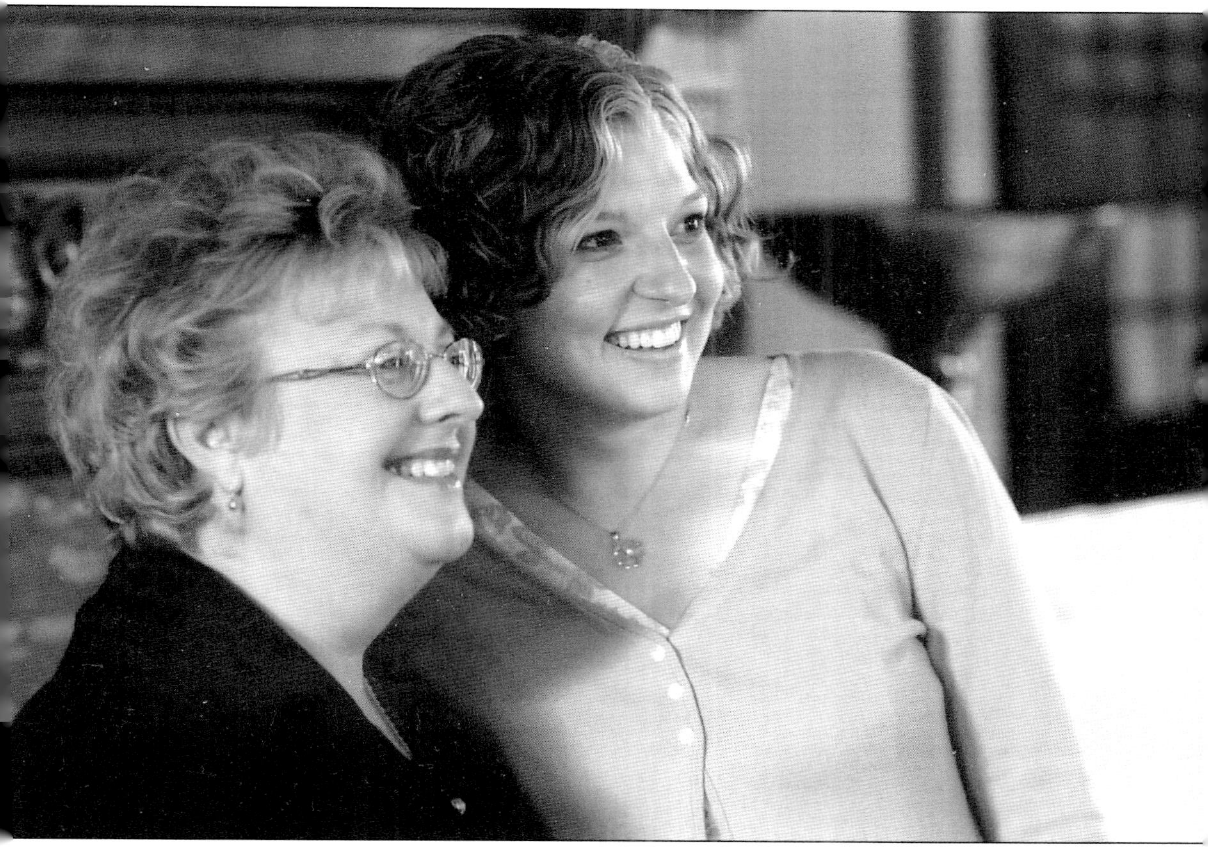

Your parents see something in you. That is why they are sending you to college. Saint Mary's sees something in you. That is why they have accepted you into this community of intelligent and energetic women. I promise that after four years you will see something in yourself that you never dreamed could be there. Prior to Saint Mary's I had always thought of myself as a girl, but now I truly see myself as a "young woman." I saw for the first time something that Saint Mary's has been seeing in its accepted students for over a hundred years and my dad saw in me when I could not.

My dad wrote something in a card four years ago that he left for me my first day of college. He said, "The quality of the student you are is not measured by grades but by the quality of the person that emerges from the college experience." Somehow he caught the essence of the Saint Mary's experience: this place doesn't just turn out smart women. It turns out women dedicated to honor, social responsibility, academic excellence, and critical thought—women who happen to be smart, too.

You are "accepted students" because we think you belong here. Welcome.

—Excerpt from address given by Elizabeth Jablonski-Diehl '04, student body president (2003–2004), to accepted students in O'Laughlin Auditorium

Saint Mary's College
NOTRE DAME • INDIANA

The Nation's Premier Catholic Women's College

January 17, 2000

Dear Kimberly:

Congratulations on your decision to join the Saint Mary's family! We are so pleased that you accepted our offer of admission to the class of 2004. The $200 deposit that you enclosed with your acknowledgement card will be credited toward your account at Saint Mary's and will reserve your place in the freshman class.

Orientation is scheduled for Friday, August 18 through Sunday, August 20. The program begins early on Friday morning so you may move into your residence hall room anytime after 9:00 a.m. on Thursday, August 17. You will hear more about orientation and your housing assignment in future mailings.

We have enclosed a list of area hotels and motels to accommodate your family for the weekend. Please note that the University of Notre Dame plans its orientation program for the same weekend so we would advise you to make your reservations as early as possible.

Several other members of the Saint Mary's community will be sending you information especially designed to help you make a smooth transition to life at Saint Mary's. We all are anxious to assist you as you prepare for your college years. Please let us know if we can answer any questions or assist you in any way.

Welcome to Saint Mary's, Kimberly.

Sincerely,

Mary Pat Nolan

Mary Pat Nolan
Director of Admission

Enclosure

Admission Office (219) 284-4587 • (800) 551-7621 • FAX (219) 284-4841
Visit our Website: http://www.saintmarys.edu

Notre Dame, Indiana 46556-5001

This is the author's welcome letter from 2000.

Orientation 2000

August 17-20, 2000

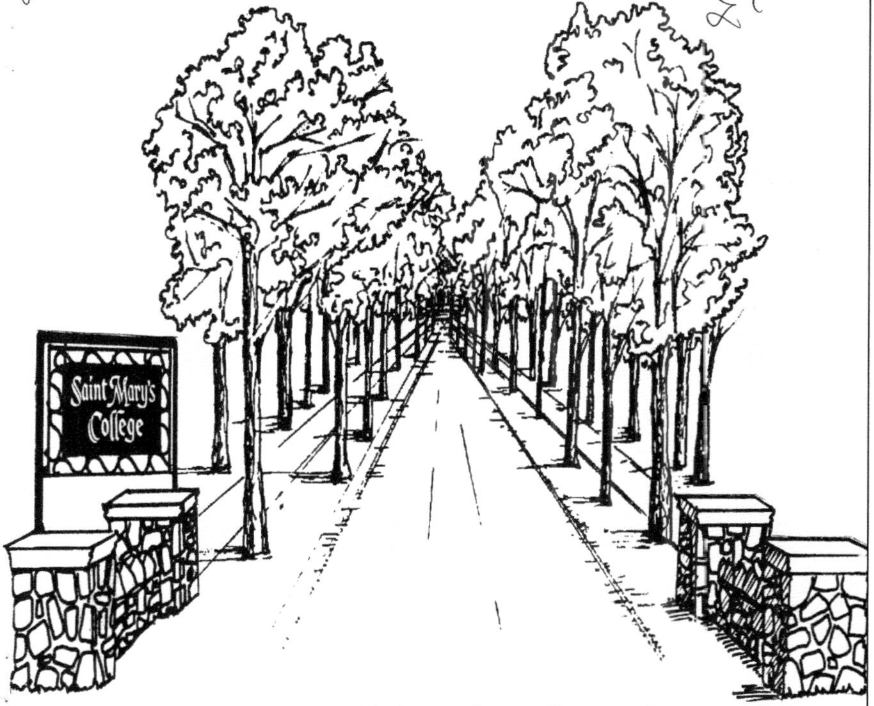

*"Do not go where the path may lead.
Go instead where there is no path and leave a trail."*

—Muriel Strode

Saint Mary's College
Notre Dame, Indiana

Dear Kymberly,

Hi and welcome to Saint Mary's! After all the effort and planning to get to this point, now the fun can begin! I'm Angela and I'm your orientation counselor. I just wanted to drop you a note to let you know how excited I am to meet you and your parents and help you through this Orientation Weekend. If there's anything I can help you with, I'll be in and out of my room (225 Holy Cross) all day or give me a quick call (x4348)—otherwise there will be a meeting tonight at 6:30 at the flagpole in the circle outside Holy Cross. Don't forget your orientation booklet! See you there!

Sincerely,
Angela Cederquist, 2002

SAINT MARY'S COLLEGE
NOTRE DAME
HOLY CROSS, INDIANA

December 27, 1943

Mr. John Powers
R.D. 1, Eagle Road
Willoughby, Ohio

Dear Mr. Powers,

It is a pleasure to have your letter advising us of your plans to have your daughter Mary Carolyn matriculate at Saint Mary's in September 1944. I thank you for check received for matriculation fee and room deposit. We have placed Mary Carolyn's name on the waiting list for a double room with bath. It is very probable that such a room will be available to her and that she will share it with another freshman. We will write you more specifically of this in the early spring.

We are particularly happy to welcome Mary Carolyn as a Saint Mary's daughter. She will carry on a lovely tradition of her mother and aunt and will have a pleasant bond, I am sure, with Notre Dame as your Alma Mater.

Kindest regards to you and all your family for a happy and a blessed new year!

Yours very sincerely,

Sister Kathryn Marie

Sister Kathryn Marie,
Director of Admissions

SKM:SBM

This is Carrie Powers's welcome letter from 1943.

DATE Augt.28 1946

SAINT MARY'S COLLEGE
NOTRE DAME
HOLY CROSS, INDIANA

TO

Mrs. John Powers
R.D. 1 Eagle Road
Willoughby Ohio

FOR MISS Carolyn

1946						
		To Entrance Fee				
Sept.	9	To Board and Tuition (One Semester)	$ 425	00		
	9	To Room " "	100	00		
			525	00		
Jan.	16	Check	25	00	$ 500	00
		Coupon book for Books and Incidentals			25	00

Seen here is Carrie Powers's tuition statement from 1946.

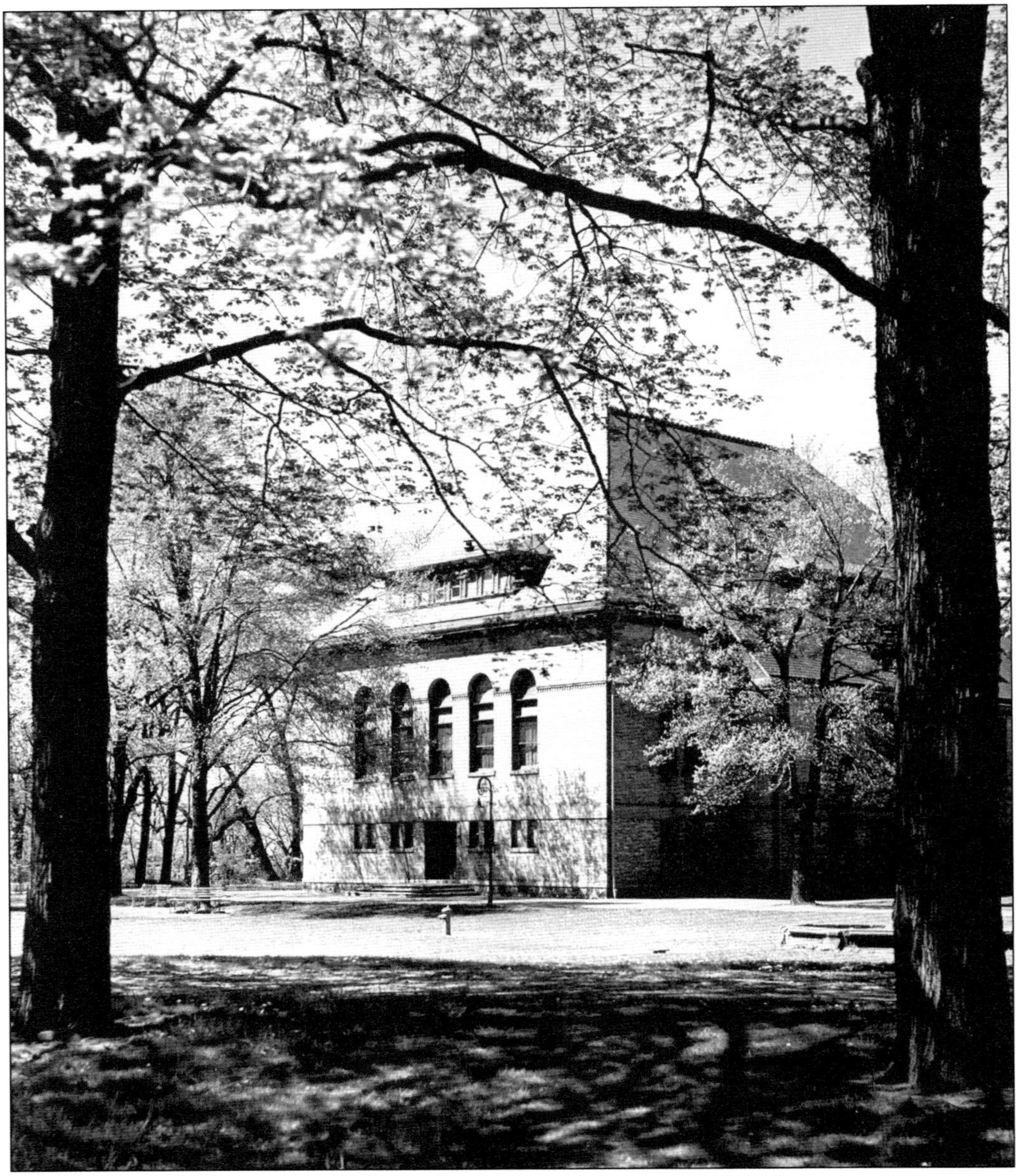

Saint Mary's was a lifeline for me the very first week that I arrived there.

On arriving at SMC, I assumed that I would have to follow my high school regimen of sports. During that first week, I visited Angela Hall and found myself laughing out loud in tremendous relief. The basketball floor was slanted so that on the south side of the gym if you shot a basket on the left side you were a foot or so higher than the right side. It was such a blessing for me. I felt that a tremendous burden had been lifted. The message was loud—Saint Mary's did not care so much about sports in that day. The pressure was gone.

I realize that sports are important. I haven't given up on them. I have been teaching Hatha Yoga for the past 37 years, twice a week in Brighton and Pinckney, MI, but at that time in my life, God was good to me.

—Judy Enright '62

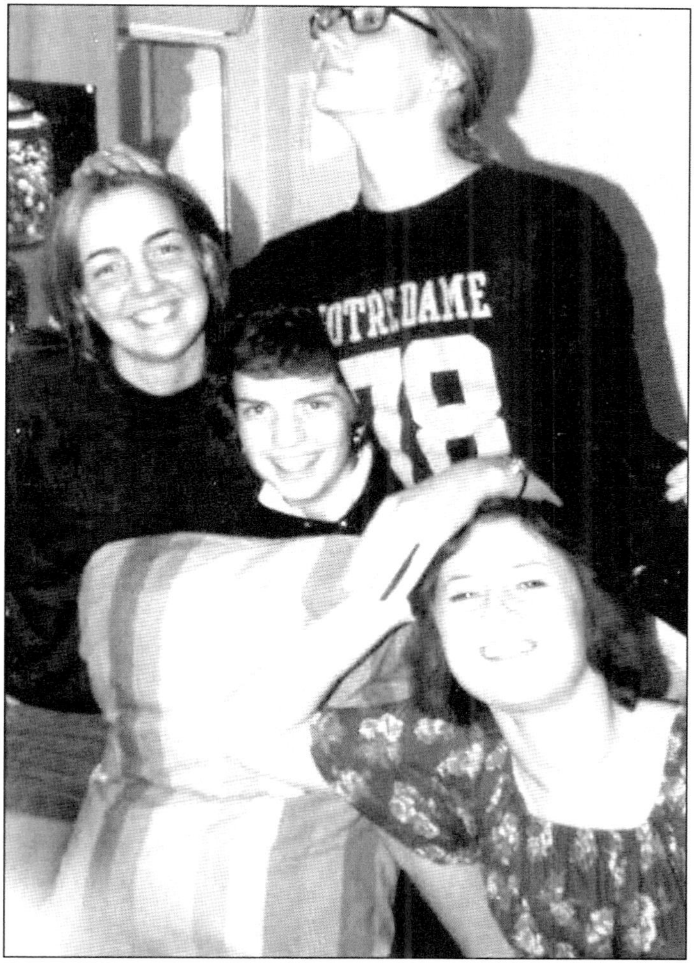

My single room in Regina before our very first panty raid. Future graduates of the class of 1978. I am on the far left, Nue (Mary Helen Nugent, RSM) is next to me, Karla is on the far right, Kathy is above.

On a Saturday morning in August 1974 my parents moved me into my room in Regina Hall. I remember watching my parents unpack my things as I sat on my bed in a fog and watched them. I know, in my mind, even though I was so excited about coming, I wondered why was I here. I soon learned that it was the perfect place for me!

Being in Regina Freshman Year was perfect because it encouraged me to leave my single and meet other girls. I remember the 1st ND football game when we all dressed up and went! We had a great time!

I remember the 1st retreat I went on that was sponsored by Sr. Karol Jackowski. I went with a few friends, and we didn't know any of the others but I remember that Friday night, they burned the Chocolate fondue, I remember Michael playing the bag pipes, I remember on Saturday us making snow angels, climbing in trees, saying God bless you as we turned off lights, and trying to walk up the painful stairs. (The sisters in residence at the retreat house were incredibly strict and put that plastic that people put on carpet upside down so it hurt when you walked on it). I remember most, Sr. Karol beginning my Spiritual Journey.

Thank You Saint Mary's!

—Annette Ruth Jenkins Hayden '78

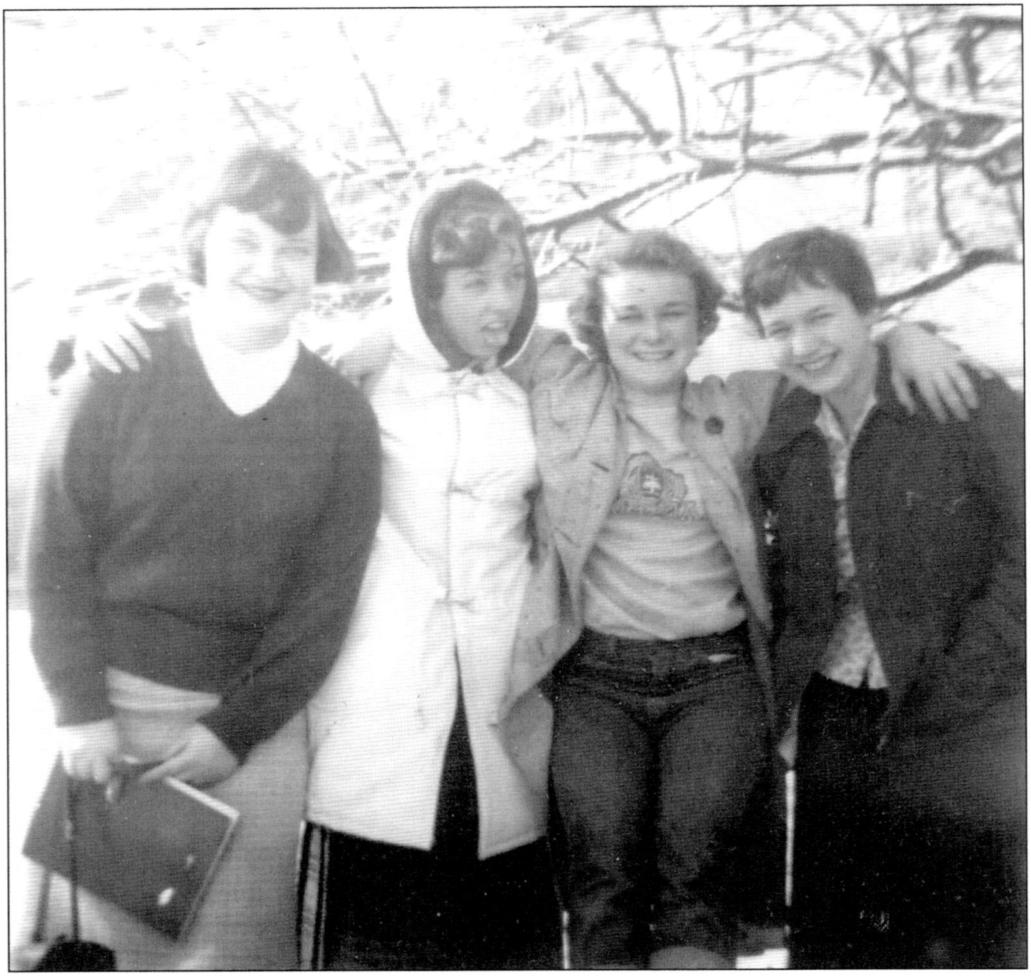

Who are The "59ers"? Who are these 137 seniors graduating on May 30th? These seniors are the champions of the 285 who arrived here in September 1955 to the greeting of Sister Maria Assunta, their new dean, and Sister Katherine Elaine, their freshman class sponsor. The new students were greeted by the first drive down the avenue which would later serve as the path to the gate, the multi-colored arch to Fall and the snowbound street. Bright orange greeted them that year, the color of steel pillars of the just begun auditorium and arts center. Their first year was a year of 'firsts'; Notre Dame Football, Victory Dances, Variety Shows, the first annual Parent Weekend, the noisy "21 gun salute," pink-carnation makers and sitting on cement steps of the nearly finished O'Laughlin for the 'first' graduation.

—Myra Hunter, *St. Mary's Static*, Senior Week 1959

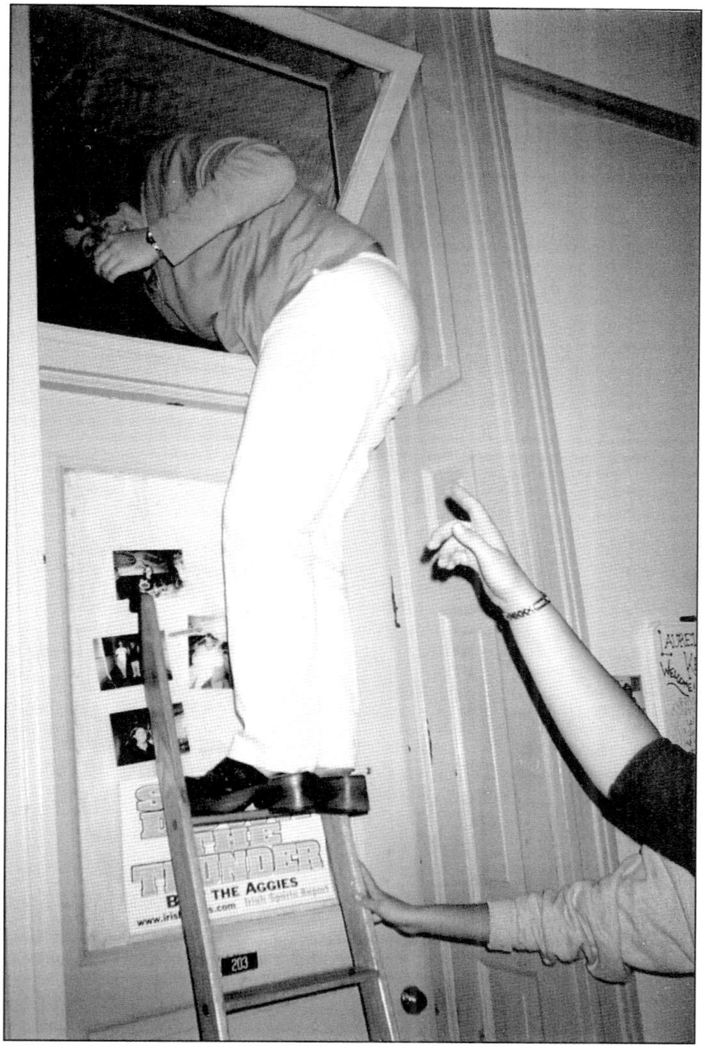

Focused as we were on mischief of the moment, exams were the furthest thing from our minds as freshmen in the fall of 1955. Between fits of giggles, my three roommates and I put on our pj's, brushed our teeth, smeared our faces with Noxema, and hurried to bed as soon as it was "lights out." We heard the dean make rounds. We lay in bed waiting. Then, around midnight, we heard it! The horrific crash of a transom, two floors above us, followed by another and another, like big cannon fire. The noise magnified four times over by carnivorous linoleum halls, vaulted ceilings and broad wooden stairwells, echoed throughout Holy Cross Hall. As soon as the room next to us fired off their salvo, my roommates and I jumped into action.

I expected the dean to arrive any second, and I prayed my father would understand my suspension, or worse, dismissal, while I watched Mary, Susie and Connie take their turns at the transom, lustily lowering and slamming. Hall monitors, class officers, and the dean raced around not sure what to do or who to blame. The police were called, and I think even a couple of fire trucks. Our hall nearly came off its foundation that night as its occupants hit their transoms in lieu of books and what would infamously become known as the "Twenty-one Gun Salute."

—Barbara Benford Trafficanda '59

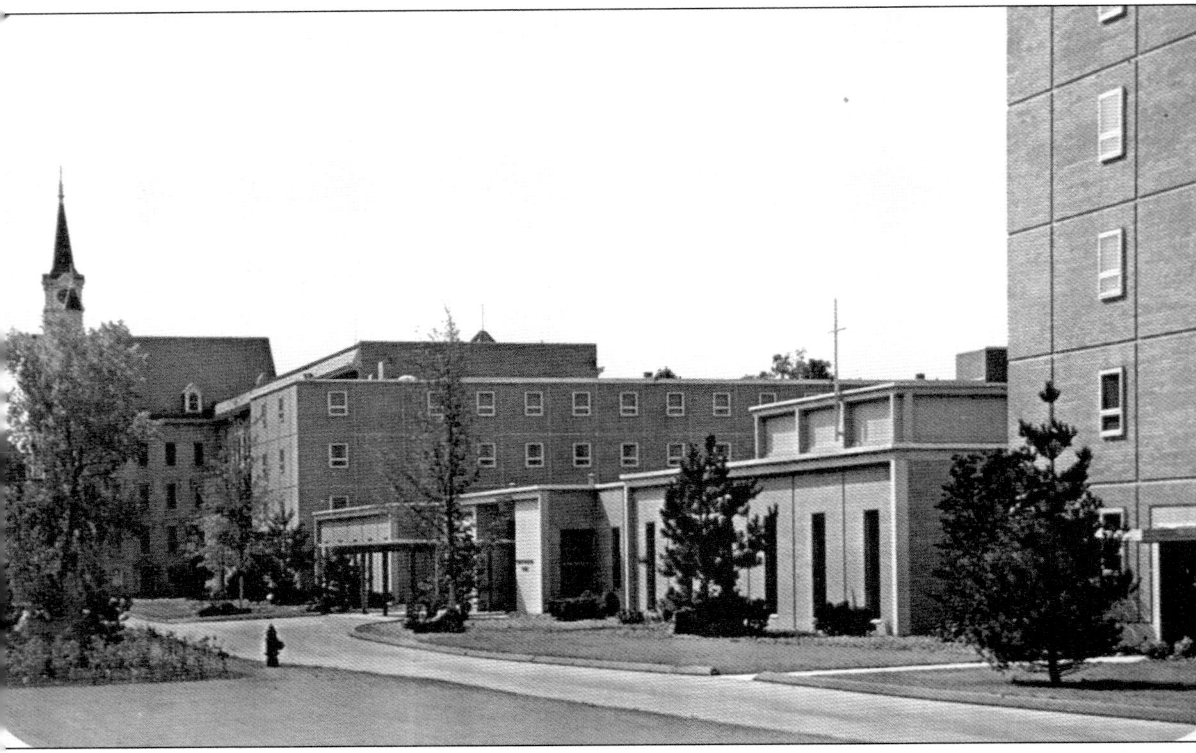

I remember receiving my acceptance letter and being so excited about Saint Mary's and all of the possibilities and doors that would now be open to me. I remember hauling my possessions up five flights of stairs in Regina Hall to my new home for the next year. But, what I most vividly remember, is meeting my first new friend.

I was sitting at my desk, arranging odds and ends and acclimating myself to my new surroundings. My door was open and I heard this sound. It was kind of like this groaning, moaning sound. The sounds were getting louder, stronger and more vocal. What I saw was this blonde girl with red lipstick lugging this rug that was twice as big as she was down the hallway. After laughing, I helped her drag the rug into her room, which was right across the hallway from me. Kelly Derrick and I became immediate friends. I remember crying with her when my parents left to return to Ohio, and I remember crying together again with Kelly when her mom made the trip back to Atlanta.

Kelly Derrick Cadman is probably my oldest and dearest friend. Even though we don't talk daily, or even weekly, when we do end up together, it is as though nothing has changed. My experience at Saint Mary's was better because of her and I am so glad she is my friend.

—Carla J. Novak Whittier '94

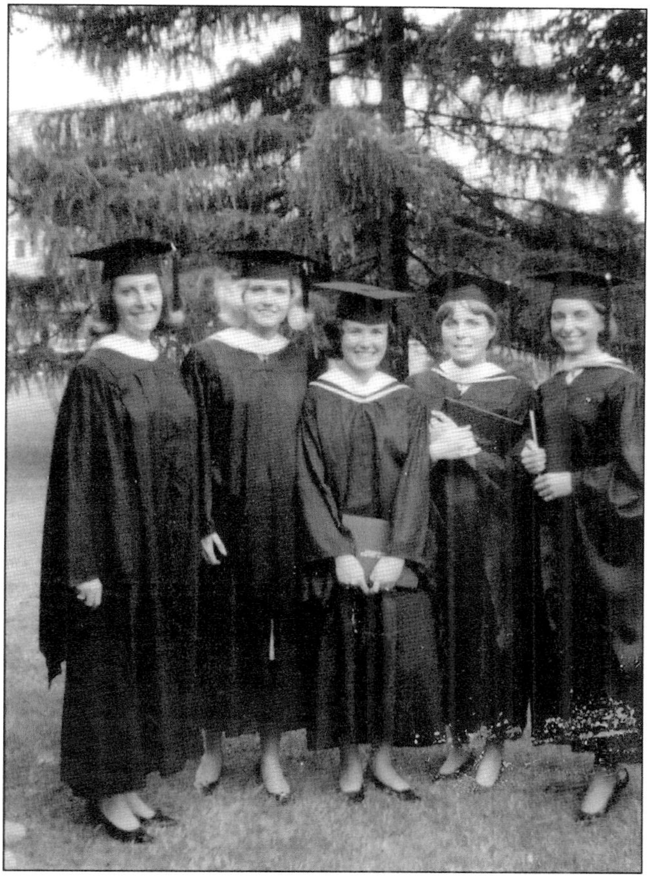

The students posing for this photograph are, from left to right, E. J. Caluwaert, Carolyn Fleming (deceased), Sheila Kelly, Elise Meyer, and Karin Vanek.

I was so nervous that first day at Saint Mary's in September of 1961. I had corresponded with my roommate, Carolyn Fleming from Dallas, but we had yet to meet. I should have never worried at all—she was warm and delightful. She was in my wedding 4 ½ years later. Her ND brother roomed with my future husband. Carolyn and I were so compatible that we lived together for 2 years, and in the same first floor room in Holy Cross Hall, number 103. She even gave me a gold charm for my bracelet in the shape of Texas with "103" engraved in it. I still have it.

My dear roommate died four years ago of heart disease. Life is somehow different without her. I have happy, humorous memories of our college days together. The time Carolyn put a crayfish in my bed! She wrapped it up and brought it home after a walk to the ND lake, and she was so proud of herself. Getting dressed for dances, double-dates, borrowing clothes, participating in retreats, laughing into the night over ridiculous things, and then talking very late as roommates once again the very night before my wedding. I look at my Saint Mary's scrapbook, and Carolyn is there so often (frequently eating chocolate chip cookies). She was such an important part of my life and I valued her friendship from the moment I met her in room 103 Holy Cross. What a great smile she had as I walked into that room freshman year and she greeted me with such friendship. How lucky I was to draw such a fantastic roommate! I didn't even mind when she short-sheeted my bed.

—Sheila Kelly Ames '65

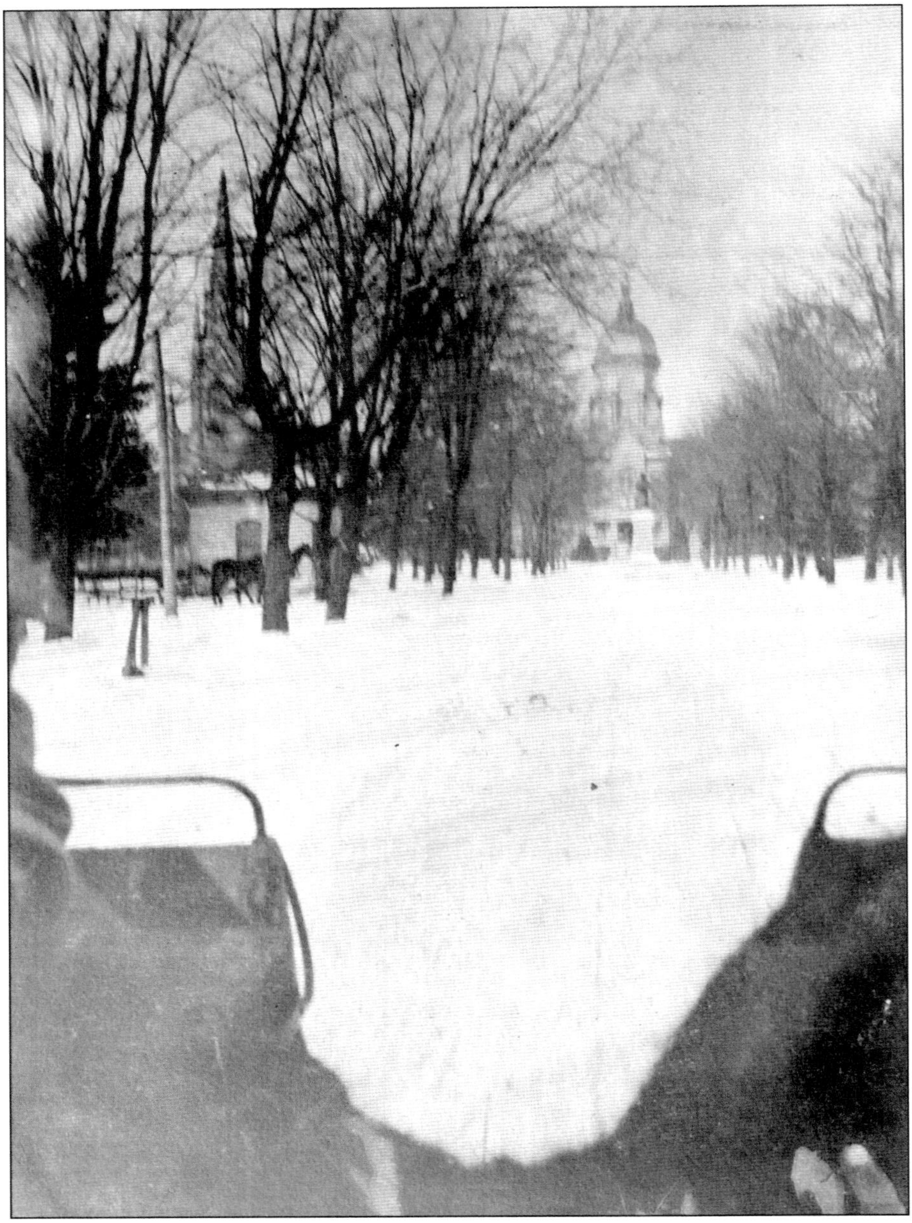

Freshman year I remember telling my cousin Don, who was a student at ND, that the ND food couldn't possibly be as horrible as the guys kept saying it was. Then, the following Monday, I went to the post office to pick up mail after the nun told it was about time that I came because she had a package for me that she wanted to get rid of. Don and his friends mailed me a Friday night fish dinner from the ND dining hall. It had been in the package three days when I picked it up. Lord, did it ever stink! I remember running outside trying to find the nearest dumpster to throw it in. After that experience, I always let the guys complain, but I was always happy to enjoy the Saga food dinners we had—complete with homemade desserts each night.

—E. J. Caluwaert McFadden '65

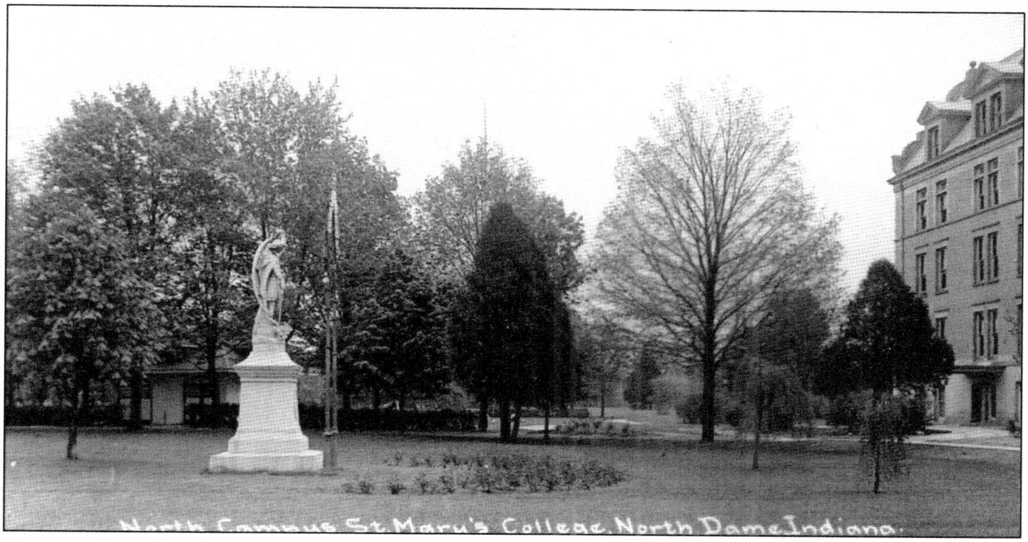

I knew I loved it there my very first year, and I knew I would love it always. I used to love to sit at twilight on beautiful evenings on the wide window ledge of our room in Holy Cross Hall and look out at the shrine of Michael the Archangel that had lights surrounding it. I'd play "Moon River" and listen to the evening sounds, feel the soft breeze and dream of my future. I loved to walk the Avenue with the scent of Sycamore trees. That smell always reminds me of Saint Mary's, even today.

—Sheila Kelly Ames '65

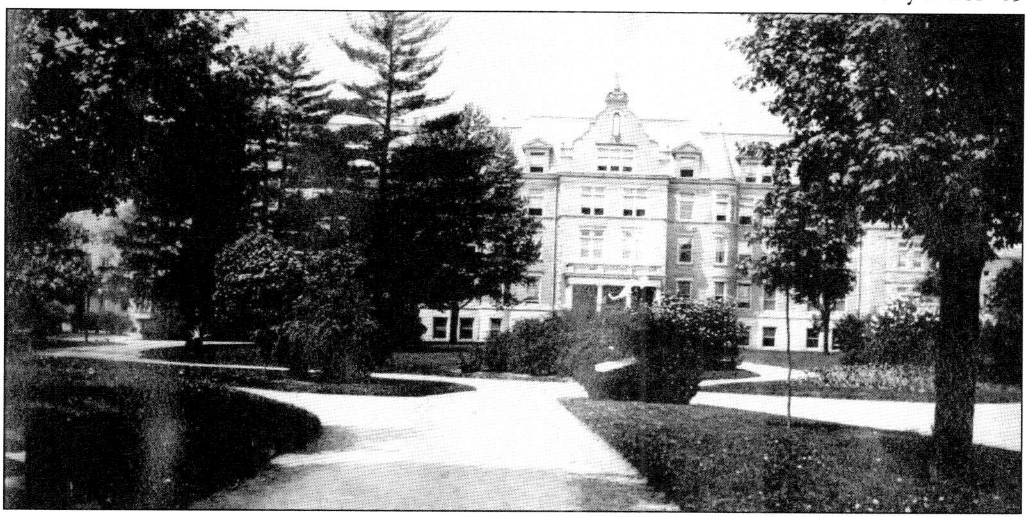

Some of my favorite things include corresponding with my future roommate, Pat Devine, the summer of 1961, then meeting her in our room in Holy Cross. Whew, you never know how that's going to be, but I was lucky and we just kept rooming together. What a first floor we had! It was a small group, and we certainly weren't clones but we all just meshed, and had so much fun. We stuck together too. When Pat and I were "busted" for smoking in our room, our wonderful "hall monitor," Betty Ann Rice, fought against her military upbringing and eventually resisted turning us in. If she had turned us in we may have been kicked out of Saint Mary's and not have gone on to enjoy three more years of special memories.

—Sheila Flynn Boone '65

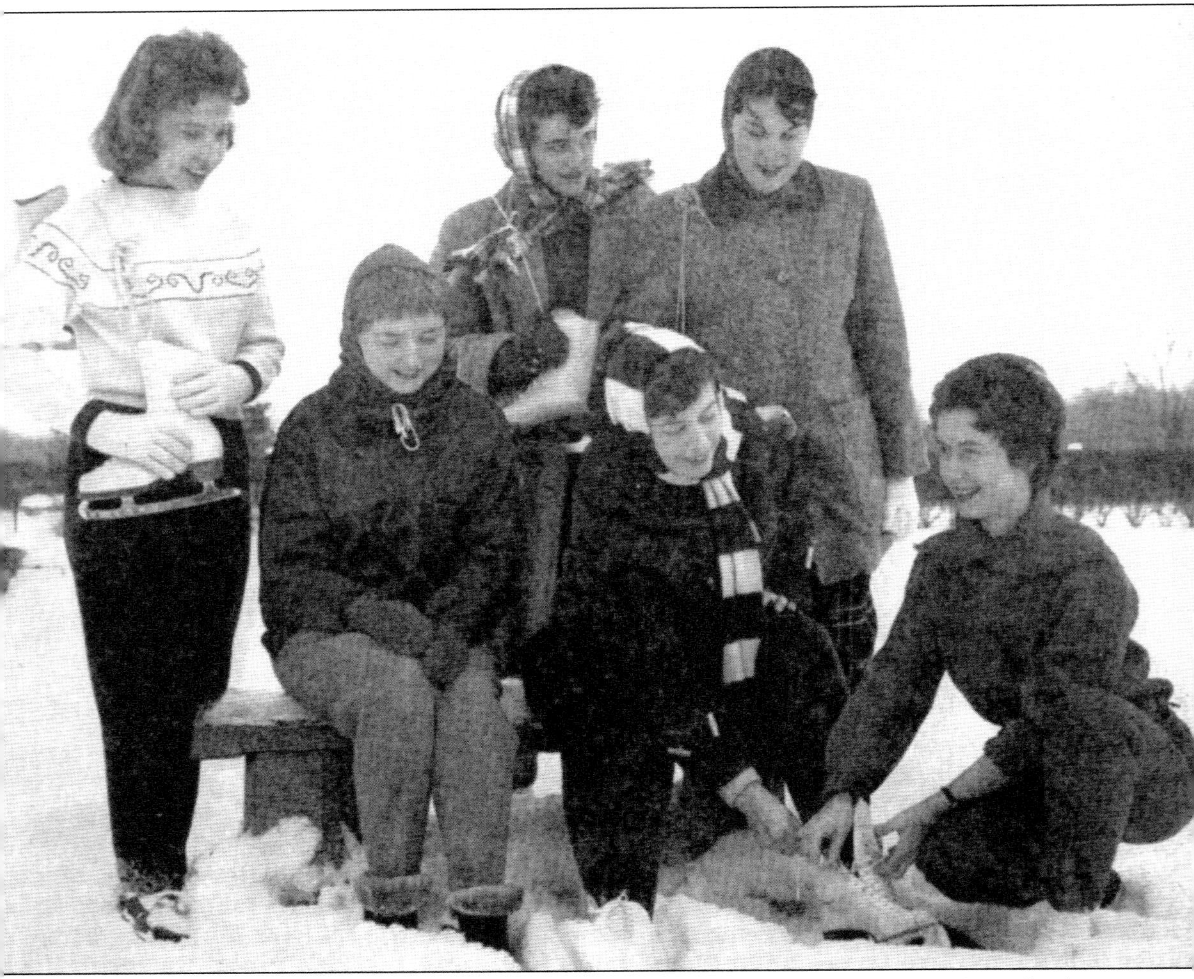

One of my most vivid memories of Saint Mary's was during winter finals week my freshman year. I was living in McCandless Hall on the 5th floor. My roommate, Maura, was a Chicago native and I was a southern girl from Atlanta, Georgia. For the first few snowfalls I was like a little kid—I couldn't get enough of the Indiana winter. During this particular exam week, it had snowed quite a bit and more was in the forecast. At about 10 Maura and I had hit the study wall—we needed a break. The dry heat of the dorm rooms had made us loopy along with reading endless study notes from "Baby Bio" class. We went to get Wendy and Annie from two doors down and were walking the hall when we bumped into our RA—K.C. Chandler. She suggested we get some fresh air so we pulled on our parkas and boots. On the way to the lobby we spied some cafeteria trays in the dorm kitchen. We all just kind of stared at each other, grabbed a tray and headed out across the snowy fields toward the access road. We ran up the hill underneath the underpass and sledded until midnight. I will never forget hearing our laughter echo across the snow, our sleds illuminated only by the moonlight. I still remember thinking what a sense of complete abandon and joy I had—sledding all our worries and cares away with the friends made that first year at Saint Mary's.

—Jeannie Sabin Barry '91

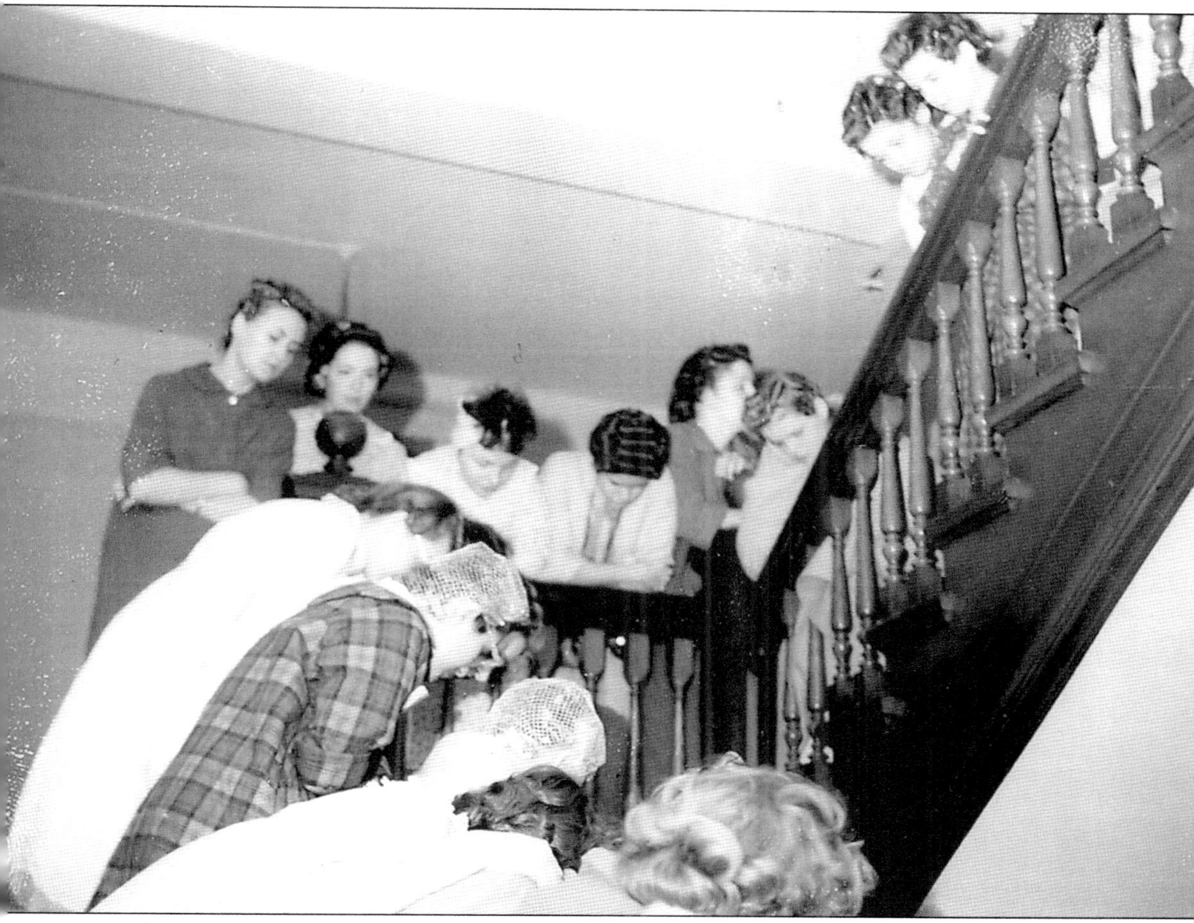

One of my most treasured memories from Saint Mary's dates back to freshman year in Holy Cross Hall. On the night before going home for Christmas vacation in 1959, we were told to line up all of our stuffed animals down the corridors and stairwells leading into the chapel. It was a beautiful sight indeed, but the real surprise came early the next morning. We were awakened at 5:30 A.M. by angelic singing. As we sleepily went from our beds to the hallways, we were greeted by our "big sisters" from the junior class, dressed in robes, with tinsel halos, carrying lighted candles as they processed through the dark hallways of Holy Cross Hall, singing the most beautiful Christmas carols I have ever heard. It was a heavenly experience that I have cherished for 45 years.

—Diana Castaldi Scheeler '63

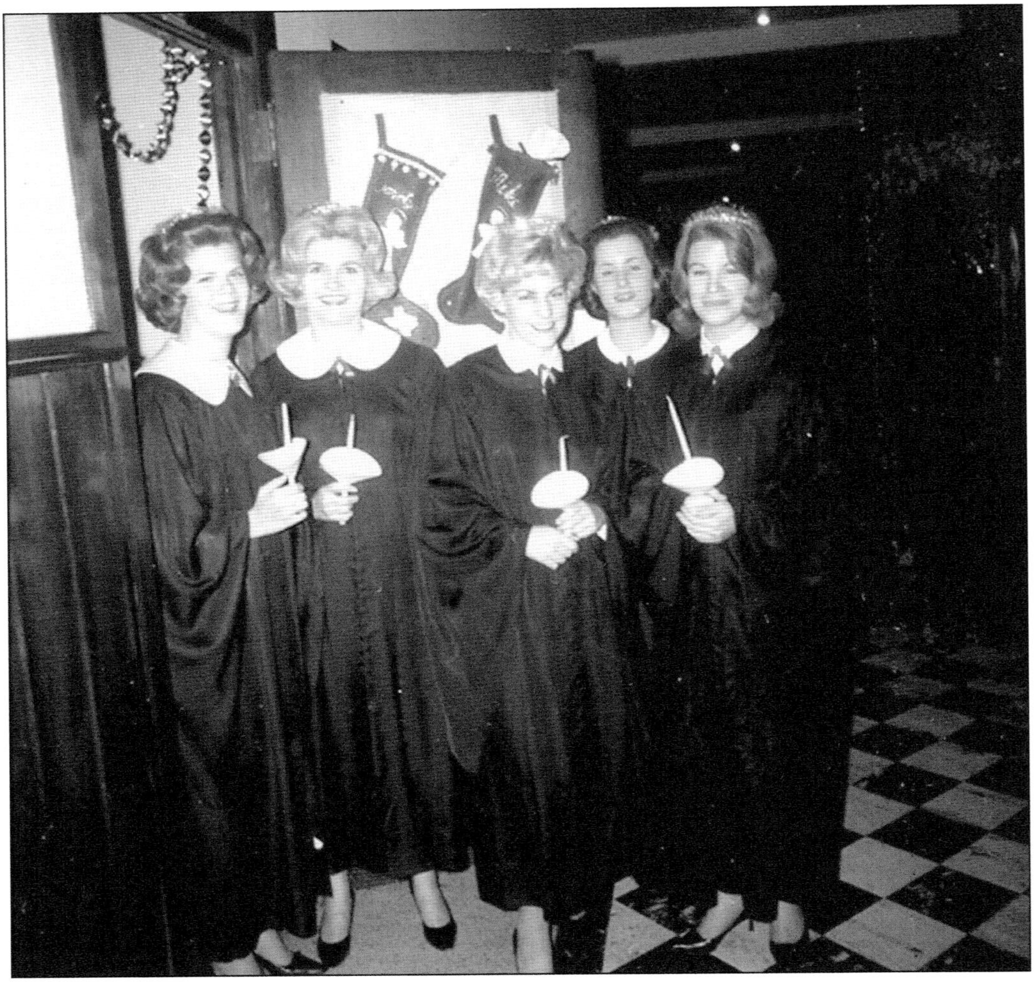

Marianne Spalding Schiavone, Carolyn Fleming Shinnick, Sheila Flynn Boone, Eileen Kelly Klehr, and Michael Pruitt wait outside their room in Le Mans to head over to Holy Cross.

One of my favorite traditions was the "big sister" program. When we entered as freshmen, an upperclassman was assigned to us, and she would do little things for us, leave us notes, answer questions...it was just so nice having someone there who knew "the ropes"!

What we really looked forward to was the Christmas parade through the halls. At midnight, our big sisters donned black gowns (like graduation robes) and went past our rooms, carrying candles, and singing and ended up at Le Mans. Our big sisters wore holly garland on their heads. When we were the big sisters, we wore silver tinsel garland. Those were special, magical nights.

After the parade, we changed into our bathrobes, and in the wee hours of the morning, we sat downstairs in the rec room in Le Mans, sang, and put on skits.

—Sheila Flynn Boone '65

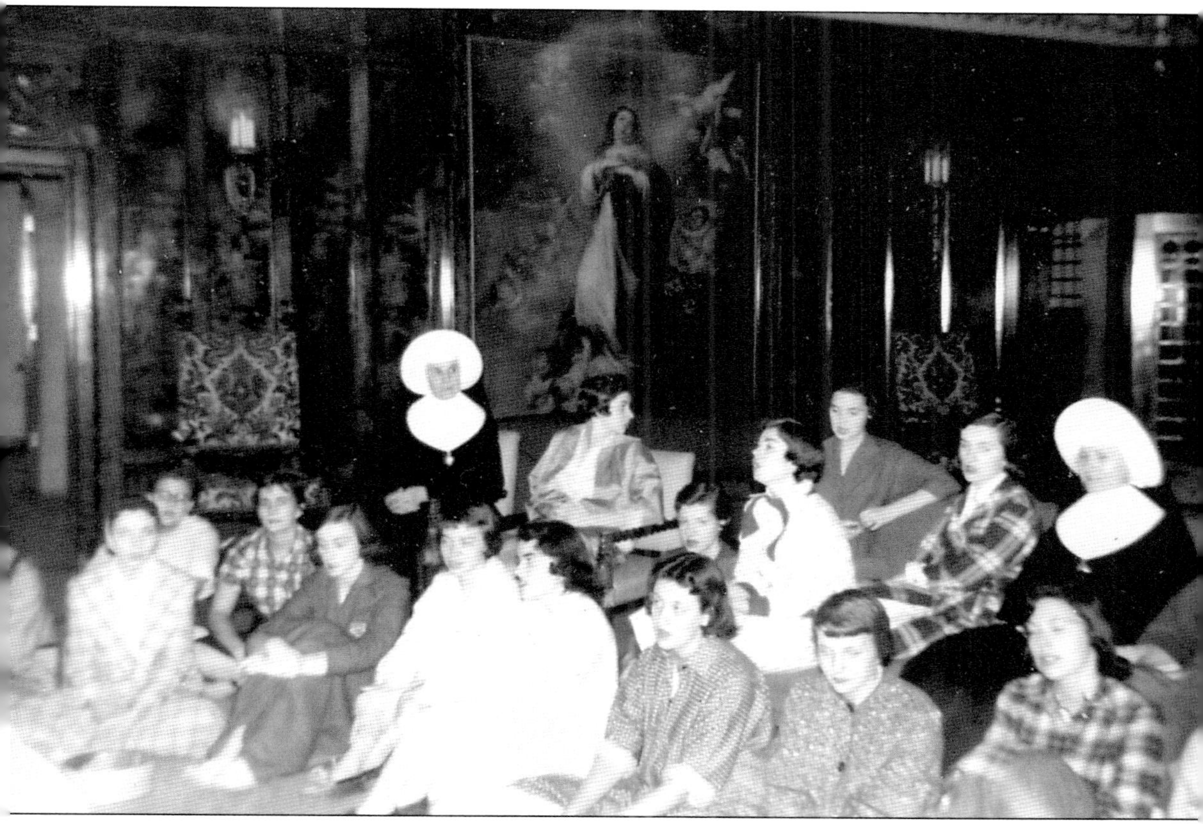

Saint Mary's becomes more amazing to us freshmen each day. The Christmas party was just out of this world in every way. We've never seen ourselves and the other classmen look so charming in yards and yards of net and tulle. The procession of juniors carrying candles was lovely, and when our big sisters came into view we were ever so proud of them.

The candlelight in the dining room had a remarkable way of flattering us—it was wonderful. During the dinner some of us noticed that bright, bright star shining over Holy Cross—the Christmas star, as someone put it. As we walked from the dining hall to the Lounge, we just couldn't help being awed by the beautiful gowns and candlelight reflected on the paneled walls.

Once everyone was seated in the Lounge, I should say curled up on the floor, the room was a blaze of color and beauty. One of the prettiest effects in the Lounge was the Christmas tree—after all, we trimmed it.

The skit, done by Lil Kearney and Mim Carroll, certainly hit home. Every one of us could have put ourselves in Lil's place-Trivium troubles, men troubles, grade troubles, and just plain troubles.

We all got a kick out of Santa Claus—that was Nancy Doyle, wasn't it? Sister Maria Renata's gift of Dewey pins sent some into peals of laughter, but then, some couldn't quite see the humor. Several freshmen wondered whether or not they'd have to dissect and draw Sister Nazareth's poor little gold fish.

After the festivities we all rustled off to our rooms and individual parties. We were all of one opinion. The Christmas party is the loveliest tradition we've seen yet and we realized even more that being a Saint Mary's girl is wonderful.

—Harriet Enneking, *St. Mary's Static*, January 1944

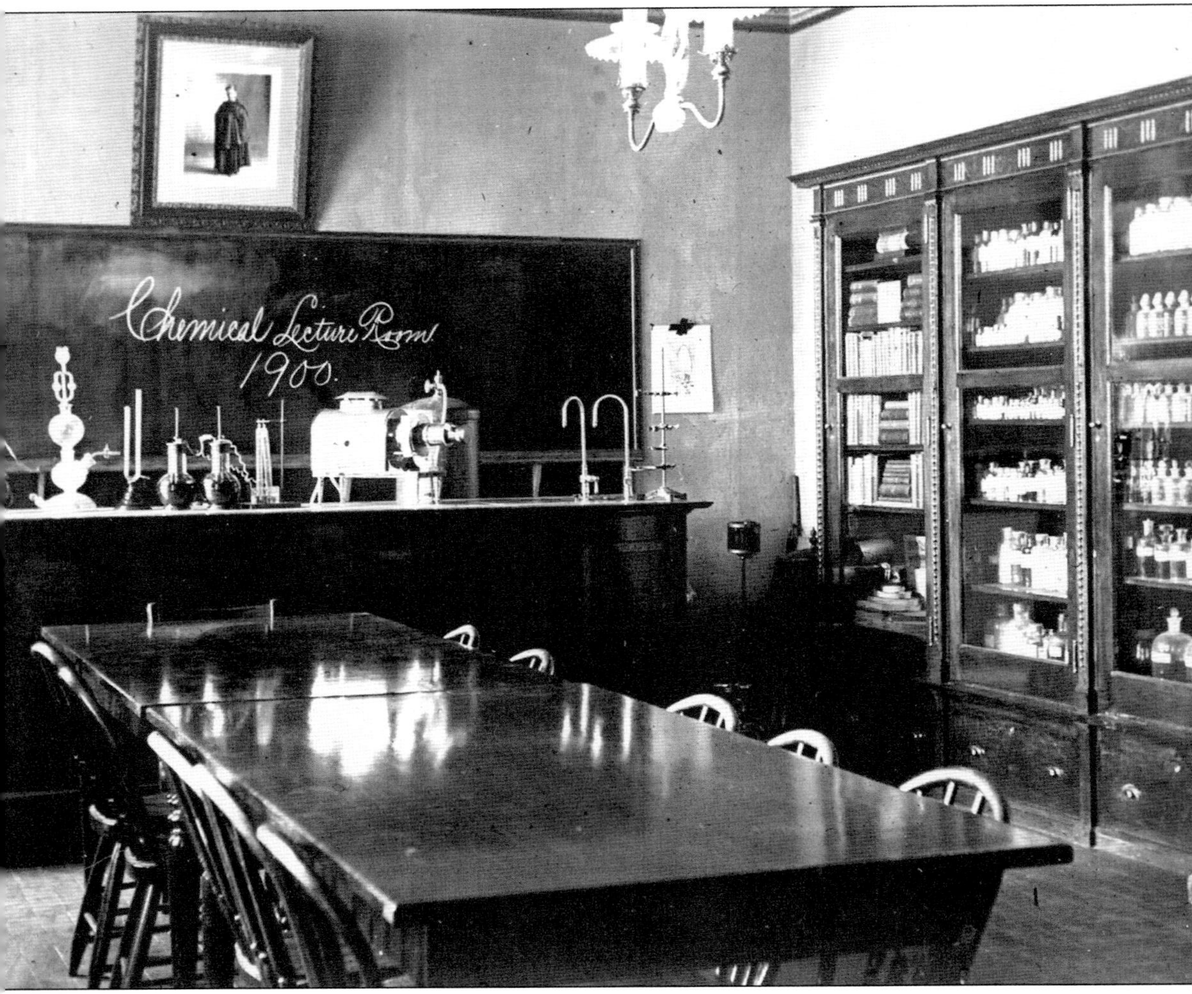

Freshman year, on the main corridor in Holy Cross right across from the Chemistry Labs—I remember the sulfur experiments!— It was the exam time nearing the end of first semester. Ann Sheridan, Carolyn K. and Mary Catherine Fitzgerald and I were hitting the books very hard, grinding under those miserable little desk lamps. A friendly fly, slow, fat, leftover from the halcyon days of October, was keeping us company, too sluggish to be annoying, just friendly enough to help us realize we were not alone.

Toward the end of the week, we discovered our animal friend dead, deceased, gone. Studying late at night in the closet by flashlight had put our emotions, if not our minds into over gear. We decided the little fellow needed a proper sendoff. Results: one small and oversized fly in a jewelry box on a scrap of satin (you do realize that the clear plastic lid conducted the light from the lowered desk lamp so that the whole box glowed)! We sang hymns, wept copiously, prostrated ourselves, and sent the fellow off with a ceremony beyond his wildest expectations. Our grief was cathartic; we approached our studies with new dignity and balance, and, happily, we all passed with flying colors. I have noted that my friends in co-educational universities and colleges did not have any similar stories to share, in fact, did not even seem to know what category this fit in.

—Catherine Opper '54

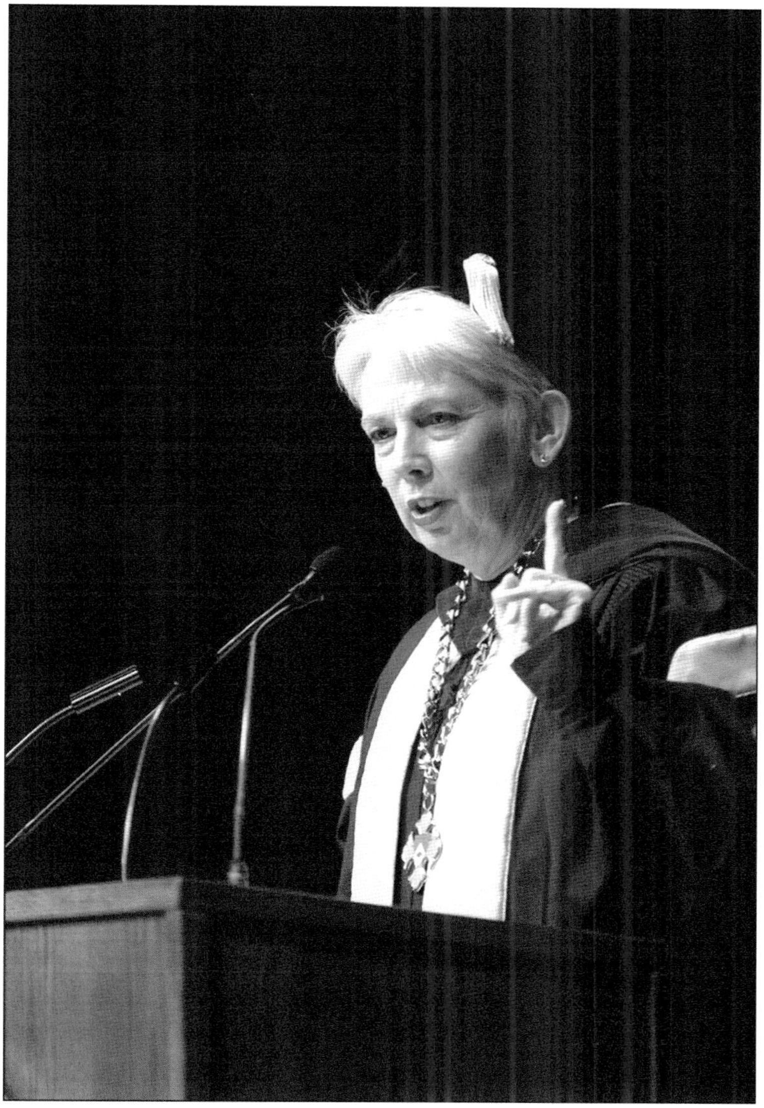

In the first years of Saint Mary's, there were 2 five month sessions each year which concluded with oral examinations. The questioning for the examinations was typically done by the Sisters. But in July 1855, Father Sorin, the founder of Notre Dame, announced that for the oral examination of Saint Mary's students, which was scheduled to take place the following day, he had asked some of his best professors at Notre Dame to question the advanced students. Professor Denis O'Leary began the examination the next morning with Mathematics. Professor O'Leary gave problems of his own devising to each girl. An account of the proceedings relates that "the girls, warming to the work, forgot fright and for two hours professor and pupils became so interested in the various branches of Mathematics that all forgot entirely that other studies had been ignored" until the noon angelus bell rang. One of those 1855 examiners told Father Sorin that the Saint Mary's students were "an honor to the thorough teaching" they had received.

—Excerpt from inaugural address given by President Carol Ann Mooney '72, Saturday, January 15, 2005. (Photograph by Matt Cashore.)

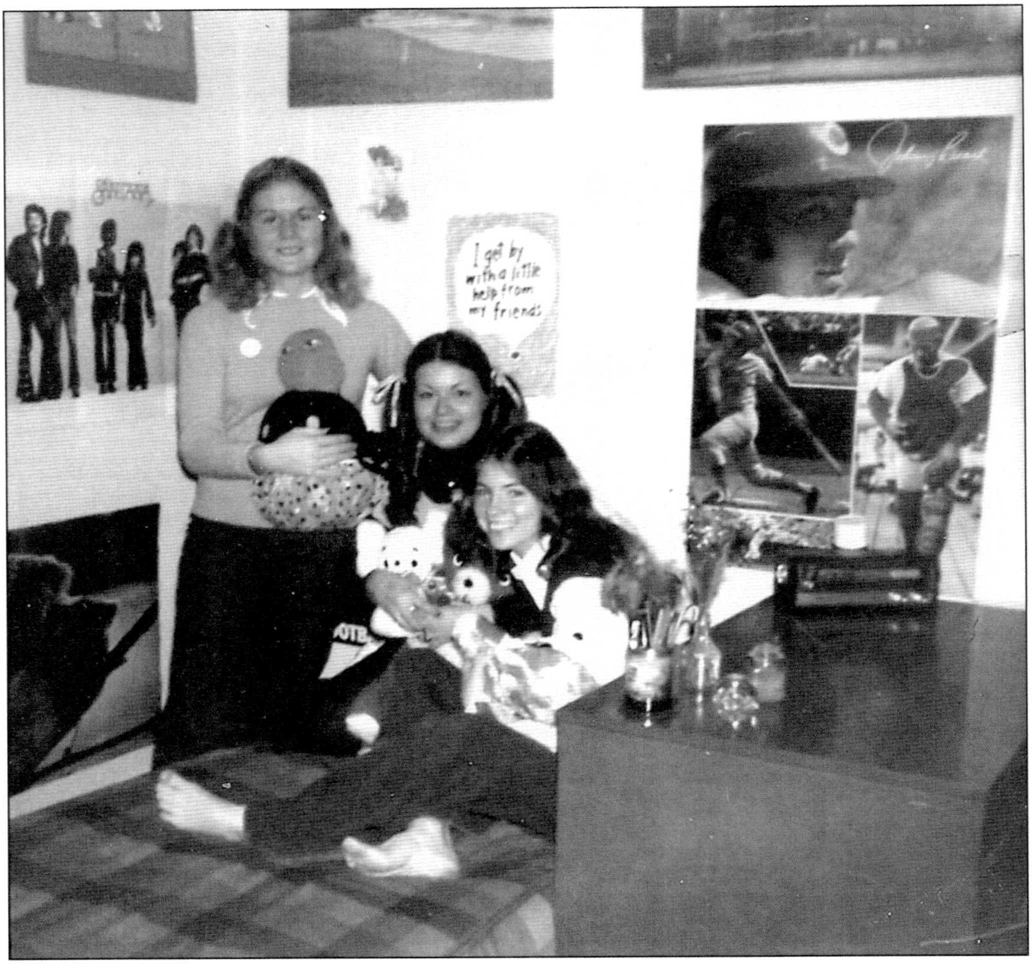

Carly Simon's voice and verse echoed through the small hallway almost continuously during the fall of 1972. Did I say echoed? I really meant that it blasted . . . loud and continuously. Of course, no one had the courage to ask Casey (Kathleen Cannon) or Sam (Mary Sue McAnallen) to turn it down! After awhile we got used to it. That song became an anthem that still serves as a reminder of that special freshman year at Saint Mary's, that time of our life and a slice of that life on fifth floor, Le Mans.

"Yes, Dad, there is a fifth floor in Le Mans...no, the elevator only goes up to the fourth floor." So started the journey to our new home...17 rooms, a hidden wing, a small hallway... a place where "everybody knows your name." Thirty freshmen (and two R.A.s) from all parts of the country, with varying interests and personalities. We became one big, happy family—someone to sit with at the dining hall, a friendly face in class...and even now, a friendly face at reunion.

—Karen Zagrocki McDonald '76

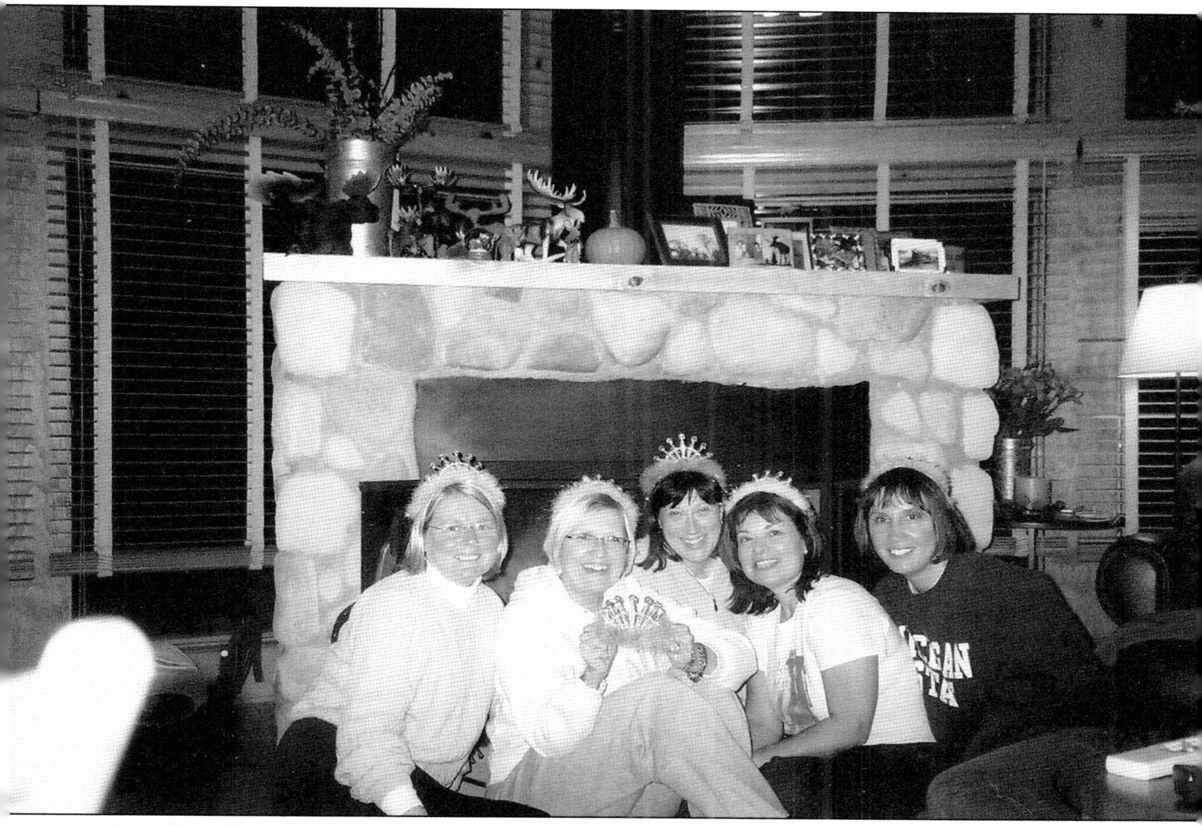

My best friends today can be traced to fifth floor, Le Mans. Many a night found us together, outside our rooms, sitting on the floor of that small hallway, doing homework, laughing, eating...and, when Carly Simon stopped, playing our Motown records. Nellie (Ellen) Lawlor, Kimi Olmstead, Mona Adamski, Barb Rapchak and Rosemarie Moulis. Soon, friends of fifth floor friends would join these late night get-togethers. Paula Tosi and Eileen Flanagan, then Cathy Strong, often found their way up to our hidden annex. Mix and match and you've got the makings of roommates and suitemates for all four years and friends for life. We celebrated our 21st birthdays together in 1975 and in 2004 most of us were able to get together to celebrate our 50th birthdays!!!

Doesn't seem possible all those years have passed, yet nothing has changed. Well, actually a few things did change. We lost Paula on her 30th birthday, we've gone through marriages, divorces, career ups and downs, child rearing, adoption, breast cancer . . . I guess you call it life. What has made the ups and downs easier is the friendship and support we provide each other. Just like that, the years melt away and we're 18 again, back on the fifth floor of Le Mans.

Thanks, Casey and Sam for providing an important part of the soundtrack for my life. Thanks fifth floor Le Mans and everyone who lived there for providing the foundation for my life.

—Karen Zagrocki McDonald '76

SAINT MARY'S COLLEGE
NOTRE DAME
HOLY CROSS, INDIANA

July 8, 1946

Miss Hallie Swift
315 Delaware
Bartlesville, Oklahoma

Dear Hallie:

I have now assigned to you room 446, a double room without bath to be shared with Ann McEniry.

The price of this room is $56.25 to each occupant.

If this assignment does not agree with your request, be assured that your name is still on the waiting list for the type of room preferred. I will make any adjustments possible before September. The fortunate thing is to have a reservation in Le Mans Hall.

Should you for any reason have to change your plan of returning to Saint Mary's, please advise me immediately. I hope, however, that we shall be welcoming you with your class on September 10.

You are enjoying, I trust, a delightful summer and sharing the fulness of Saint Mary's spirit with your associates. That generous giving and sharing can be a true apostolate, fruitful of much good for you and others.

Sincerely yours,

Sister Kathryn Marie

Sister Kathryn Marie
Dean of Women

SKM/dml

Hallie dear, we have a very new saint in Heaven: Loretta Stemp died July 9.
Hope you are enjoying every minute at home.

The dean of women informs Hallie Swift of her room assignment for the 1946–1947 academic year.

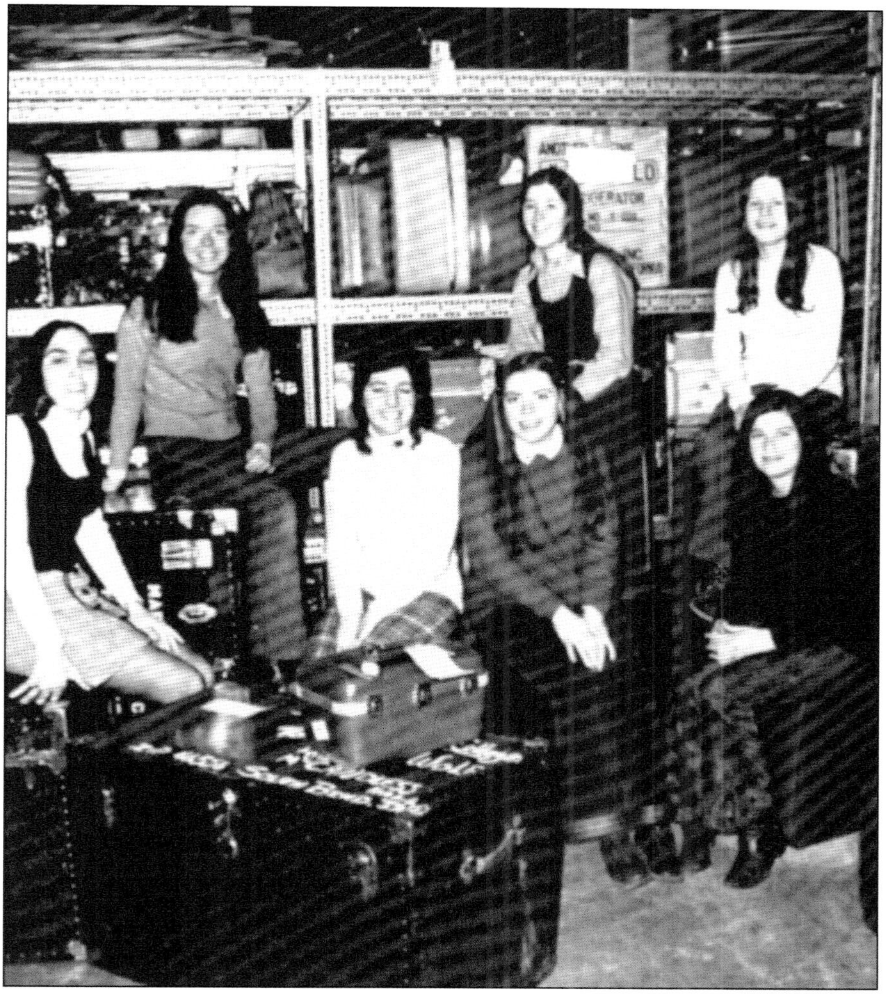

Half of the fun of coming back to college in the fall is seeing the new freshman class. You can always tell a new freshman by the look of perplexity and wonder about her. It begins when she turns from the Dixie Highway into the entrance. The long avenue of trees seems endless and she is startled to find a railroad track running right through campus. From her first glimpse of Le Mans Hall to the time she manages to find her room she is in a complete daze.

Our freshman makes mad dashes between classes down to the trunk room. Her letters home are frequent, full of detailed descriptions about campus and her college life. She thinks the lake is lovely. The library, too, is wonderful, but she doesn't think she'll spend much time there—just wait!

Her first Sunday at college means her first tea dance. The morning is spent discussing its possibilities. At 1:55, looking like something out of Vogue in her new black dress, she is full of expectations. At 5:05 she is a confirmed skeptic.

She soon learns that "freshman" and "trouble" are synonymous. She finds out it's just not a good idea to be late for meals or to have too many midnight parties. Perhaps the college would run on smoother wheels if we didn't have to allow the freshmen a few weeks to learn the ropes, but there wouldn't be half of the surprises and laughs.

—*St. Mary's Static*, October 1945

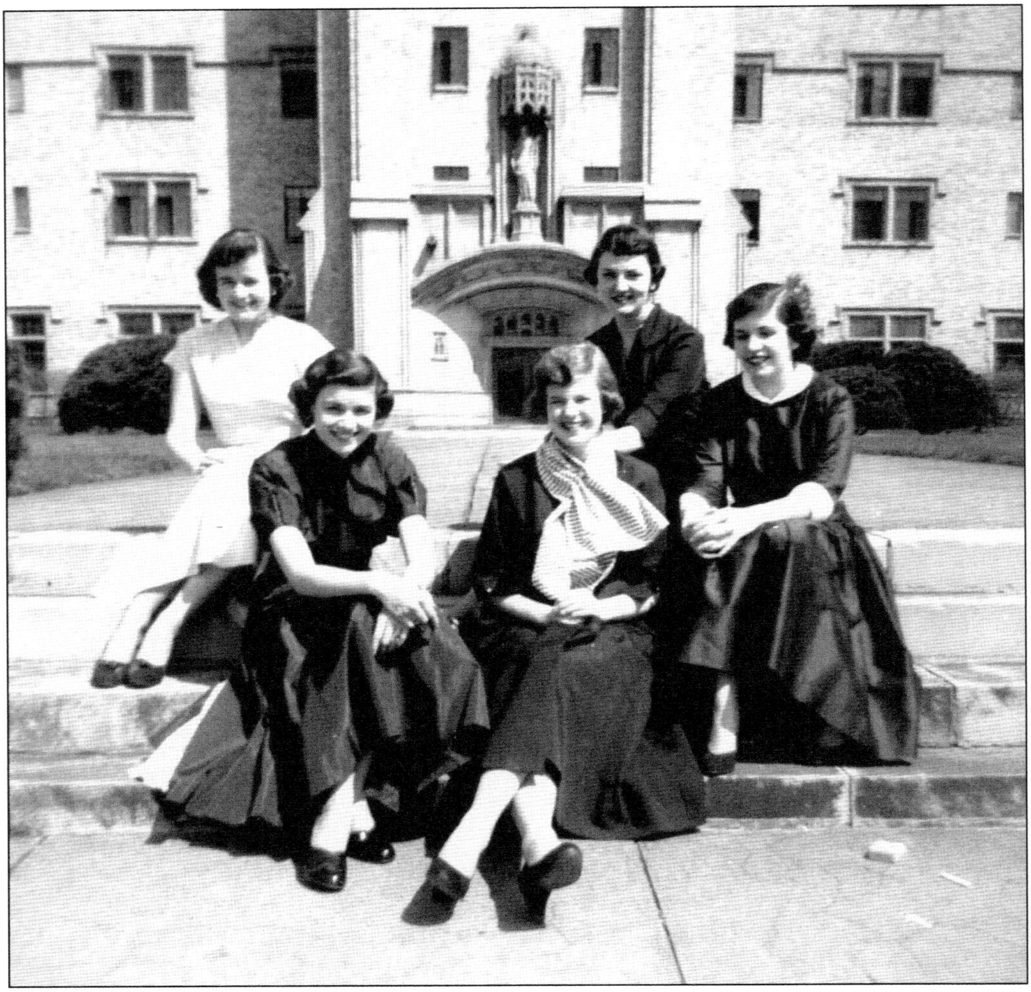

It was a night filled with firsts in 1958. It was my first date with a Notre Dame man. Exciting, I thought as I tripped, literally, into the Pebble to wait for him—but not for long. It seems he had been in the parlor for twenty-five minutes. I flew up the stairs, ran into the parlor, and stopped very dismayed. Impatient crew cuts crowded the room. It was the first time I had ever had trouble finding my date after he arrived. But there was no alternative, so I casually searched each face till I discovered my date, deeply engrossed in "Have Gun, Will Travel". Two commercials and many gunshots later I charmed him away from Paladin and we were on our way. Or we were until I discovered I had forgotten to sign out.

—Sheila Lejeune, November 25, 1958

SAINT MARY'S COLLEGE
NOTRE DAME
HOLY CROSS, INDIANA

Feast of Saint Anne, 1946

Miss Carolyn Powers
Eagle Road, R. D. 1
Willoughby, Ohio

Dear Carolyn:

As you know, one of the first privileges that comes to you as a junior is that of being Big Sister to one or several of our incoming freshmen. Your own freshman days are not so far removed that you have forgotten how much it meant to you to know that some particular girl among the old students would be looking forward in an especial manner to meeting you and to doing for you the kind and thoughtful things a big sister would do.

I am enclosing, herewith, the names of the Little Sisters that are assigned to you. Will you kindly write to them at your early convenience? Most of them have heard of our Big Sister plan and they are looking forward eagerly to hearing from you.

I hope that a pleasant correspondence with them will make the remainder of your vacation more enjoyable than it would otherwise be. I hope, too, that your interest in them will not terminate with the summer. There will be many ways in which you can make their college days happier during the next two years.

Yours very sincerely,

Sister M. Madeleva

President

Sister Madeleva informs Carolyn Powers of her role as a Big Sister to the incoming freshmen.

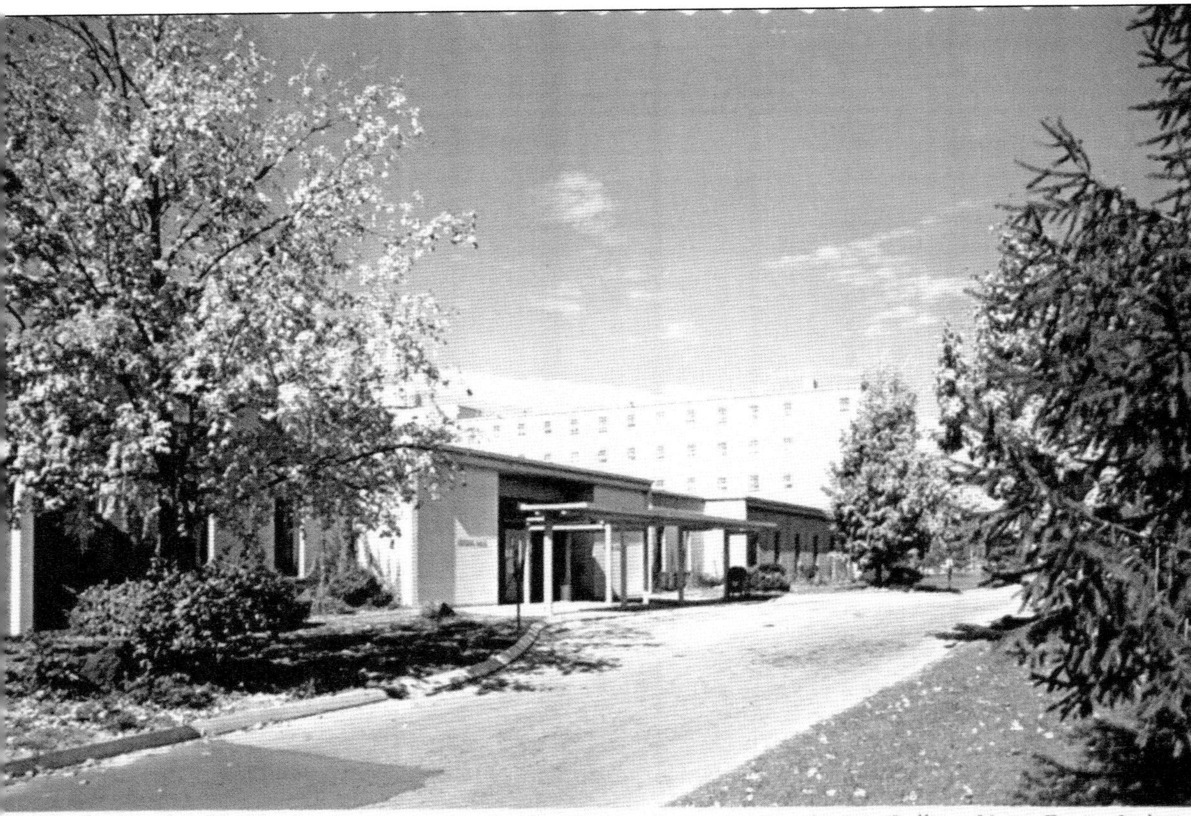

Regina Hall Saint Mary's College, Notre Dame, Indiana

We arrived in the Fall of 1970, a bunch of wide-eyed 17 and 18-year old girls. We settled in our new homes: LeMans and Holy Cross. Not McCandless. That was the "Rock Castle," the dorm where seniors picked out china patterns. Or so we were told. But what did we know? After all, we were freshmen.

Cut loose from apron strings, we asserted our independence. But restrained by curfew, that independence expired at midnight on weekdays (2 a.m. on weekends). We signed out for destinations off-campus, like the "Running Bear Nudist Camp." We thought that was funny. Again, we were freshmen.

We survived our first year. With newly-forged friendships, coupled with lousy lottery numbers, we headed to the austere accommodations of Regina Hall.

But Regina wasn't without its plus side. Each floor had a laundry room. And on a Saturday night, if there was a concert at ND and we weren't going, that laundry room became our mini-Convo or Stepan Center. A stereo would be set up. Albums by the featured artist would be pooled. Roma's would get the call to deliver refreshments, most often one small cheese pizza and a dozen or so bottles of Boone's Farm. We were sophomores, after all, "wise fools."

—Natalie Dwyer-Haller '74

Two

Across the Dixie

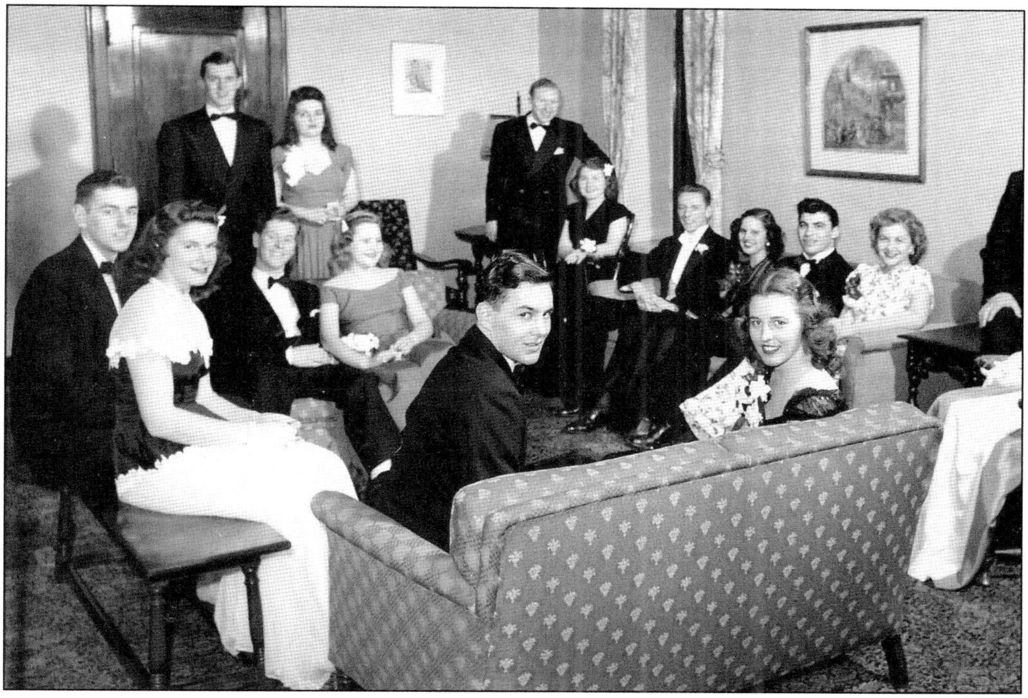

I went to Saint Mary's College from 1946–1950, right after World War II. Most of the Notre Dame guys we knew were veterans, several years older and wiser. I need not tell you how they felt about the rules at Saint Mary's.

One memory that generated the most jokes was The Rug Fund. When a Saint Mary's girl had a date to attend a ND dance, we had to submit 25¢ in an envelope labeled with the name of our date. We were told the money was for the wear and tear on the carpet on which those guys stood and waited for us.

—Mary "Mudd" McHale '50

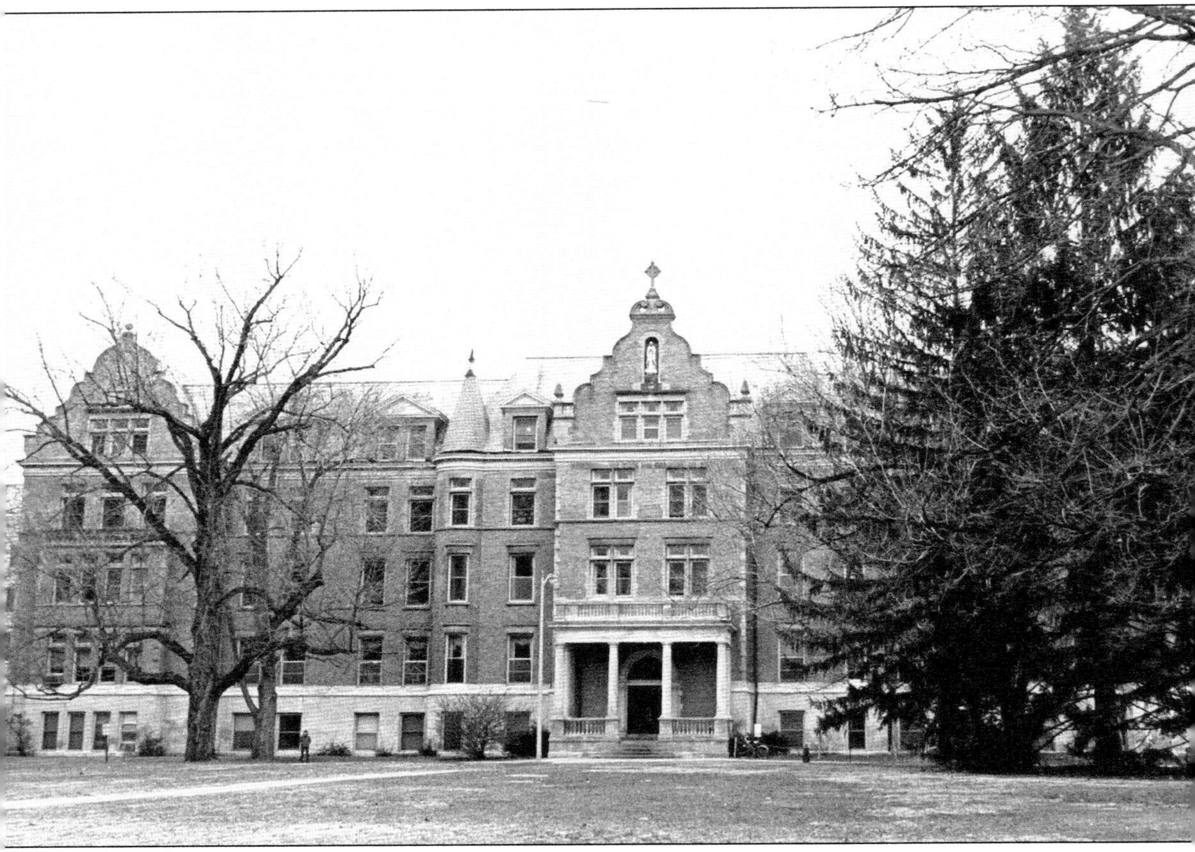

One of my fondest memories while at Saint Mary's College was my first night as a student. My friend Michelle Rowe, who I had just met that morning, and I were walking down the hall to our rooms in Holy Cross after attending the Graffiti Dance at ND. We had met many people and in particular a guy, Jonathan, from my home town in Oregon and his friend Sam. They had walked us back to our hall that night. While heading to our rooms, Michelle and I were talking about the evening and she turns to me and says, "You're going to marry him." I liked Jonathan, there were definitely sparks, but being just eighteen, marriage was not even in my thoughts. I just wanted to enjoy my freshman year. I looked at her and said, "Yeah right. Whatever. "Less than four years later, Jonathan and I were married, the day after our senior year finals in the Basilica with all of our college friends surrounding us.

—Rachel Verdick '94

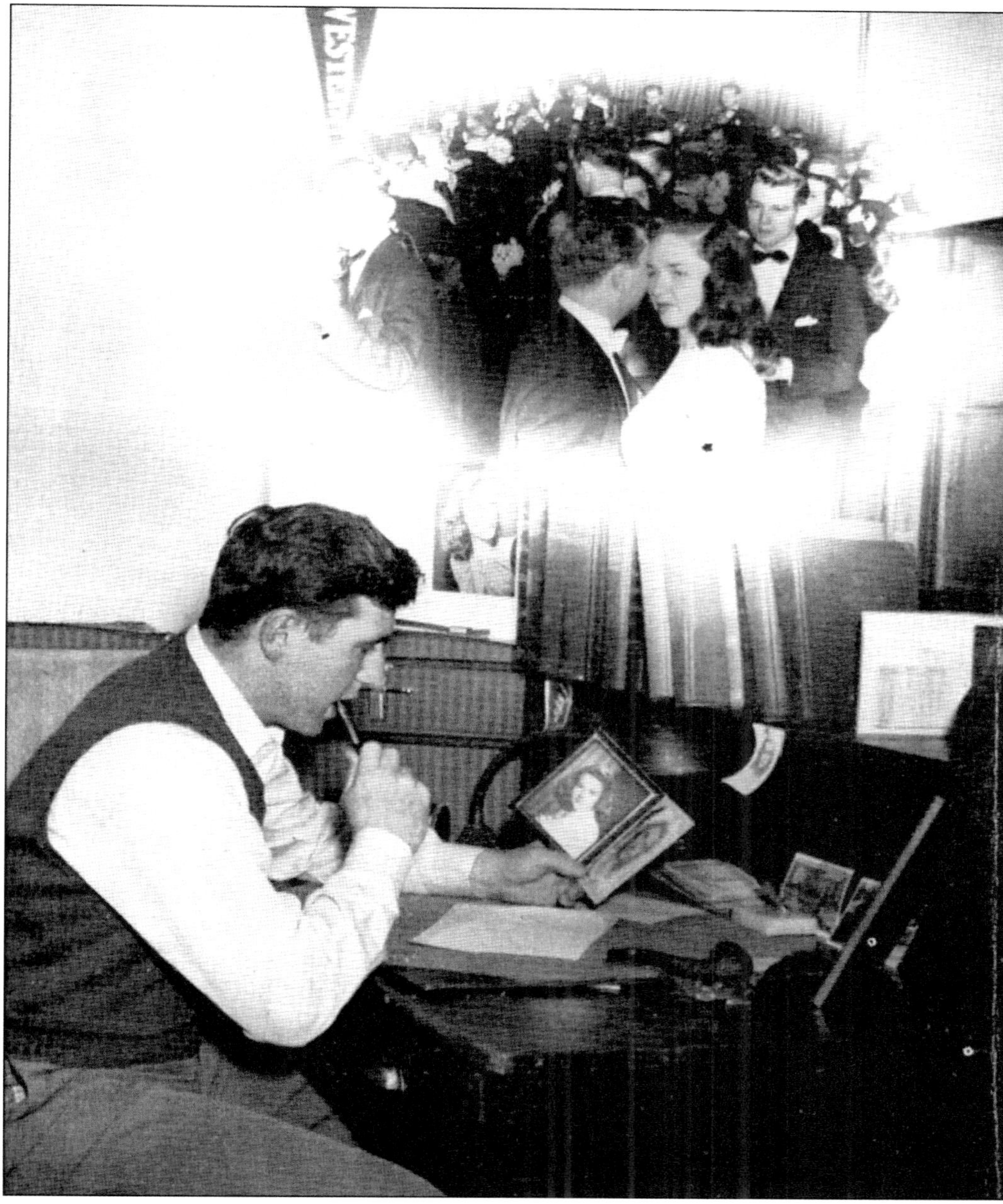

Dr. Susan Alexander's class on "Women and Class." It was an evening class and a number of ND men decided to join it, clearly not thinking it would be hard or ready to take it seriously. They soon learned that SMC students took their classes seriously, worked hard, and expected them to do the same. The discussions and lessons from this class were lively and to this day I still refer to them.

I can still remember my husband-to-be getting upset that I did not want to take his name. After asking why I should (his only response was tradition), which was not good enough for me, and why wouldn't he take mine (he got it then). The discussion ended and it was never talked about again.

—Rachel Verdick '94

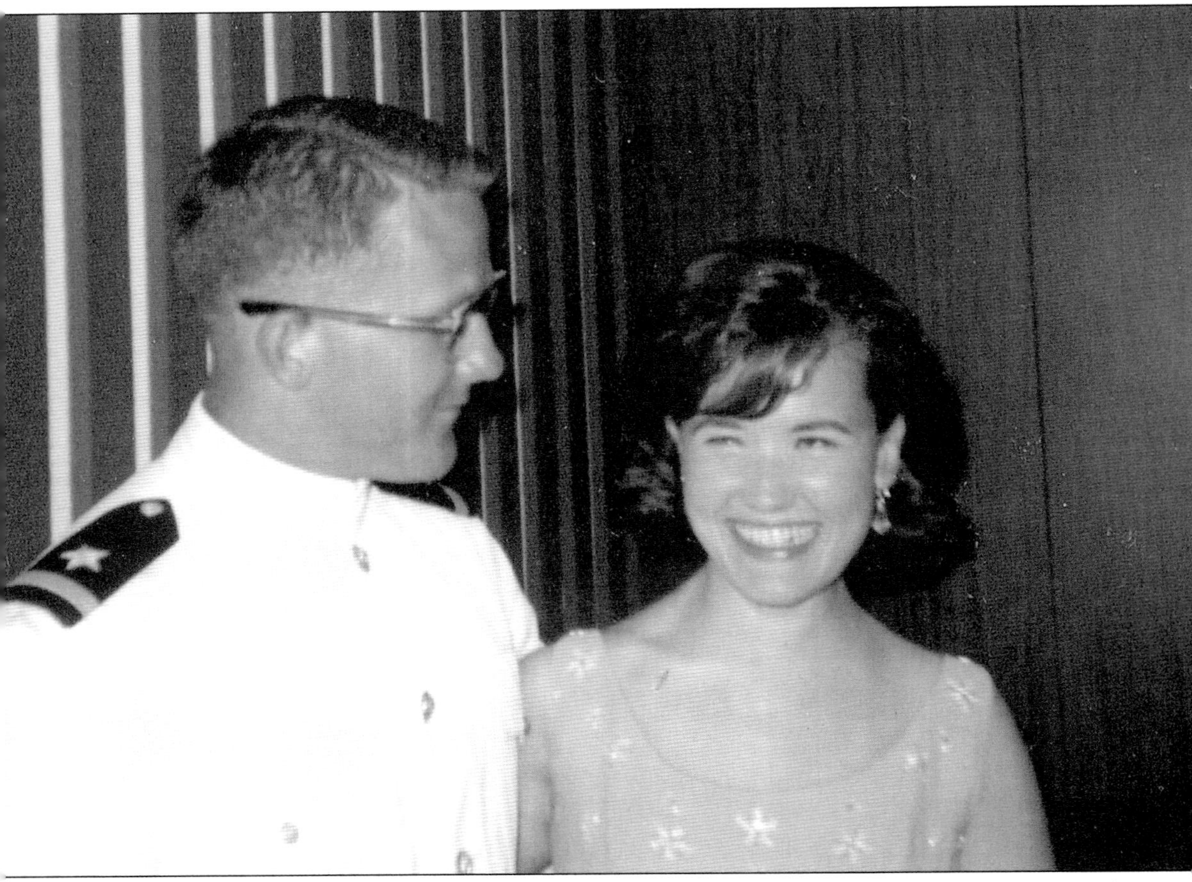

David Ames, my husband to be, flew in from the Mediterranean for SMC Senior Prom in early June '65 and my SMC graduation. It was his 6 month leave. I hadn't seen him since the previous December, when he had a short Christmas leave. That Christmas in 1964 was when we became engaged. We saw each other so rarely, that my mom asked me if I really knew him well enough to actually marry him. I think today that I would be asking my daughter the same question.

Dave was 2 years ahead of me at ND, so it made for a pretty quiet Junior and Senior year at Saint Mary's.

After graduation he had about a week left of leave, and then he left for his aircraft carrier in the Mediterranean Sea, where he was a navigator. I did not see him again until 3 days before our wedding in November '65. My mom was a basket case. Looking back, I certainly can't blame her.

—Sheila Ames '65

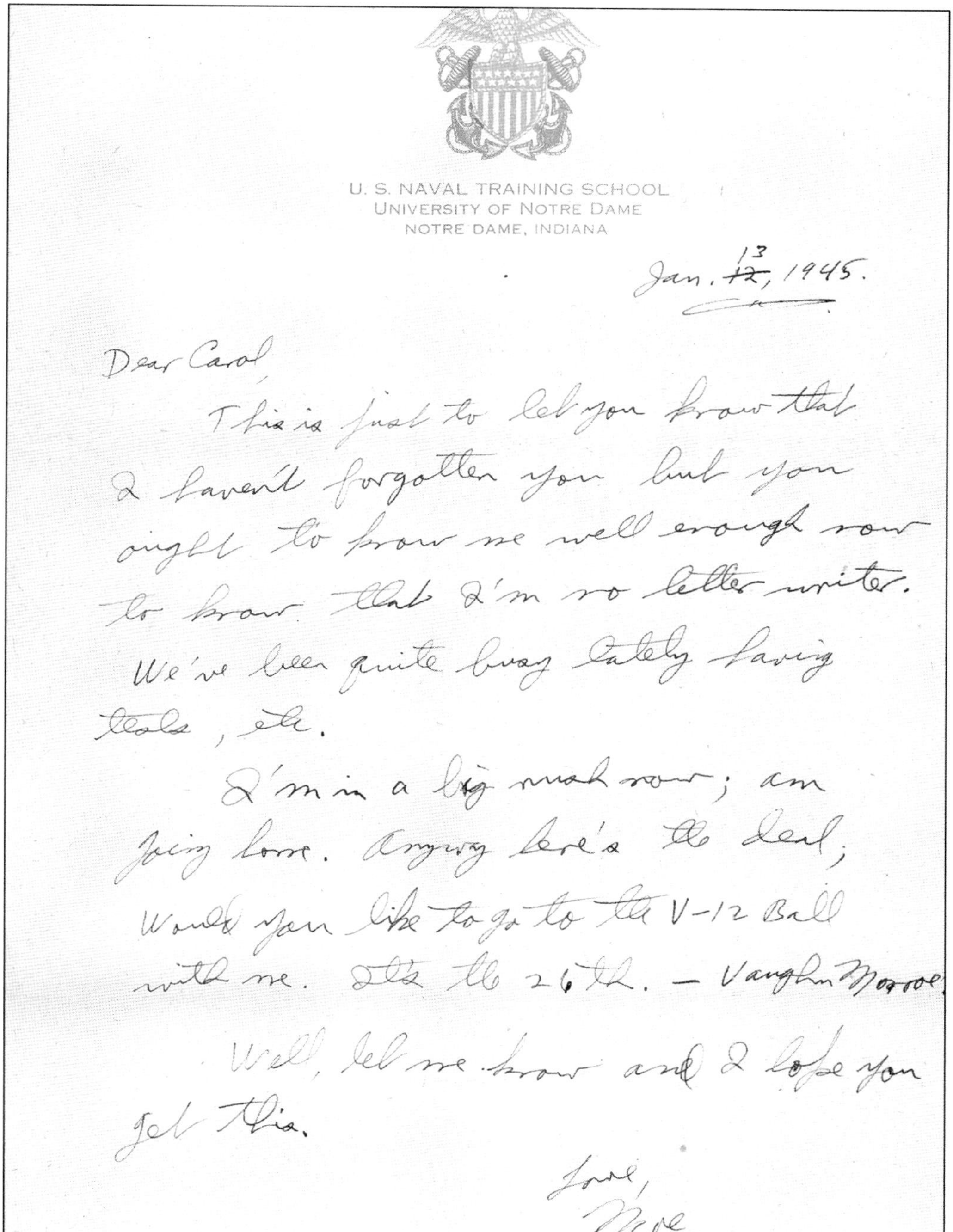
U. S. NAVAL TRAINING SCHOOL
UNIVERSITY OF NOTRE DAME
NOTRE DAME, INDIANA

Jan. ~~12~~ 13, 1945.

Dear Carol,

This is just to let you know that I haven't forgotten you but you ought to know me well enough now to know that I'm no letter writer. We've been quite busy lately having tests, etc.

I'm in a big rush now; am going home. Anyway here's the deal; would you like to go to the V-12 Ball with me. It's the 26th. – Vaughn Monroe.

Well, let me know and I hope you get this.

Love,
Moe.

Dear Carol, This is just to let you know that I haven't forgotten you but you ought to know me well enough now to know that I'm no letter writer. We've been quite busy lately having tests, etc. I'm in a big rush now; am going home. Anyway here's the deal; would you like to go to the V-12 Ball with me. It's the 26th. Well, let me know and I hope you get this.

Love, Moe

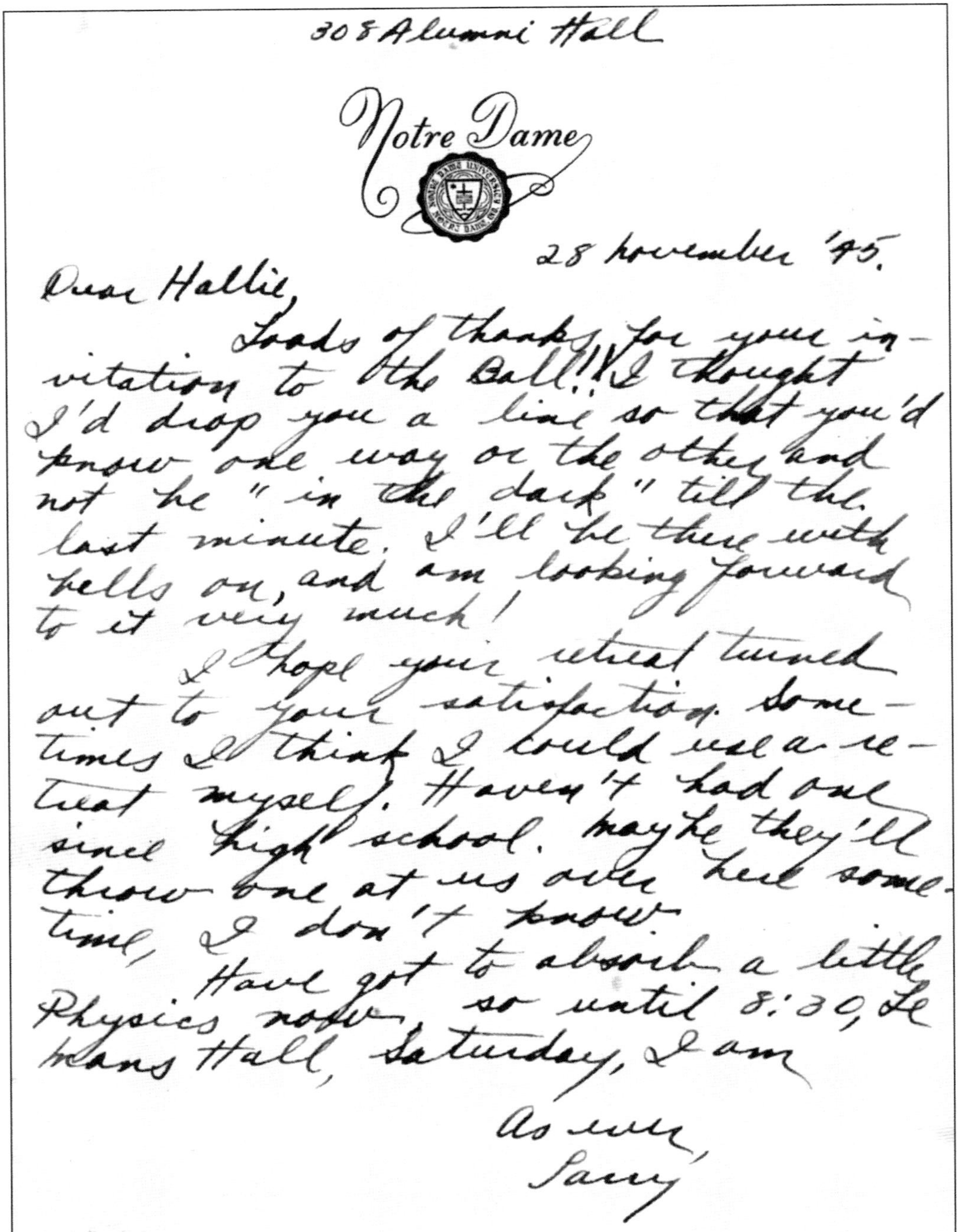

308 Alumni Hall

Notre Dame

28 November '45.

Dear Hallie,

Loads of thanks for your invitation to the Ball!! I thought I'd drop you a line so that you'd know one way or the other and not be "in the dark" till the last minute. I'll be there with bells on, and am looking forward to it very much!

I hope your retreat turned out to your satisfaction. Sometimes I think I could use a retreat myself. Haven't had one since high school. Maybe they'll throw one at us over here sometime, I don't know.

Have got to absorb a little Physics now, so until 8:30, Le Mans Hall, Saturday, I am

As ever,
Larry

This is one of many letters sent between Saint Mary's women and Notre Dame men during the forties when telephones were few and far between.

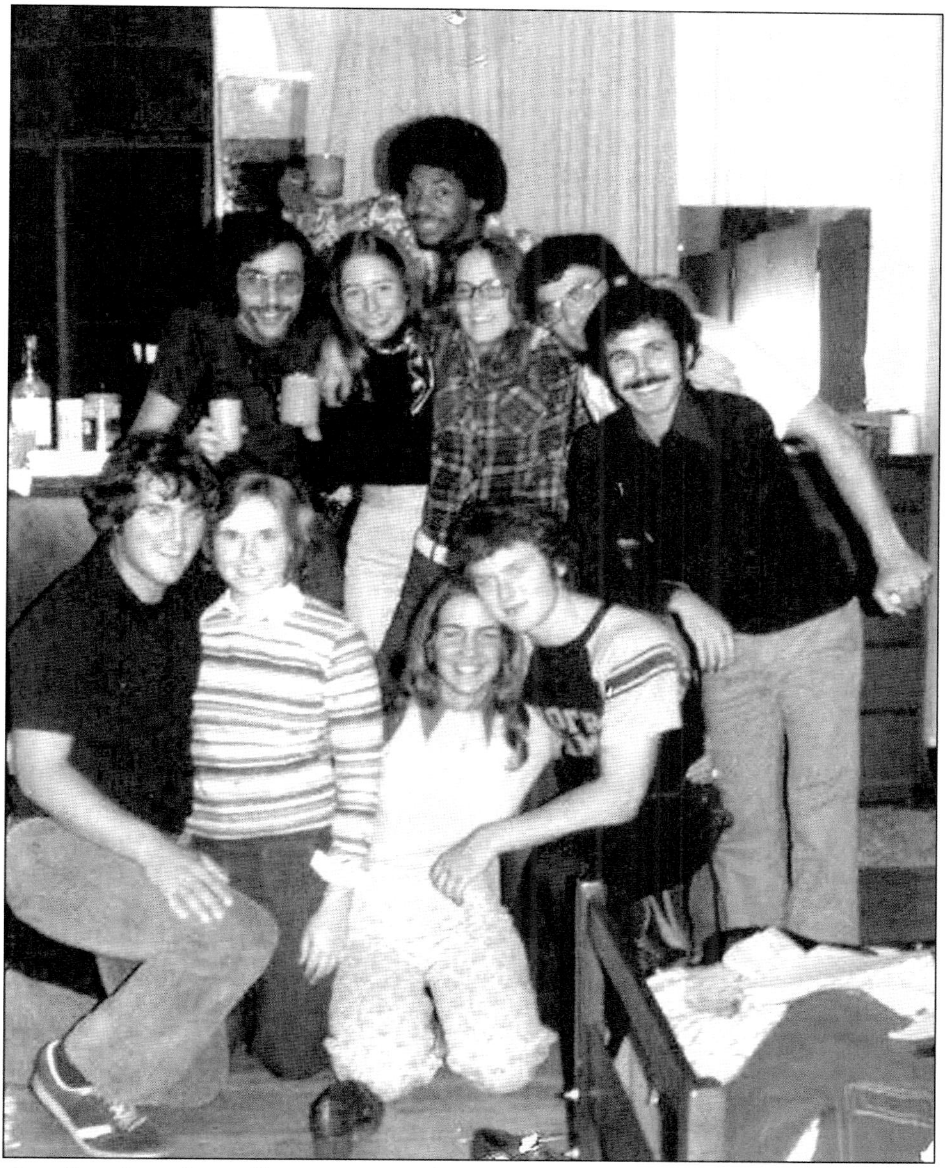

I am kneeling down in a yellow sweater with Dan who has been my husband for 25 years. The rest are some of my friends from LeMans Hall and Dan's Friends from Holy Cross Hall.

I lived in Regina freshman year, LeMans sophomore year (that is when I met the love of my life, Dan—you can see the picture of all of us in our triple) and senior year, and Holy Cross Junior Year! The friends near my rooms as well as those in my major are the friends that have meant the most to me and I continue to keep up with many of them.

Saint Mary's was such a good beginning for the real world. I graduated with a BSN in Nursing in 1978 and my Dan is a 1977 ND graduate. Every year we return to both campuses and sometimes with our children. Both campuses still feel like home. We are thrilled that our daughter, Deirdre Ruth Hayden, who graduates from Father Ryan High School in 2005, wants to come to Saint Mary's this fall.

—Annette Ruth Jenkins Hayden '78

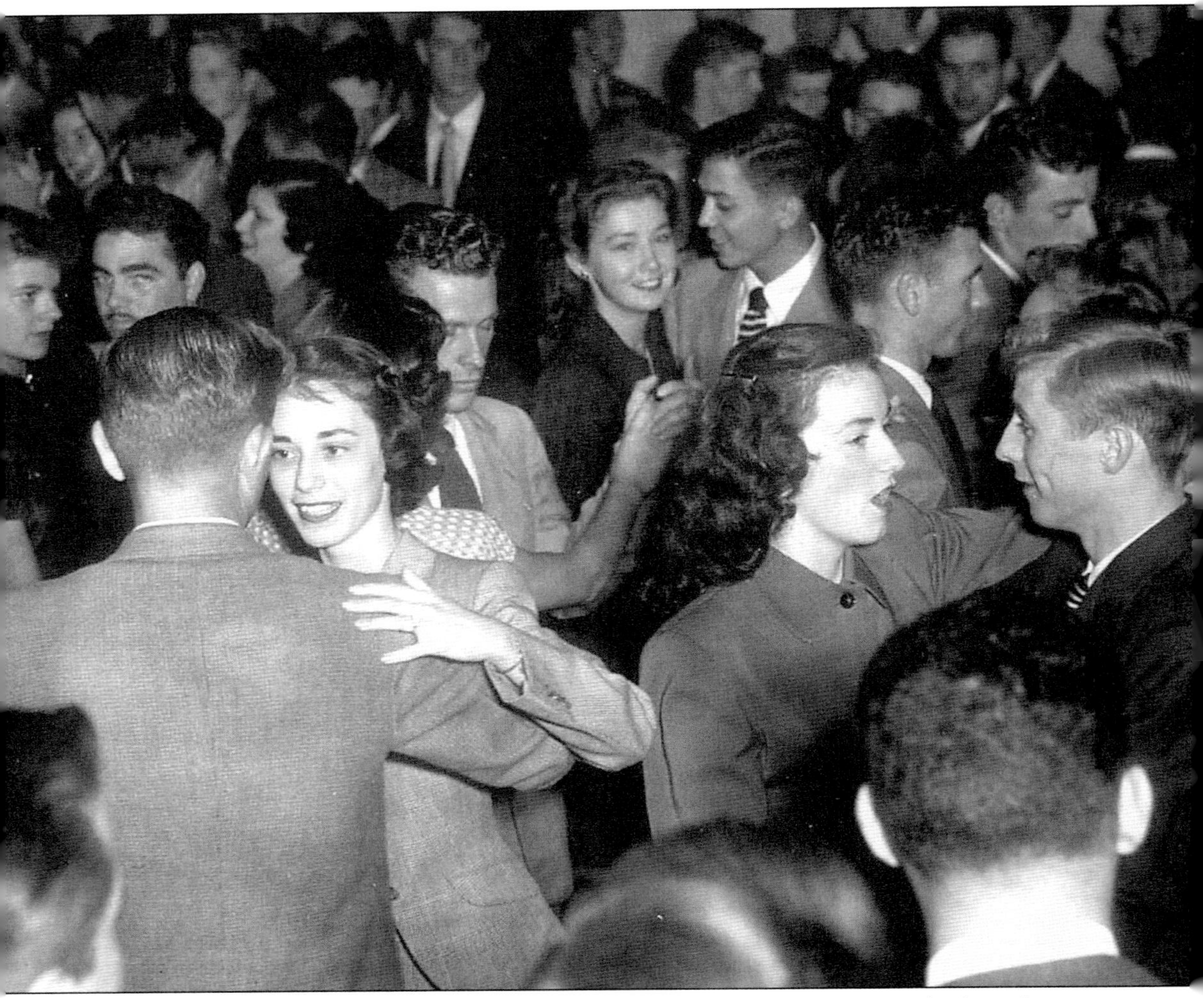

I met my future husband, Jack McHale, at a Tea Dance freshman year. We had tea dances on Sunday afternoons in the Social Hall. Someone would plug in the Victrola, and the Saint Mary's girls would line up on one wall and the Notre Dame guys along another wall. Then some of those guys would get brave enough to ask a girl to dance. Jack asked me.

On the next date we walked into South Bend. We did a lot of that. We never had much money but we ate at the Philadelphia, and more often at Kewpie's, the Eagle Nest, and Rosie's. We went to lots of movies, and sometimes sat in the bowling alley and watched the bowlers. No money to play.

Jack was a World War II Navy veteran from Houston, Texas. He gave me a miniature in my junior year and we were married the year after graduation. We settled in Houston but he left his job on The Houston Press to join the FBI. He died last August and I miss him so much.

—Mary "Mudd" McHale '50

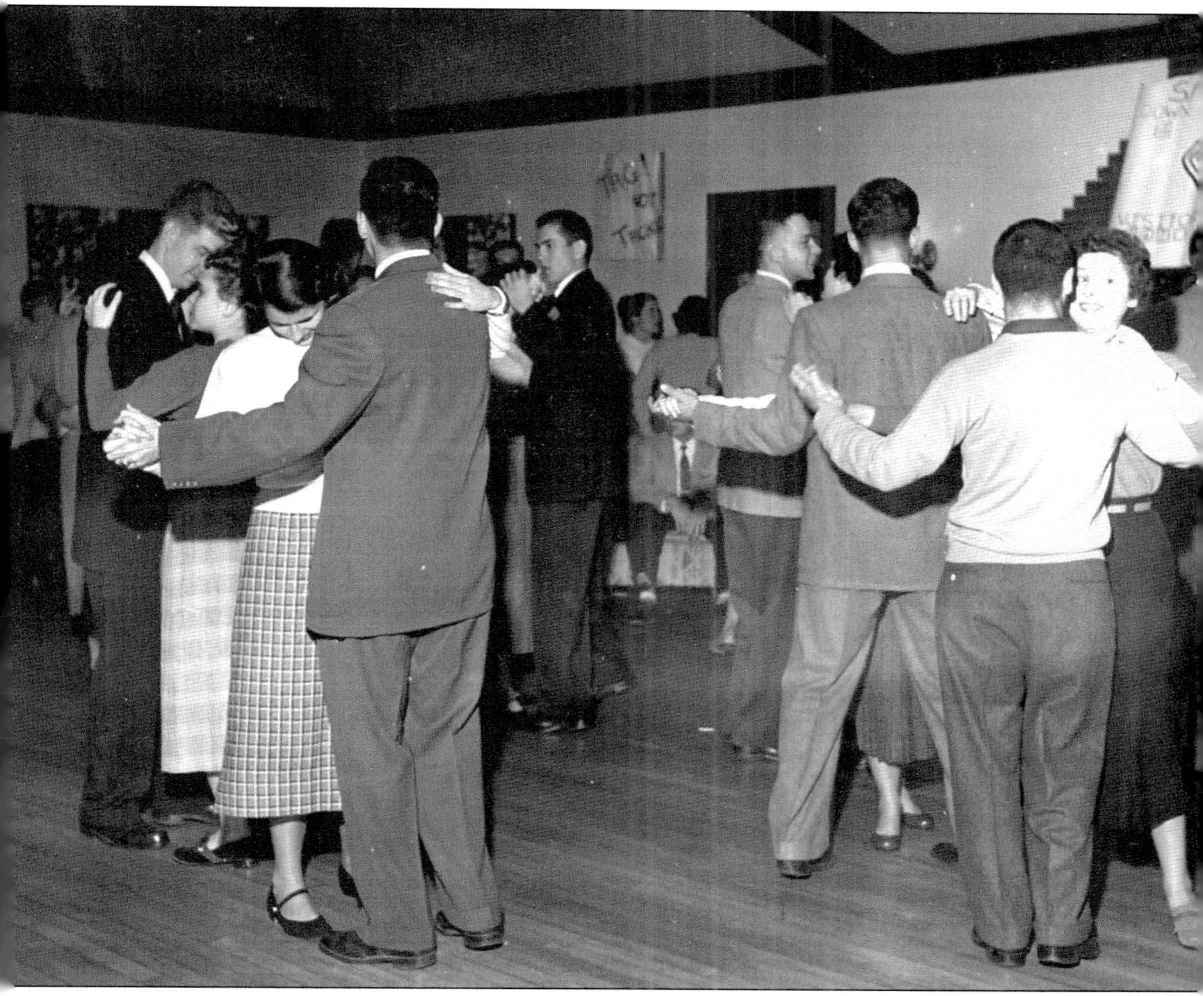

Not even a whipping rain and the tail end of that disastrous southern hurricane could keep some Notre Dame men away from the inaugural tea-dance at Saint Mary's last Sunday. Drenched and wind-lashed, a mob of cologne-scented N.D. men braved northern Indiana's humidity and the pelting rainfall to jam Le Mans Hall for the season's opening toe-crusher.

Only the social lore experts know why they call them tea dances. They never serve tea, and a great many men don't dance. For most of the N.D. men who get the Sunday habit, the tea dance means pleasant hours of charming feminine companionship. To those who strike up friendly acquaintanceships it seems that later on the queens will reciprocate by inviting them to prominent Saint Mary's functions.

Outstanding feature of last Sunday's session was the pall-like parade of new fall styles. Long black dresses slinked in and out of the babbling halls. Hose in all shades of black, smoke, gray, and dusk, drew varied comment from N.D. observers.

In the waning hours of the afternoon, as is customary, the dance crowd thins out. Couples pile onto the Red Rocket and roar downtown for a soda. Those N.D. men still in the stag line crunch down the cinderpath towards the highway, and back to their halls to wrestle with the idea of dialing 30567 or 30684 before the next tea-dance rolls around.

—John O'Connor, Notre Dame *Scholastic,* September 26, 1947

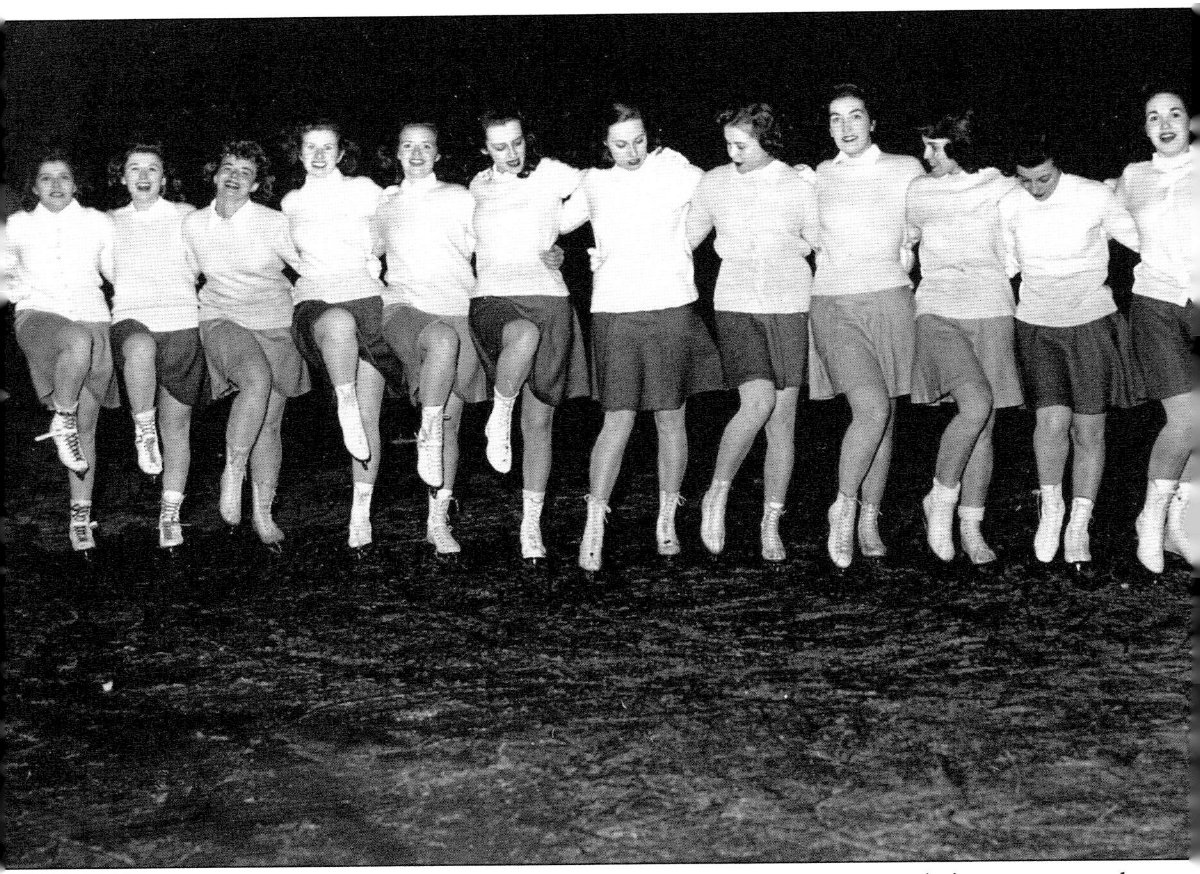

A poet has said that Mary is a grand old name, and Saint Mary's was a grand place enraptured in the gayety of the annual Winter Carnival, January 19. Recalling previous experiences at recent tea dances, we didn't expect much as we wandered across the Dixie Highway. To our surprise and pleasure, we found a wonderful time awaiting us there provided by a chance bit of sophisticated sophomore intuition. We met our equals for the evening in the Pine Ridge Lodge located in the sub basement of the fabulous College building. As usual, even though we were late ourselves, we had to wait on the misses.

We liked what we saw when our friends arrived and journeyed with them to the swelling lines around the banquet tables. We stood in line, recalling vivid chow hall memories. These memories vanished when we sampled the food. It had a strange taste. We had tasted food like this before, never in the chow hall but perhaps at home. Since there wasn't any snow, we huddled around the bonfire, waiting for the haywagon to return. Penny George was vocalizing the Hong Kong Blues when we reentered the Pine Ridge Lodge for the floor show. She ought to have had a talent scout watching her because she was a star among the torch song vocalists. Ten o'clock rolled around quickly as we danced away the fleeting hours. Our Saint Mary's adventures were finished as we said farewell regretfully and headed for our own unromantic dorms.

All in all, we had a wonderful evening and long for more. Might we add that as a result of this carnival, one of our fellow bachelors lost his way in snowdrifts where there were none and is now planning how to major in homemaking.

—Jack Hummel, *Scholastic*

During a month full of exciting football weekends, Charity Ball, quarterlies, the Sophomore Cotillion and Thanksgiving vacation, almost anything can happen.

In the diamond department—Clare Slattery and Jeanne Wick. Both received their rings at the Grotto on the Notre Dame campus. Jeanne's engagement was followed by a ceremony in the Sacred Heart Church. The juniors are finally coming into their own with Fran Delahanty and her newly acquired N.D. ring.

It isn't enough that Carrie Powers should receive twenty American beauties for her birthday. A special greeting representing each year was attached to each rose.

—Harriet Enneking '48,
St. Mary's Static, November 1946

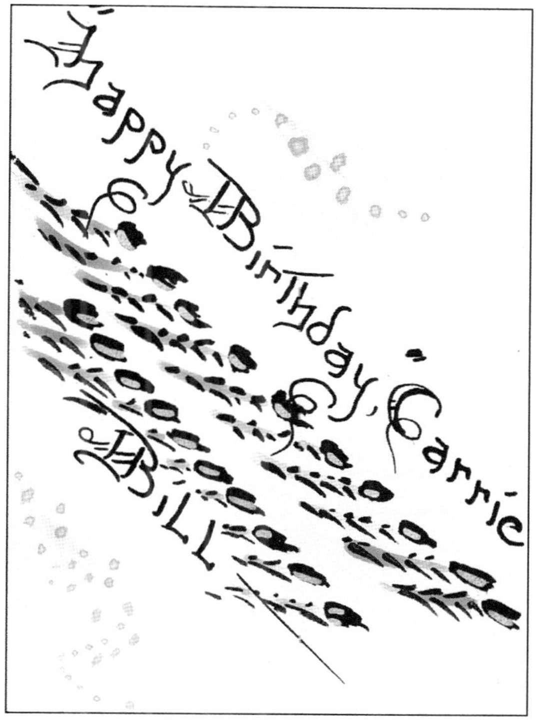

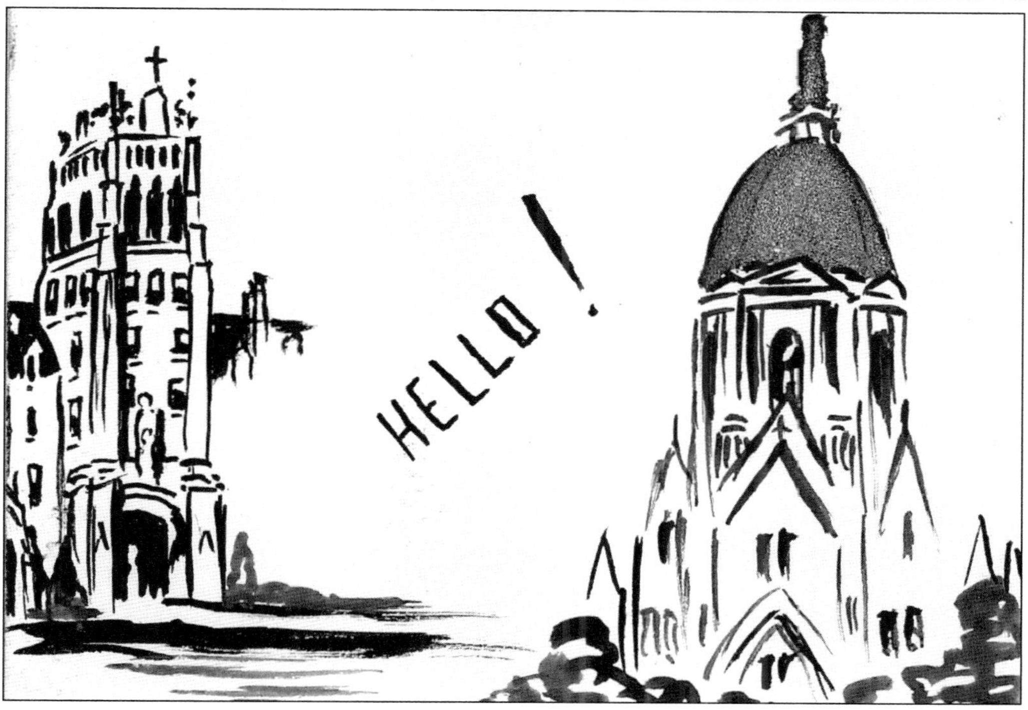

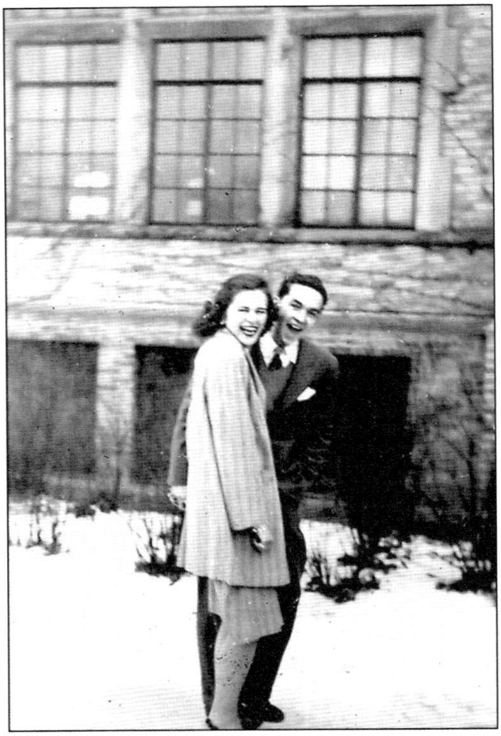

To go to Notre Dame without explicit permission from the Dean of Women is forbidden. We may not walk about the campus with our "boys" during the week; Saturdays and Sundays only. Men visitors are never to be taken above the first floor and may go to the Oriole only in the basement. Your guests may come at 2 on Sundays afternoons, and must leave at 5. Please be in the rectangle when you are expecting visitors. It is too difficult to reach every girl in her room.

—Student council bulletin, 1944

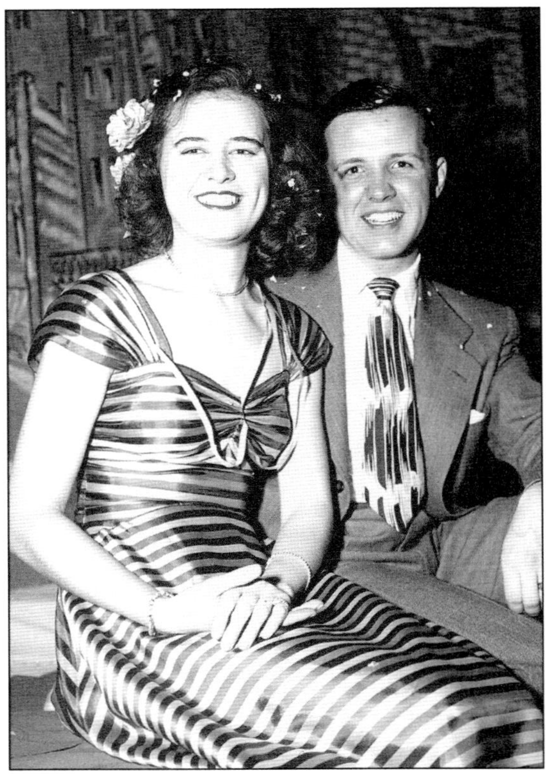

Carrie Powers and Bill celebrated their first Mardi Gras together along with the rest of the student body at the Palais Royale. "The Rebels," an organization of 700 Notre Dame students whose hearts lie below the Mason Dixon line, inaugurated another Notre Dame tradition with the 1948 Mardi Gras.

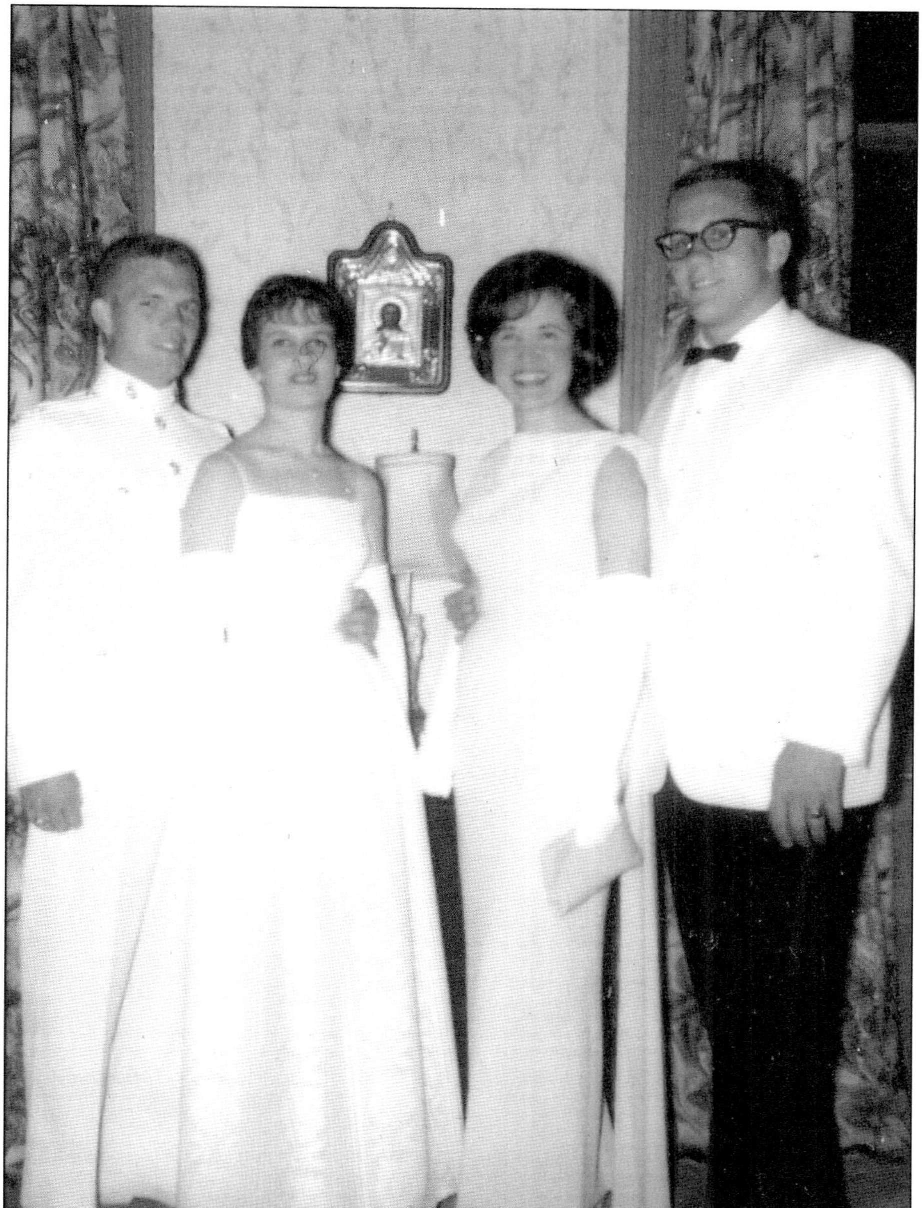

Freshman year the guys at ND were trying to sell lots of tickets for their Frolic. The day tickets were to be returned if your "import" couldn't come, they had me get a beautiful Saint Mary's woman to dress up in a Prom dress and be displayed in a spot light to let the guys know what they had "across the Dixie". Then we ran a blind date desk to fix up as many (almost 100) guys who wanted a date. Neither Pat nor I had a date and we were asked to the Frolic by two of the guys seeking dates. Since there were so few of us compared to the number at ND if a guy had a date to a large affair—11:30 curfew—he would be awaken in the morning by all the lights and radios in his room blaring at 5 a.m. That's when the power came back on and his friends had turned everything on to retaliate.

—Sandy Barlett '61

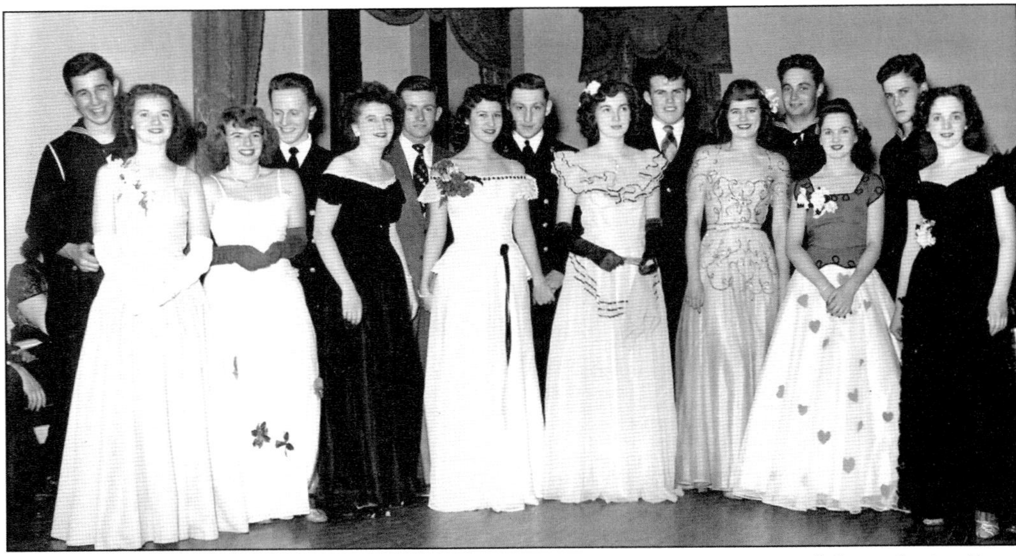

For the dances at Notre Dame and Saint Mary's, we wore long dresses with lots of crinolines. A friend of mine told me that during a dance at the field house of Notre Dame, something happened that one of her crinolines loosened and fell to the ground. She quietly stepped out of it and placed it on a chair.

The rage was strapless gowns. It was a must that we wore straps, no spaghetti straps, and they had to be one inch thick. I remember my mother bought ribbons and sewed them on to my dress. We just did what it took to get to the dance.

—Jean Giddens Cass '57

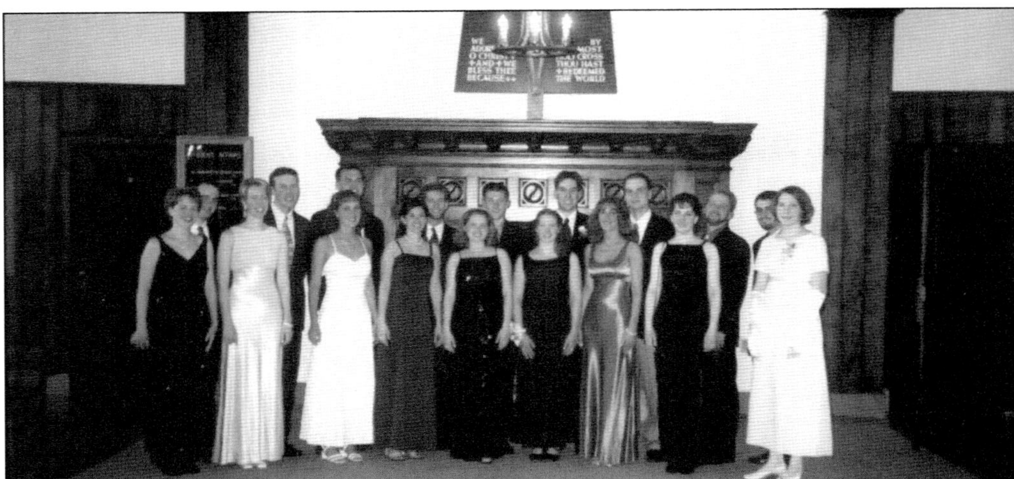

The group of friends grew and solidified to a fantastic group of women pictured here at the 1999 Senior Formal. This was just the first of many occasions—graduation, weddings, housewarmings, picnics—where we would all gather together for a photo opp. The women in this photograph, from left to right, are Rachel Reynard Prickman, Jen D'Anastasio Prickman, Jaime Sessions Kammerzell, Mary Hubert, Maureen Gill, Anne Eckert Yearsich, Jennifer Sessions Kramer, Brooke Lawrence, and Erin Emig LaCourt.

—Erin Emig LaCourt '99

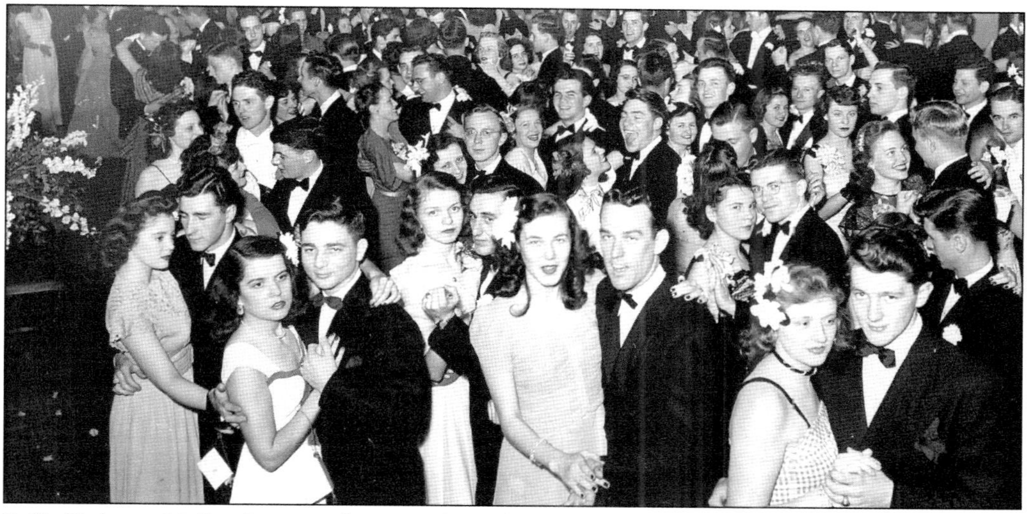

Polly Dale and I lived across from Kathy Zeller and Connie J. our freshman year in Holy Cross. The twist was the new big dance and only a select few very "in" people knew how to do it at Victory Dances and Mixers. Kathy Zeller knew how! We all went out in the hall one night and someone with music (most of us did not have music let alone Boom boxes then) turned it up loud and Kathy took over as teacher. She had us all get bath towels and hold them behind our fannies and pull them back and forth to get the right hip motion!!! It was hilarious.

—Therese McCaffrey McConville '65

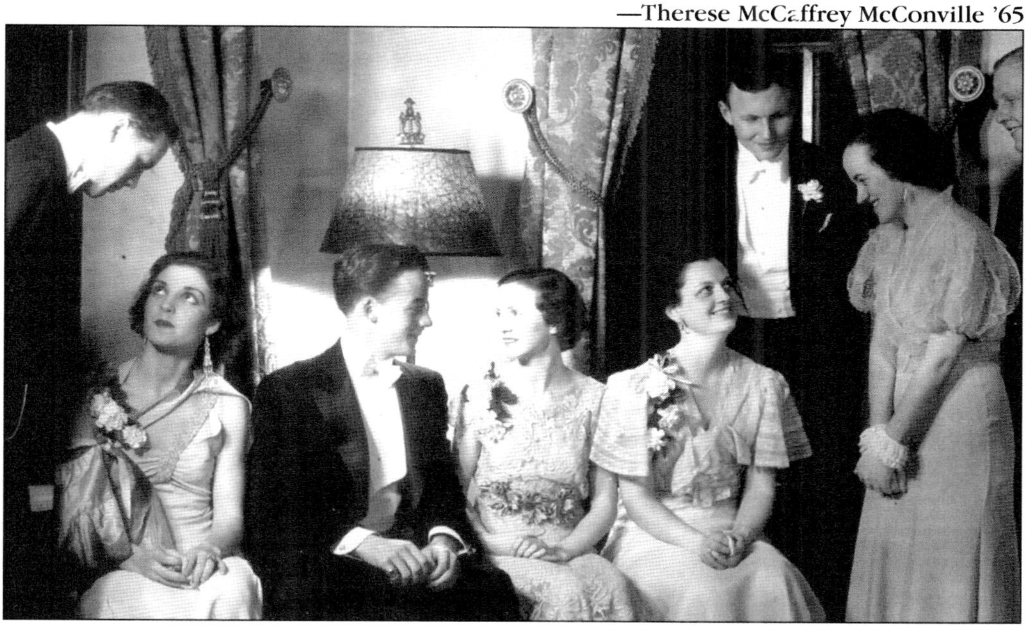

Ah, the mixers at ND! So many boys, so little time. What fun they were. A pack of us would walk over and back. The chatter was incessant—all about the cute guy we had met. Who would ever guess that we might marry one of them? I don't think we even minded the "hours" that we had, or "signing in and out" with our dates name on the line and telling exactly where we would be. We were an amazingly innocent bunch then, and it worked so well for us.

—Sheila Kelly Ames '65

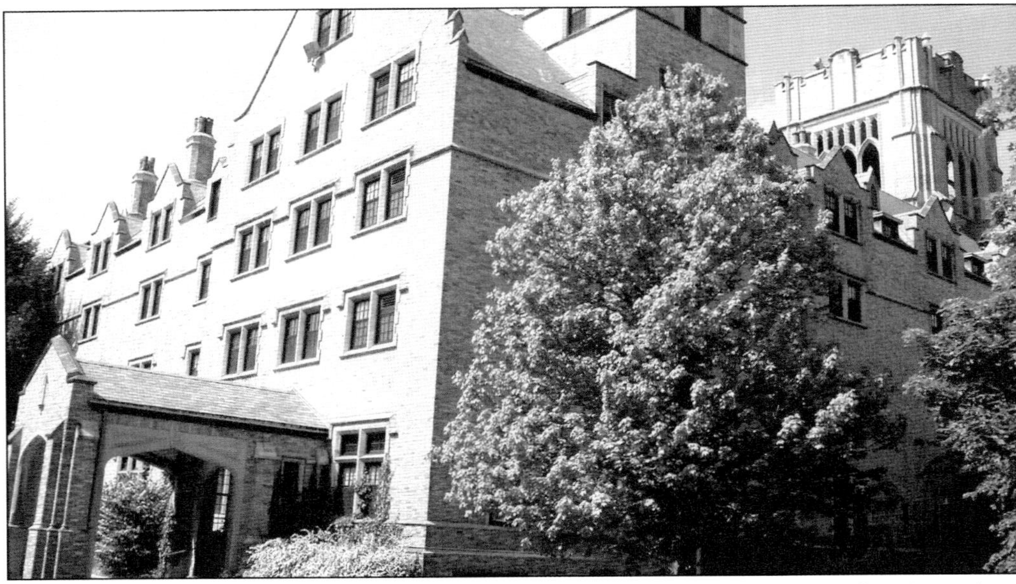

The boys across the "Dixie" have dubbed our school "the Rock." Some of us here don't exactly know the origin of the term. However, we have always had a vague notion that it was originally a sly joke aimed at our disciplinary regulations and undergraduate permissions not entirely in harmony with what our "dates" consider educational "freedom."

—Carrie Powers Powell '48, Holy Cross *Courier* 1945

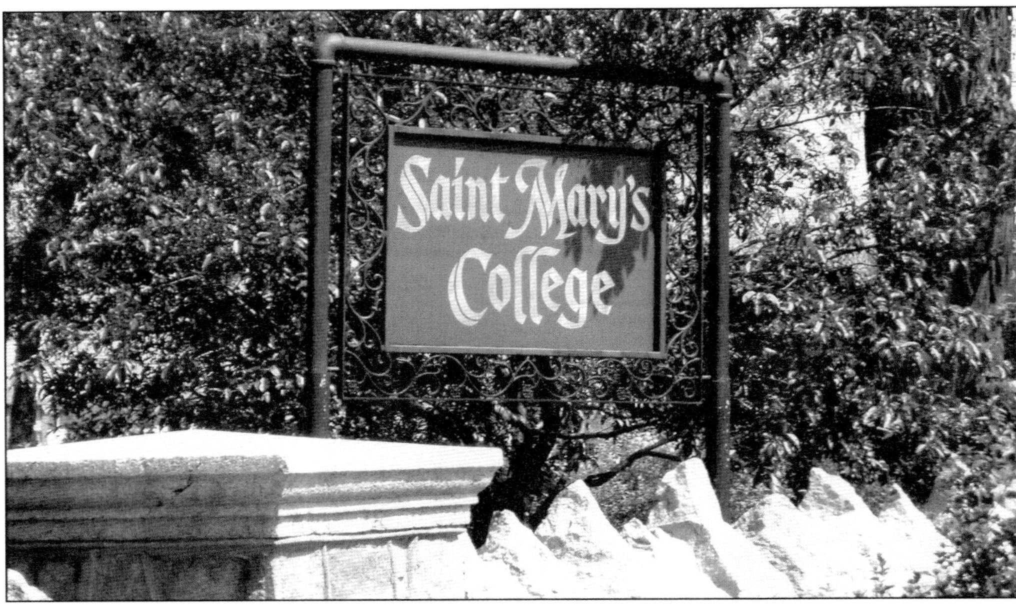

When a Saint Mary's woman had a beau at Notre Dame, they would write each other frequently because telephone use was sharply restricted as was leaving campus during the week. After dinner each evening the girls would walk down The Avenue and leave a letter tucked into the niche between the stones of the stone gate. Each girl had a particular stone. Their beaus would walk over later to pick up the letters and leave one of their own.

—As told to Molly Mannino '65 by her aunt Rita Fitzpatrick '35

Three

THE SAINT MARY'S WAY

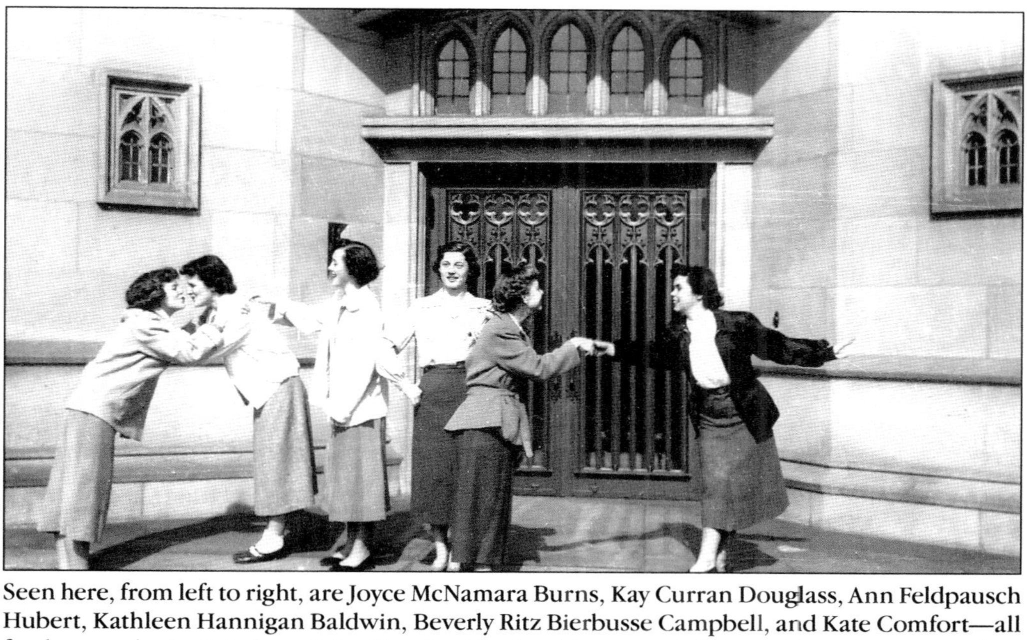

Seen here, from left to right, are Joyce McNamara Burns, Kay Curran Douglass, Ann Feldpausch Hubert, Kathleen Hannigan Baldwin, Beverly Ritz Bierbusse Campbell, and Kate Comfort—all freshman who imitate how Saint Mary's girls should say goodnight and how they wanted to. Ann says "no kissing" as she taps Kay Douglass on the shoulder. Kathleen Baldwin poses as Mother Superior. Beverly and Kate say goodnight the Saint Mary's way.

—Kathleen Douglass '54

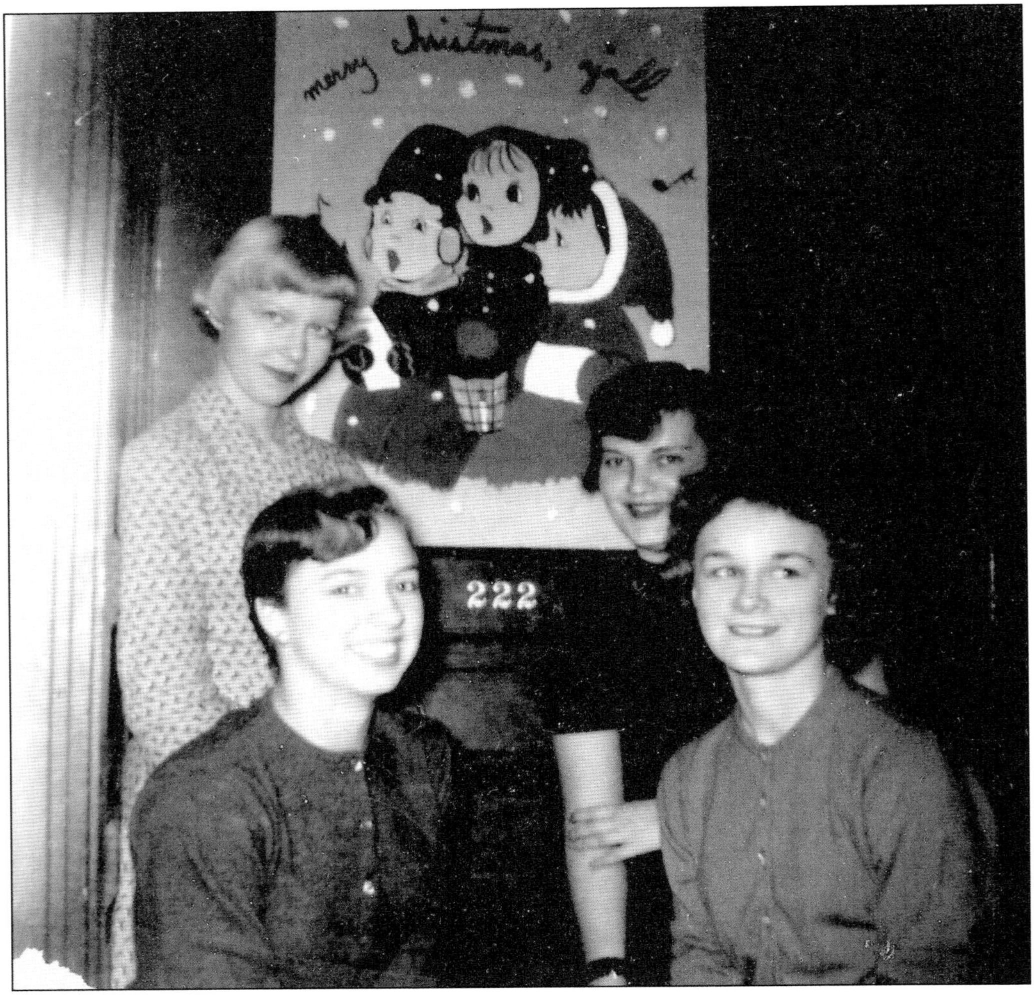

Seen here, from left to right, are the following: (first row) Barbara Benford Trafficanda and Sue Brown Bapst; (second row) Connie Roller Curtin and Mary Carpenter Erler as freshman roommates in a Holy Cross Hall quad, 1955.

This note was left in our room when we arrived as freshman in 1955. These reminders would really put the Saint Mary's students of today in a tizzy! Remove all bottles – take them downstairs. Empty waste baskets daily. Have nothing under beds. Have no Scotch tape on walls, woodwork, or furniture. Have nothing on closet floors. Straighten closet shelves. Make your beds neatly. Draw curtains when dressing or undressing. Never leave clothes lying about if you plan to leave campus, or rooms. Turn off all lights in rooms and baths. Close windows in wet weather or before you leave campus. Straighten and clean drawers. Always keep a scarf on each dresser. A clean blotter on each desk.

—Barbara Benford Trafficanda '59

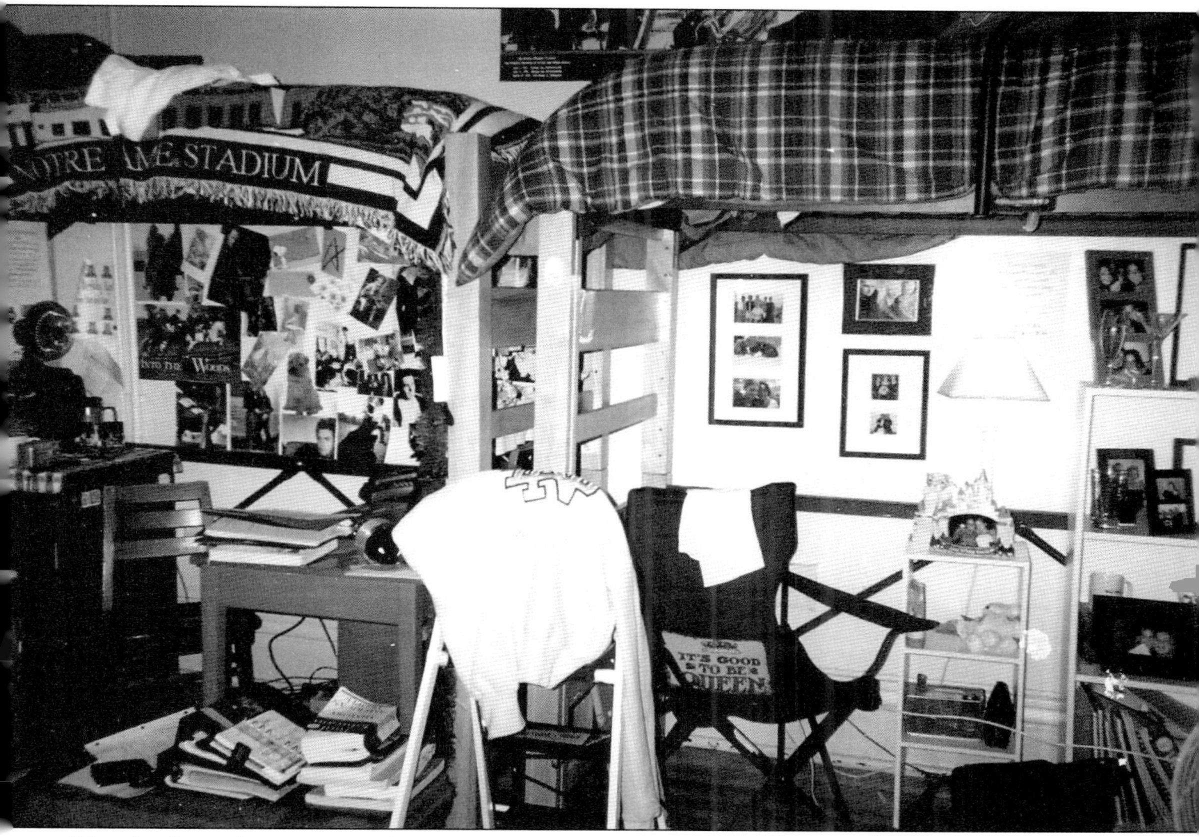

This freshman's room in Holy Cross Hall in 2000 would not have passed room inspections in the 1940s.

1. Have beds carefully made, 2. Have floors clean and furniture dusted, 3. Leave upper ledges of windows clear, 4. Place only small plants on lower sills of windows, 5. Have wardrobe closets in order and leave them open at night for airing, 6. Arrange shoes in rack or holder, 7. Keep lavatories and bath rooms in order, 8. Be careful to place laundered lingerie and hose on hangers only, not on radiators, furniture, or window drapes, 9. Place empty valises in trunk room, 10. Keep bookcases, magazine racks, and room details in order, 11. Hang up all clothing, 12. Keep all food in tin boxes, 13. Empty waste paper baskets. Obviously this freshman's room in Holy Cross Hall in 2000 would not have passed inspection.

—Suggestions on room inspections for students, 1944

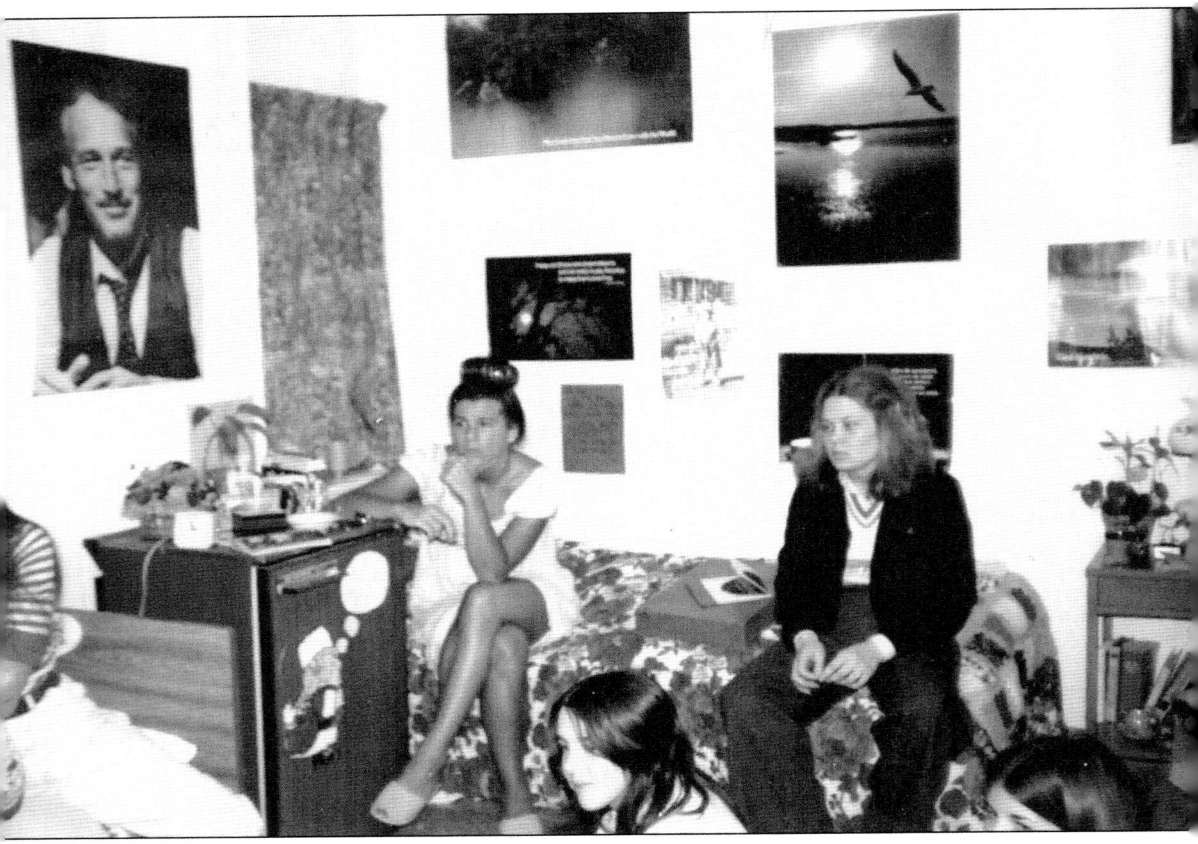

Saint Mary's College believes in "the personal touch." Hence, even room assignments are personalized. And the persons responsible are the deans, Sister Michaela and Sr. Maria Concepta. Here are some notes culled from the files of the deans, illustrating tried and true techniques on how to get your room assignment changed and/or cancelled.

Salutations should be warm and pleasant, but no sugary; keep it simple. Suggested: "My dear Sister,"

The body of letter should include effective themes. 1) The "I have health reasons" theme. Suggested: "My sinus condition will not allow me to remain on the East Wing in Le Mans due to the breezes off of Lake Marion." 2) The Veiled Threat. Suggested: "Since my father is the president of..." 3) The "Pull Rank" Theme. Suggested: "But Sister, isn't it Saint Mary's tradition to put seniors in..."

The complimentary close should be pleasant, but firm. Suggested: "Trusting in your unfailing ability, I remain, Hopefully yours," If your letter writing fails to produce the desired results, you can resort to the long distance phone call. Do not, however, call collect, as this immediately alienates the dean.

—*St. Mary's Static*, September 1960

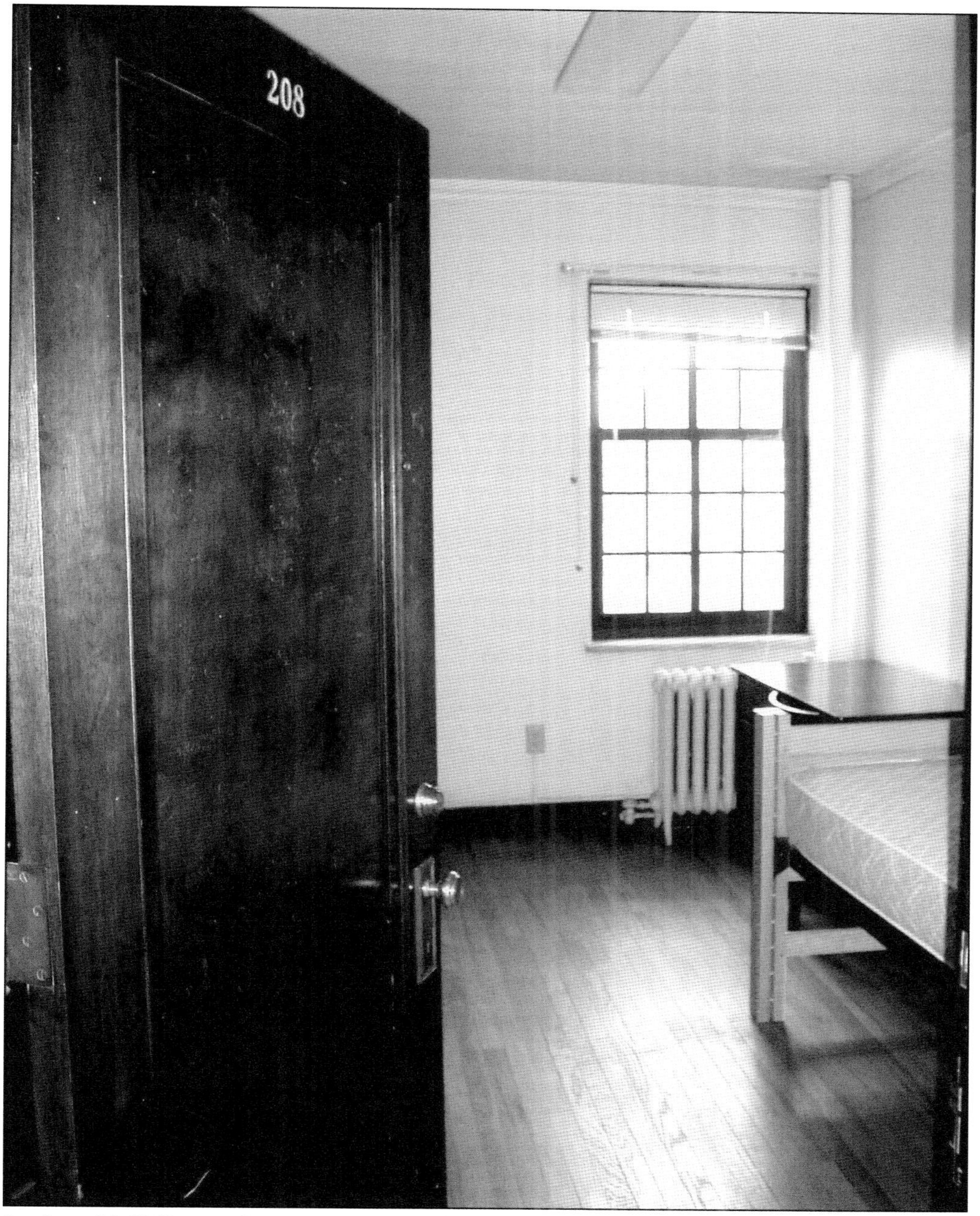

In the mid-1940s, students were required to observe certain rules as soon as they moved into their rooms. Nails, paste, and tacks were not to be used on walls, wood work, or furniture. All damages were charged to the student. Pictures had to be suspended from the molding. House draperies could not be replaced by others. Windows had to be closed when the student left campus. Seven lights, not to exceed 40 watts, could be used in single rooms; nine lights could be used in double rooms. Male visitors (friends and relatives) were not allowed in the private rooms, except at the opening and closing of school when permission was granted to fathers and brothers who carried baggage and furniture.

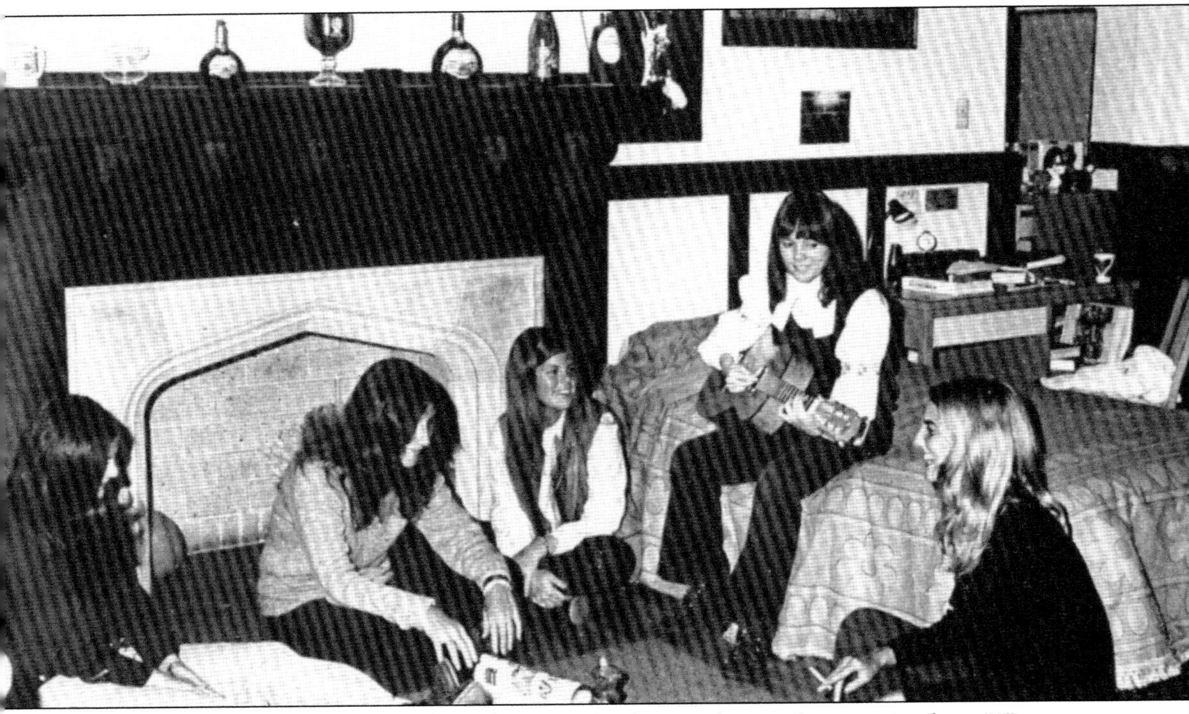

Carolyn and I were some of the few people that we knew that received an "A" on room check. We were pretty proud of that. Room check was random, weekly room examination for neatness by Mrs. Randall. Of course no one locked their doors then. It just wasn't done. So everyone knocked and simply walked in.

We also have a great housekeeping gal, Virginia, who brought us sheets once a week and dusted our rooms, so I guess having a neat room wasn't too difficult. She would also keep the hall floors cleaned of dust and our large communal bathroom clean. Once, someone taped a pair of stuffed knee socks in shoes to the toilet seat in one stall. Then they locked the door and crawled out. It sure looked like the stall was "taken", but we wondered who had such skinny legs. After a day or so Virginia figured it out and opened the door. A goldfish was swimming in the bowl!

—Sheila Kelly Ames '65

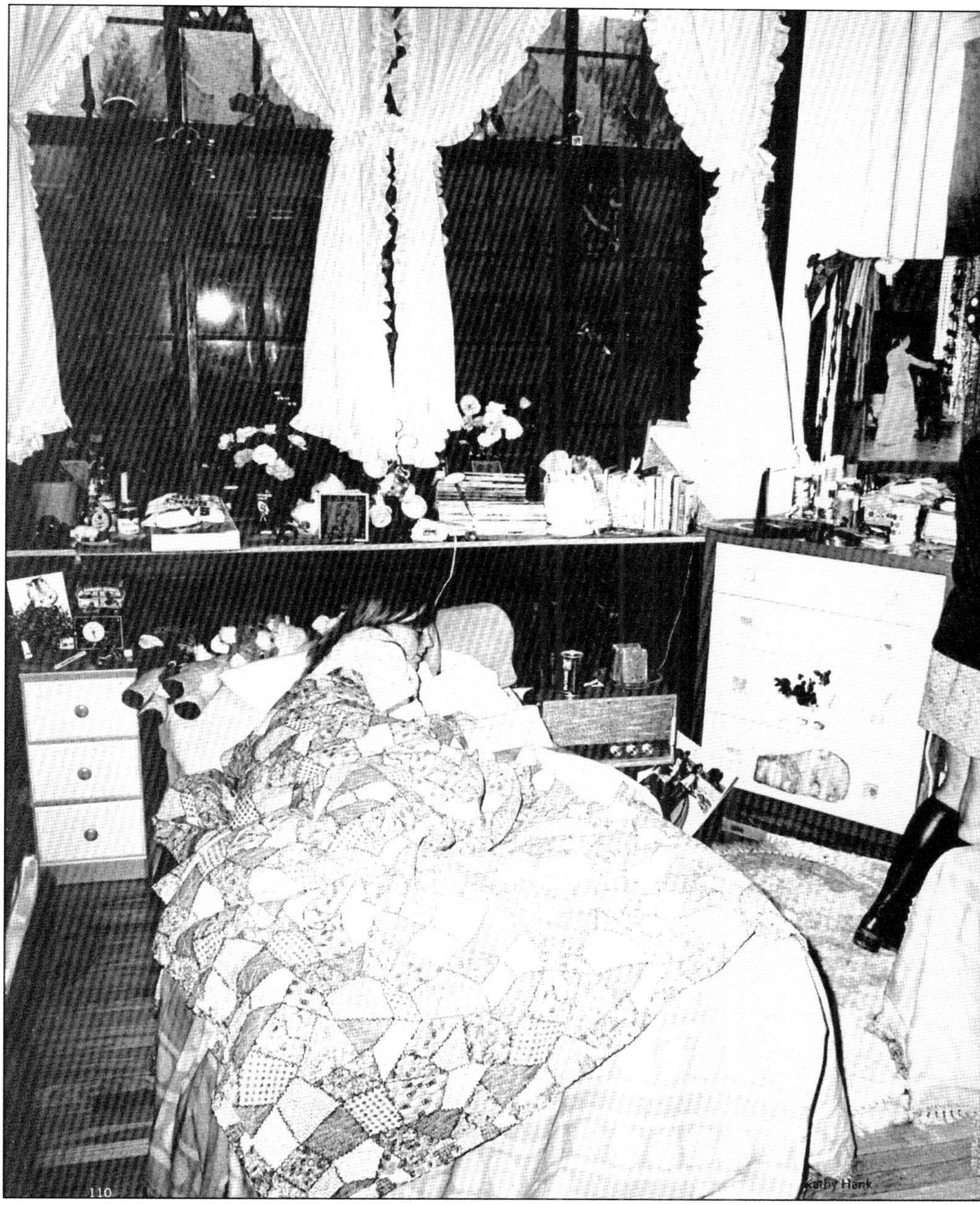

I do remember that we had to be in our rooms at certain time and the lights out. That was wonderful because it kept Mary L. out of our room. One day Joanne and I moved all of the furniture out of Marci Murdock's room and Mary's room and hid it in the ironing board closet.

Remember when Joanne Bonk and I put the notes on the door to the first floor Holy Cross hall telling the nuns not to step on the white squares because they were just painted. Then we stood by the door peeking out from behind the blinds and watching the postulants tip-toe down the hall till they realized they had been had.

—Junie Miller Smith '65

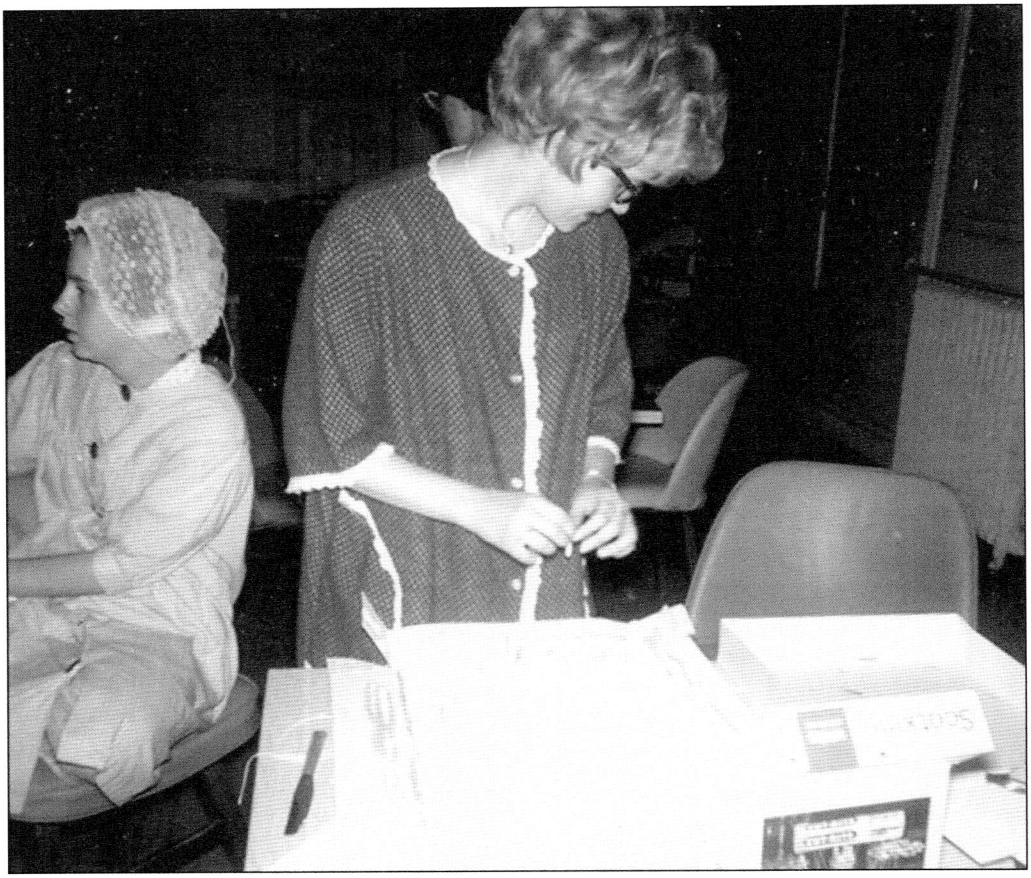

Indiscretion almost got me into trouble at college. Saint Mary's had rules upon rules. The proximity of Notre Dame made the nuns extra careful to protect our innocence. I understand there's much more freedom today, but back in the forties you could be restricted to campus for all sorts of infractions, like talking after lights out. I resented the short leash, and for that reason alone, had little compunction about what I did.

It started out innocently enough. It was Friday night, and I wanted to see Saturday's menu posted on the kitchen wall. If they were having French toast, it was worth getting up for breakfast. If it was just Cheerios, forget it. Problem: the kitchen was off-limits to students (one more rule.) Flashlight in hand, I made my way through the unfamiliar area behind the darkened dining hall. Where was the menu? Forget the menu. Something eminently more interesting caught my eye. Brownies. A whole tray of brownies. A serendipitous surprise, just sitting there saying "Eat me!"

What moved the caper from merely foolish to potentially dangerous was the unexpected appearance of the kitchen manager. I heard her lumbering through the pantry, calling: "Who's there?" What to do? I couldn't eat them all on the run, and I sure wasn't going to throw them away. So I bolted out another door, evidence in hand, hoping she wouldn't recognize me. Glory be to God if she didn't make chase. Fortunately she was older (a lot) and heavier (a lot.) She made it up two flights of stairs, but I made it up three.

Funny thing, I can't remember whether the brownies were that good. But I'll never forget the sound of Mrs. McEcheran, pounding after a scared, homesick teenager who just couldn't resist some comfort food.

—Emily Bott, student 1940–1941

Marshall Field & Company

Official Outfitters

ST. MARY'S COLLEGE 1944-1945

Notre Dame, Indiana ***Holy Cross post office***

1 black wool suit with cardigan jacket. Sizes 10 to 16.................... $27.50
White sport shirts. Each.............. 2.15
1 two-piece white cotton broadcloth dress 8.00
4 two-piece cotton dresses same style as white one but in colors. Peach, light blue, aqua, light yellow. (These are not available at Marshall Field & Company. Suggest purchase of material and dress-making at home.)
1 gym suit.*
Beige hose.
Black or brown sport shoes to wear with suit.

For your convenience in delivery before school opening, we suggest that orders be placed by July 20. When you come in, please ask for Miss McHugh.

High School Shop—Fourth Floor, North, Wabash

On purchases to be delivered in Illinois, 2% should be added to quoted prices of all merchandise to cover additional expense due to the Illinois Retailers' Occupation Tax.

The prices of articles offered herein do not exceed maximum prices as determined under Office of Price Administration regulations. As required by that Office, we will inform you upon request of our maximum prices for any of the articles listed.

* Price will be given later.

When my acceptance letter came announcing my membership into the freshman class of 1953, along with it was a brochure to order uniforms. At first though, the charcoal grey suit and white blouse seemed a bit ridiculous to me as I had graduated from a public high school. The attire for warmer weather was "golfers." These were dresses buttoned down the front and buttoned on the sleeves. They received this nickname because there was room on the arm sleeves to swing a golf club. They came in pastel colors and white. The white "golfer" was to be worn only on special occasions such as parades to the Church with Sodality or whenever there was an event the Sisters deemed important enough for white. But woe unto you if you wore the white one for just class.

Uniforms were to be worn during the week in the classroom. You had to "dress" for dinner and it was unacceptable to wear a uniform at dinner. Stockings were also required. At this point in time, knee highs were our answer to stockings. I remember Sister Sophia said that if you wore knee highs, you should never cross your legs. She looked down at the front row with girls from my class and told us how awful it looked to her to see our knee highs with crossed legs.

—Jean Giddens Cass '57

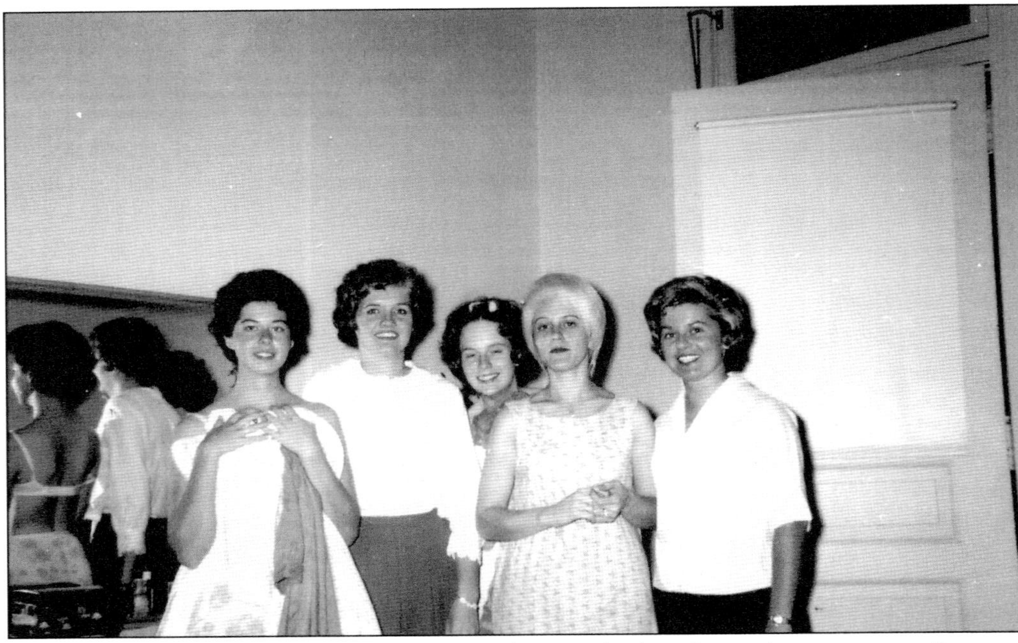

We had what I would call bloomers for gym class. We had to change in our rooms of course. We wore a rain coat as we walked across the campus to the field. The purpose of the raincoat was to hide the bloomers and our bare legs so we wouldn't embarrass the nuns.

—Jean Giddens Cass '57

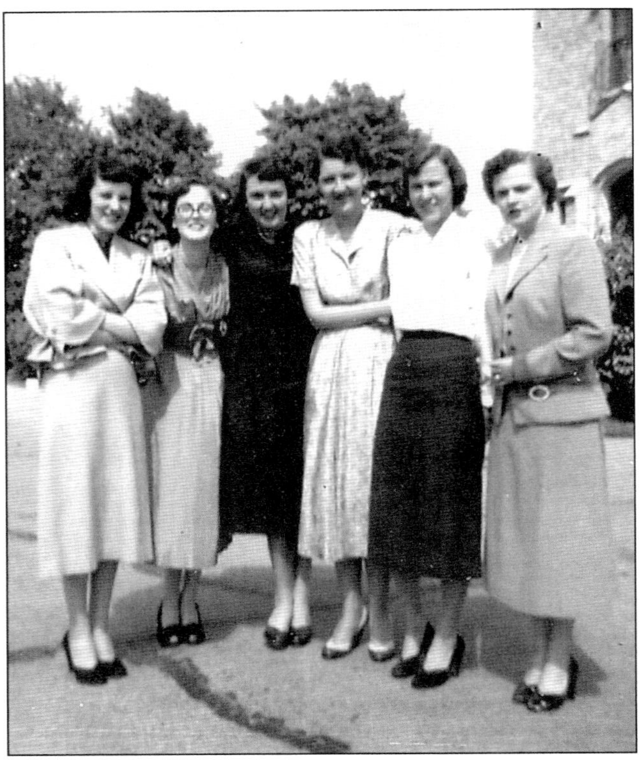

On the one occasion I tried wearing slacks, I took a short cut across the great hall. Who should enter it? Sister Madeleva! SMC was so small that all but the library was connected by steam tunnels. Having never seen snow falling until college (I felt like I was inside a Snow globe for months) I was a tunnel rat.

—Sandy Barlett '61

We were not encouraged to spend time outside our rooms wearing jeans or shorts so instead we stayed dressed in the clothes we wore to Sunday Mass. It was not a special occasion but just a typical Sunday. In the spring of 1953 we relax on a Sunday morning on the quad in front of Le Mans.

—Joan Sharpe Burke '53

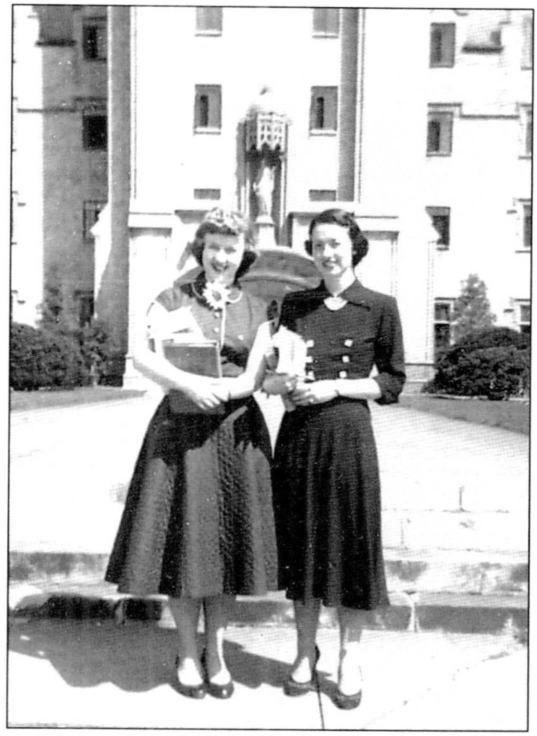

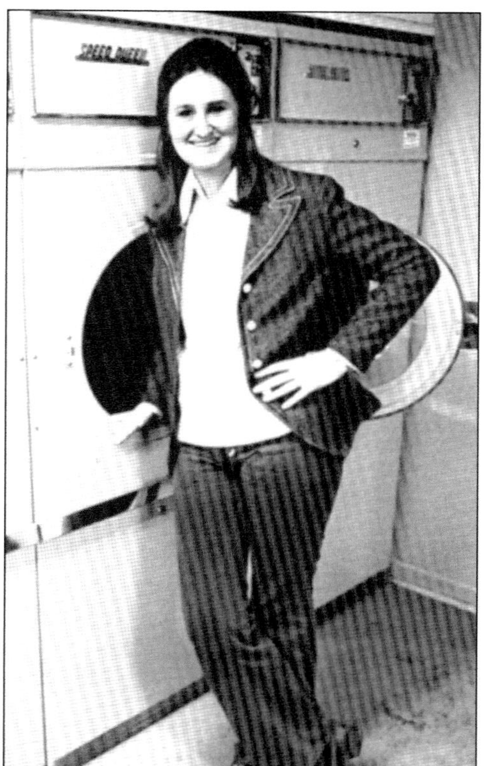

Laundry may be sent home by express or parcel post in regular laundry kit, or it may be sent to Slicks Ideal Laundry in South Bend where a special rate is given to our students. There is a laundryette in the basement for the convenience of those who may wish to do some pieces themselves.

—Carrie Powers Powell's scrapbook, General Regulations, 1944

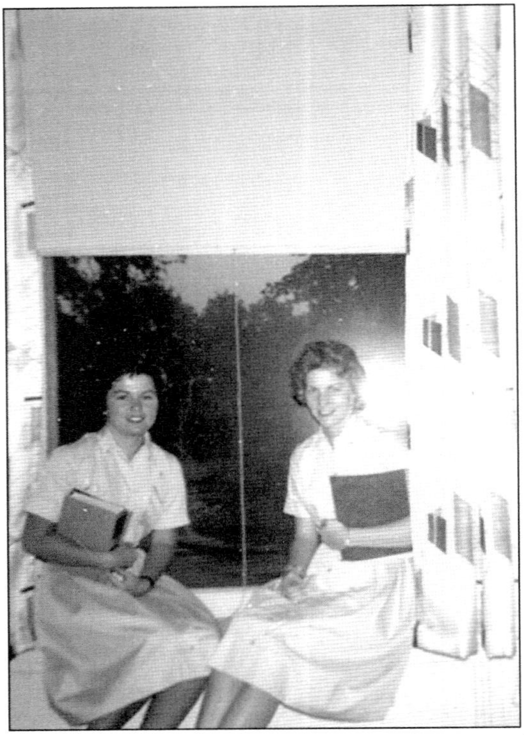

I graduated in 1961, the last days of Sister Madeleva. Rules were very strict. 5:30 and 8:30 PM curfews, signing in and out at the front desk, lights out at 10:30; however, ND shut off electricity to rooms so no possibility of hiding in closets like we did. Uniforms, fruit must be cut with knife and fork, one phone for each large section of a floor, and no slacks unless going sledding.

—Sandy Bartlett '61

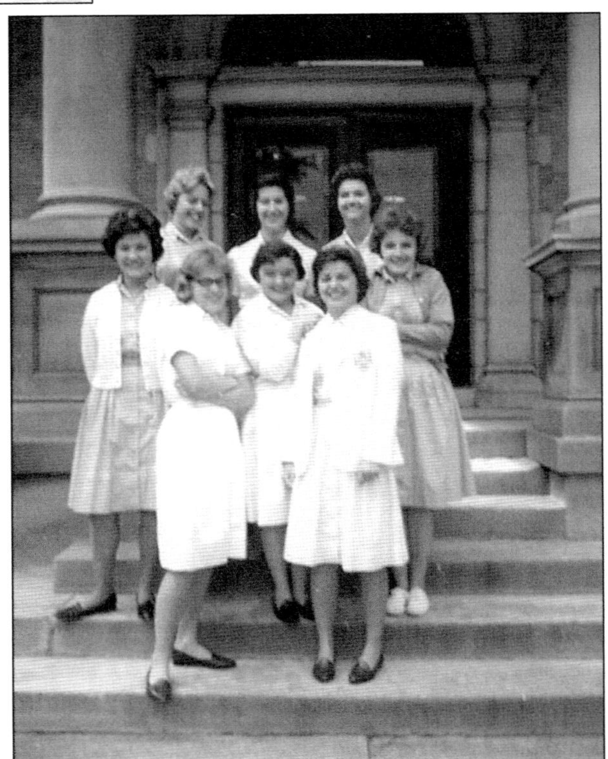

Freshman and sophomore years, we wore uniforms. In the spring and fall we wore pastel shirtwaists, and in the winter we had grey wool pleated skirts and navy blue blazers. The student body voted them out for the 1963 school year. I kind of liked them—it made life very easy!

Pictured here, from left to right, are the following: (first row) Sheila Flynn Boone, Pattie Massalotti, Pat Devine McCarthy; (second row) Sheila Kelly Ames, Janice Batkiewicz Kraniak, E.J. Caluwaert McFadden, Carolyn Fleming Shinnick, Kay Denig Fleming, in our uniforms on the steps of Holy Cross in 1962.

—Sheila Flynn Boone '65

From 8:30 p.m. to 9:45 p.m. every evening is a period of quiet and study. Each student must be in her room. If anyone works in the library till 9 p.m., she gives the reason for her absence to the Student Council supervisor of her floor as soon as she returns. The bell at 9:45 p.m. is to prepare for bed-time; subdued recreation may be had. The bell at 10:15 p.m. is for quiet, lights out, and so to bed.

Be sure to set your alarm or have someone call you for morning Sacrifice of the Mass at 6:45 a.m. It's not obligatory but the best "Saint Mary's way."

—Student council bulletin, mid-1940s

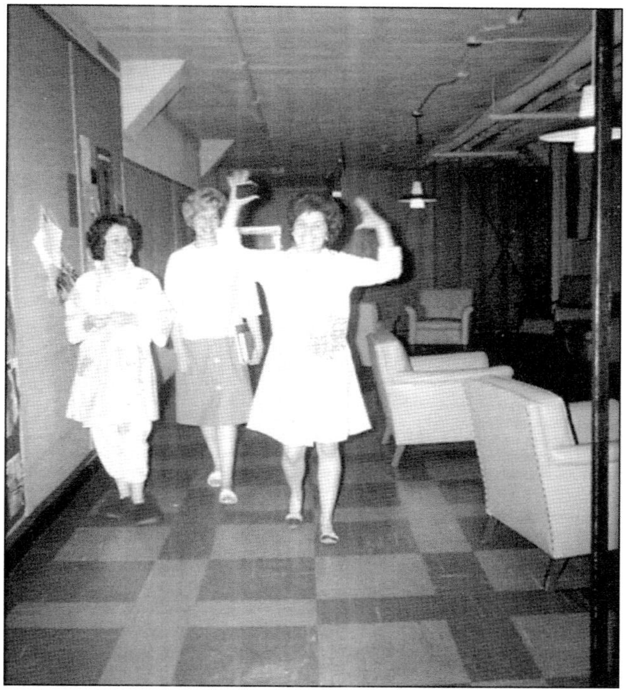

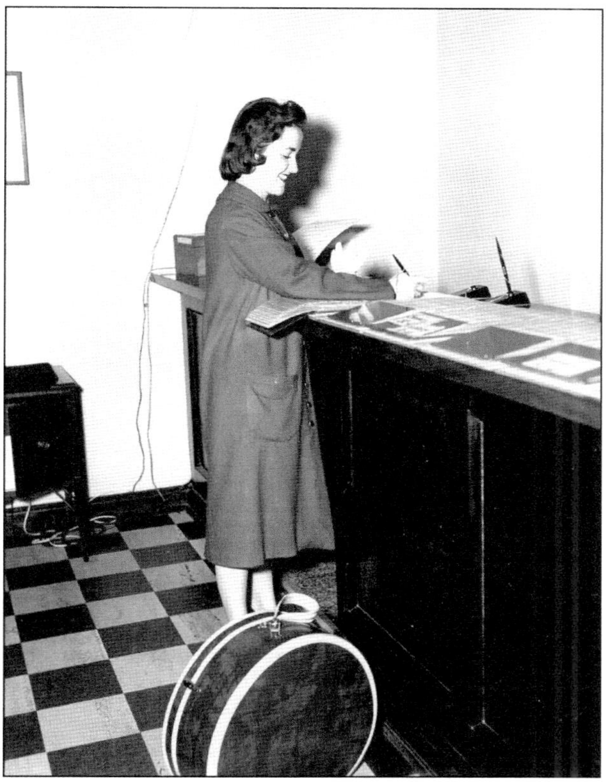

We needed to sign out in the Dean of Students' Office whenever we left campus. After an evening date we signed back in the east parlor. The catcher was that the nuns used the room south of "our" room as a social area. No one ever knew when a nun would walk through our parlor to their room. In those days everyone was polite and stood when a nun entered the room. It was hilarious at times.

Sr. Sophia was our dean, was as tall, if not taller than Sr. Rebecca. Sr. Sophia and a student would stand behind a sign in table and on the wall behind them hung a huge painting of Salome holding the bleeding head of St. John. We tried not to avert our eyes up behind Sr. Sophia.

—Nancy Brozovich Lucey '57

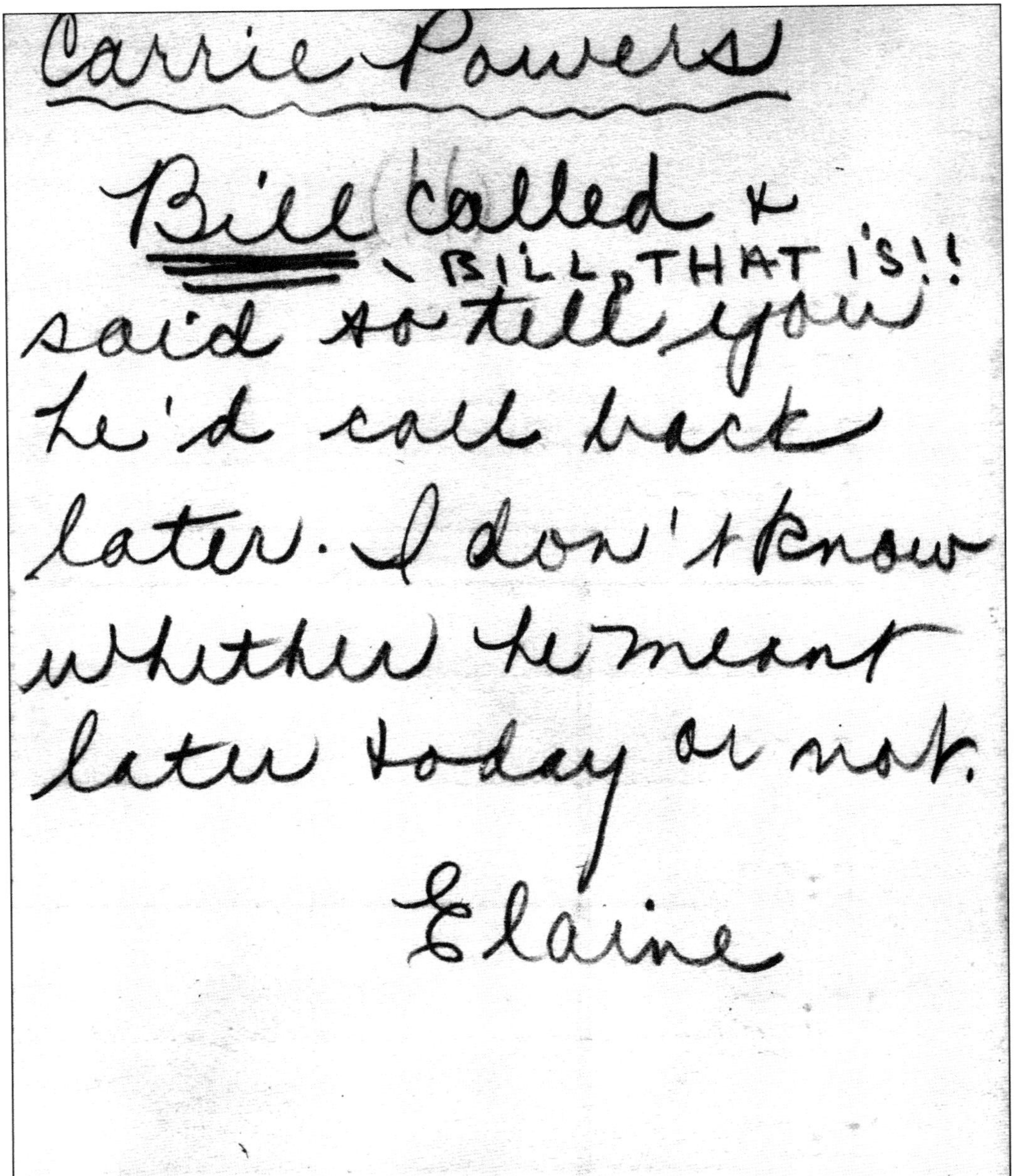
Carrie Powers

Bill called &
BILL, THAT IS!!
said to tell you he'd call back later. I don't know whether he meant later today or not.

Elaine

In Le Mans Hall there are three phones for receiving calls in the P.O. lobby. The phones on the second, third, and fourth floors of Le Mans Hall are for outgoing calls only. You may be in the habit of giving your phone number. If so, be certain that you give the numbers of the first floor phones only. Residents of Holy Cross Hall will use the phones on the third and fourth floors; arrange to receive your calls there before 8:30p.m. These phones are for use of Holy Cross residents only.

Remember also that there are only eight phones for almost five hundred of us. Your good common sense will tell you that phone chats must be brief. Three minutes will do for short distance as well as for long.

—Student council bulletin, 1944

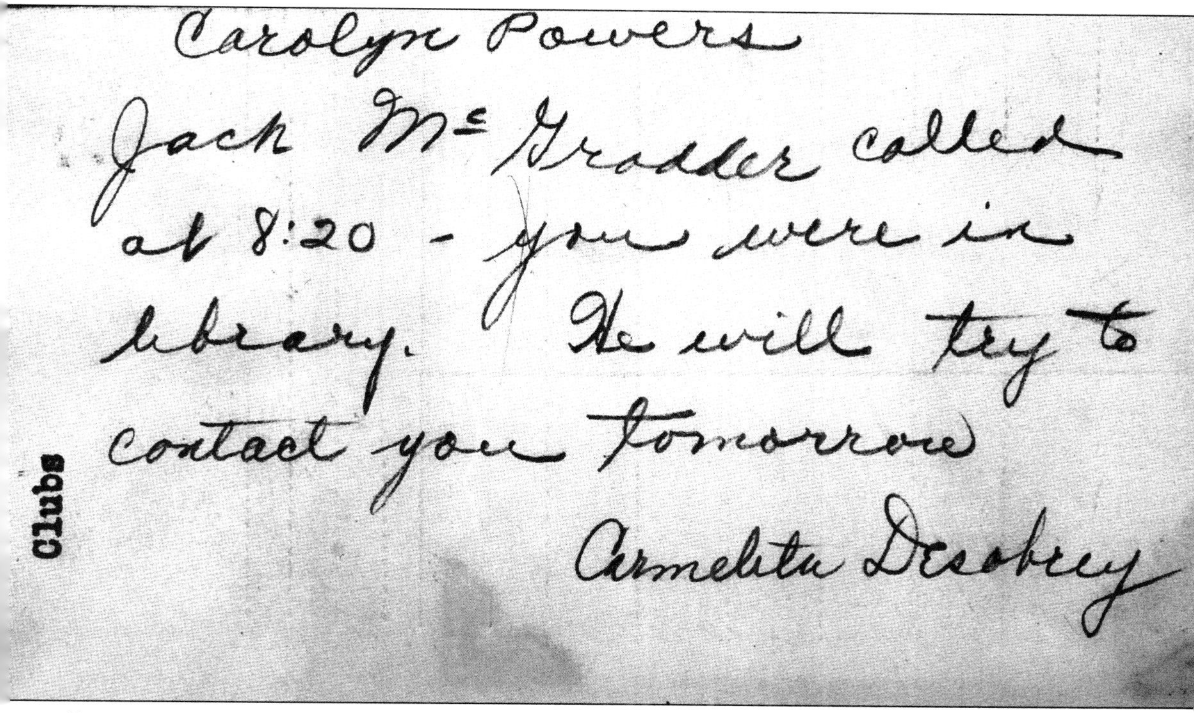

Carolyn Powers

Jack Mc Gradder called at 8:20 - you were in library. He will try to contact you tomorrow

Carmelita Desobry

Be courteous in answering the phone. If you're unable to find the person asked for, please be so kind as to write and file in the phone file: the name of the person asked for, the name of the caller, the time of the call, the message, and your name. When you hear the house phone ring, don't take the "Ring, telephone, ring" attitude. It may mean a call for you. Even if it doesn't you should be courteous enough to answer. Ask the girl's room number then walk, don't run, and tell her; don't yell at her, that she has a phone call. Such yelling forfeits the privilege of house phones.

All telephone calls are to be taken care of before 8:30p.m. Only with special permission from the Dean may you call after that time. You may receive necessary long distance calls after 8:30p.m. House phones are not used during class hours. Report to the Dean of Women long distance calls during class hours. She will relay them.

–Carrie Powers Powell's scrapbook, student council bulletin, 1944

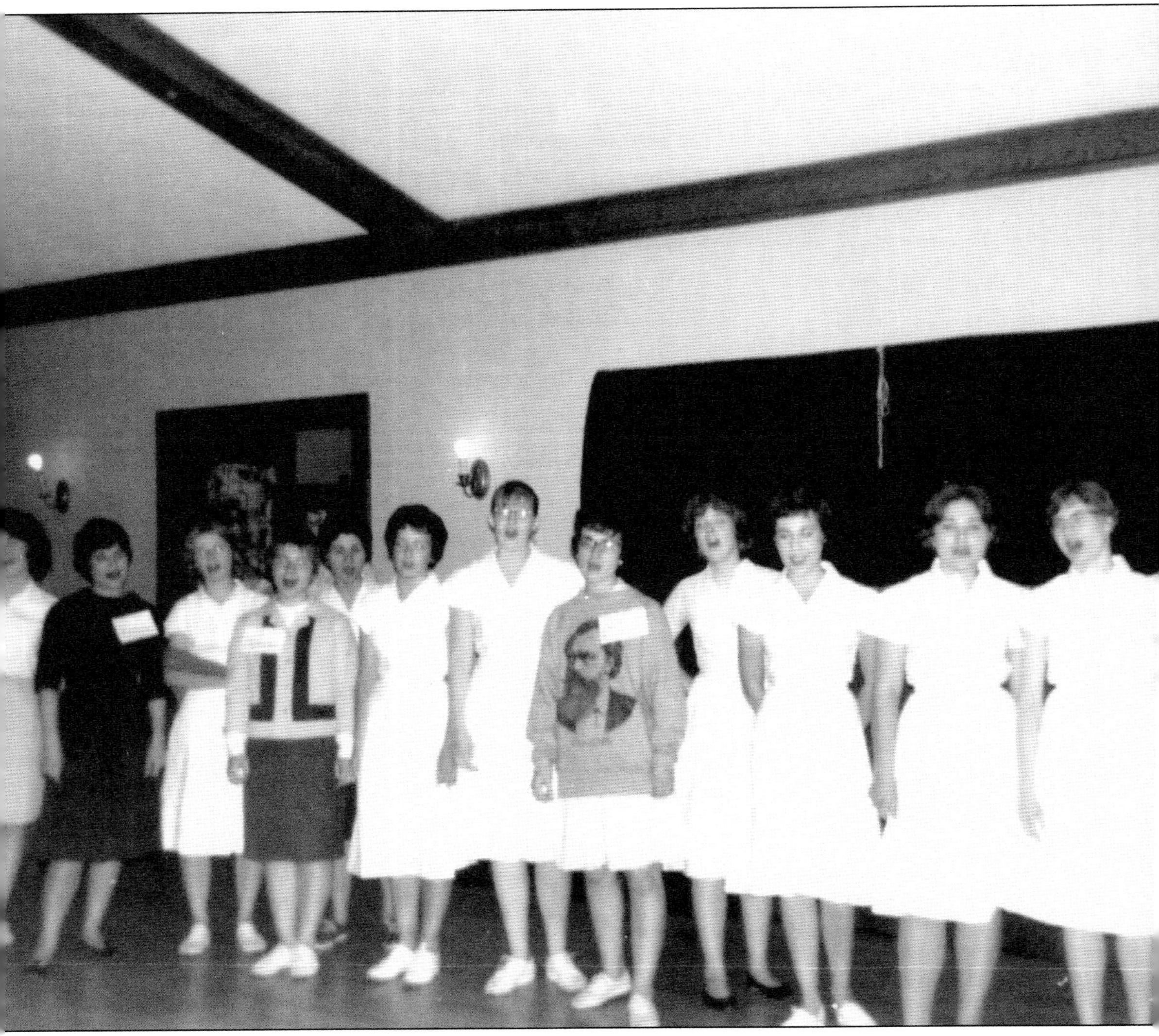

Your service is a privilege and an opportunity for professional training. To fulfill your contract, you have these responsibilities: 1. Punctuality. Know your service schedule. Report promptly; leave only at the close of your assigned period. 2. Efficiency. Perform your duties as directed and perfectly as possible. Your contract calls for fourteen hours of work weekly as scheduled by your director. Excused absence must be made up hour for hour. Unexcused absence and tardiness involve forfeiture of your position. 3. Courtesy. Refinement and graciousness are essentials of satisfactory service. Genuine and unfailing courtesy toward your directors, your associates, and all patrons is imperative. 4. Dependability. Keep your word. Word reliably, not as you prefer, but as you are directed. Learn by the daily experience of your job. Develop good judgment and use it. 5. Proper Grooming. Personal cleanliness, taste in dress, conservative use of cosmetics, regard for manicure, hair arrangement, and similar details are all important. Complete uniform is to be worn during the hours when the college group is so attired. Appropriate costume for the day and hour is required at other times. Chewing gum is absolutely prohibited.

—Bulletin to students in service, 1944

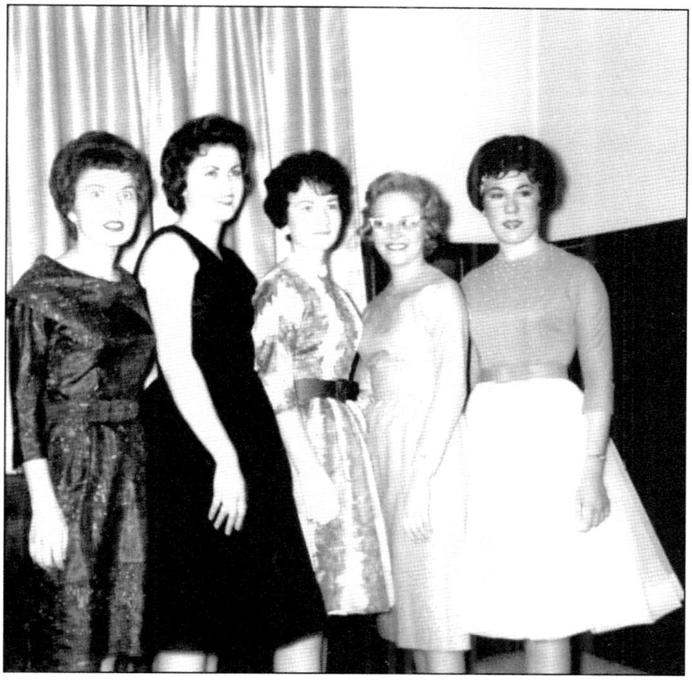

Seen here, from left to right, are Lois Reith, Eileen O'Brien, Ann McMillan, Kathleen Kiefer, Sandra Kudnowski, who were able to forget about staff student responsibilities for a few hours and dress up for the Notre Dame Charity Ball on January 6, 1962.

When I arrived (by Greyhound bus from Atlanta) at Saint Mary's in September of 1961, I was a staff student. Staff students were on full scholarship at Saint Mary's. Our education was free—as long as we worked 26 to 30 hours per week in the Le Mans dining room. We worked for Saga Food Service. We had fewer vacations days than the other SMC students. We all lived on the fifth floor in Le Mans, and we usually used the back stairs to and from the kitchen. At times we felt like Cinderella, but for a free education at SMC, it was worth trying to balance our classes and work. We all grew very close. We even got $50 per semester for books!

Meals were served family-style in the dining room. Staff students rolled out carts with serving platters to be passed around the long tables. It was important to serve the nuns properly and also Miss Marion McCandless. We also cleaned up those tables after the meals. We often sang as we wiped, particularly attacking the blueberry pie globs. We wore white uniforms which were, thankfully, supplied by a laundry service. Staff girls who had class conflicts would work in the Oriole, the snack bar in the basement of Le Mans.

In 1964, I worked summer school. When the alumnae came for reunion in 1964, I realized that they could have alcohol in Le Mans in student rooms for the occasion! Even at age 19, I could see how much the alumnae enjoyed being together again. Sadly, that summer, Sister Madeleva passed away. It was a great loss to Saint Mary's.

Due to our work schedules, most of us staff girls needed 9 semesters to graduate. I am listed in the class of 1965, but I finished in January, 1966.

In 1965, a new dining hall was opened at Saint Mary's. Food was served cafeteria-style. The students could choose what they wanted to eat. No more family-style service gave the students more freedom to eat when they wanted. This convenience foretold the end of the labor-intensive staff student program. In 1965, we scarcely realized how very expensive our education was at Saint Mary's.

—Eileen Fitzgerald Harris '65

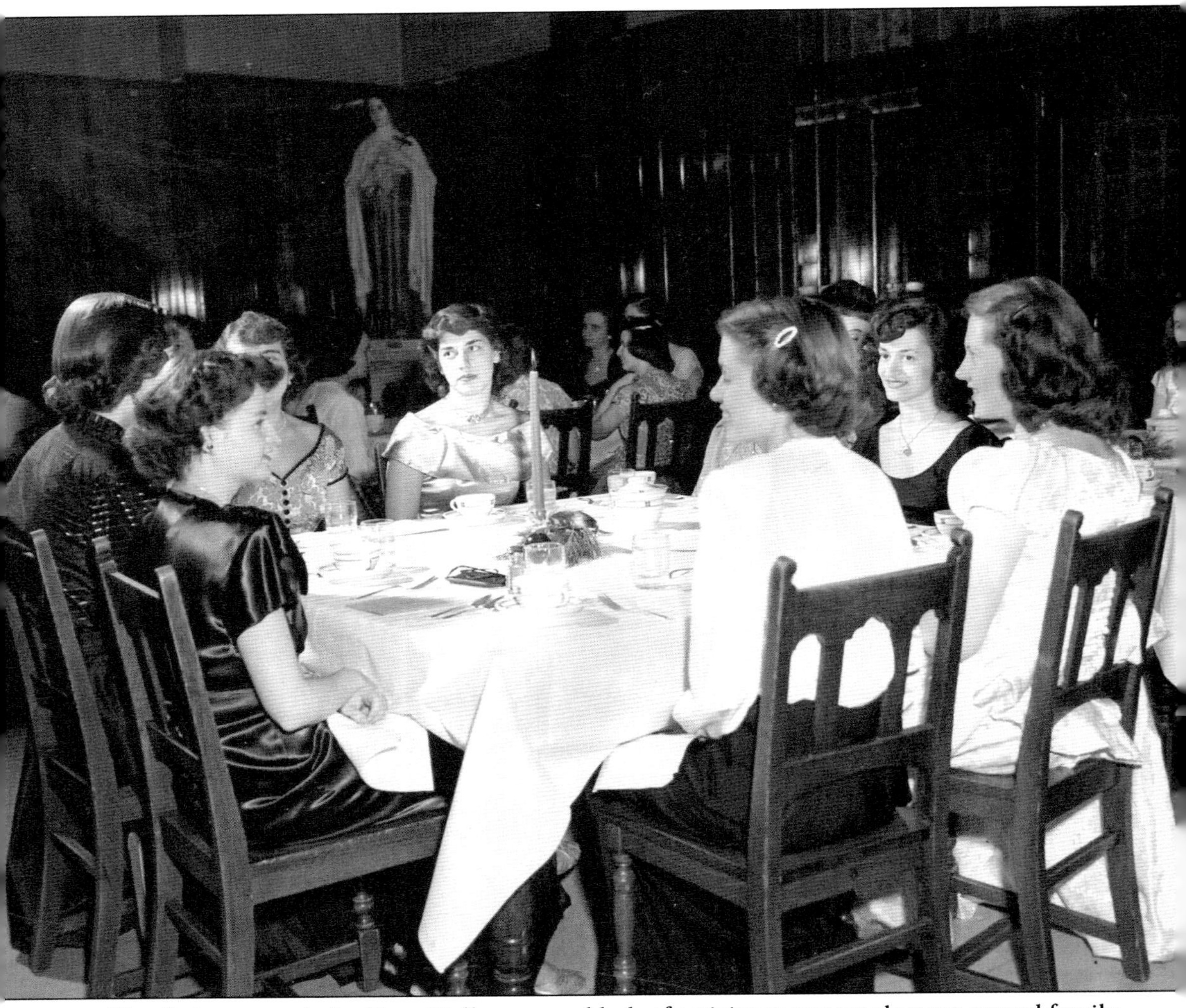

The dining room in Le Mans Hall was a real hub of activity as our meals were served family style to us. During the week you could sit wherever you wanted to for breakfast. If you sat near the end, you would probably pour the coffee. If you sat to the left of the head, you were the last to be served and we termed that seat, "starvation corner."

Table assignments were made about every four weeks. All of the class years were included so you could get to know the girls in different years. A nun or lay professor sat at the head and we would file in. Before lunch we recited the Angelus together. Sister Madeleva sat at the head table of the dining room. Students were able to sit with her their senior year. There was a French table where we spoke only French. Many of us would wait before we filed in to make sure we would not sit right next to our professor. On weekends we sat anywhere we wanted. If we planned to go elsewhere besides the dining room on Saturday or Sunday, we signed out for dinner. From time to time we ordered out for pizza.

During Lent we listened to religious readings and maintained silence. Every evening when Sister Madeleva was in the dining room, she led out and we followed and formed a circle as we all prayed the rosary. This was not mandatory, but many did join in.

—Jean Giddens Cass '57

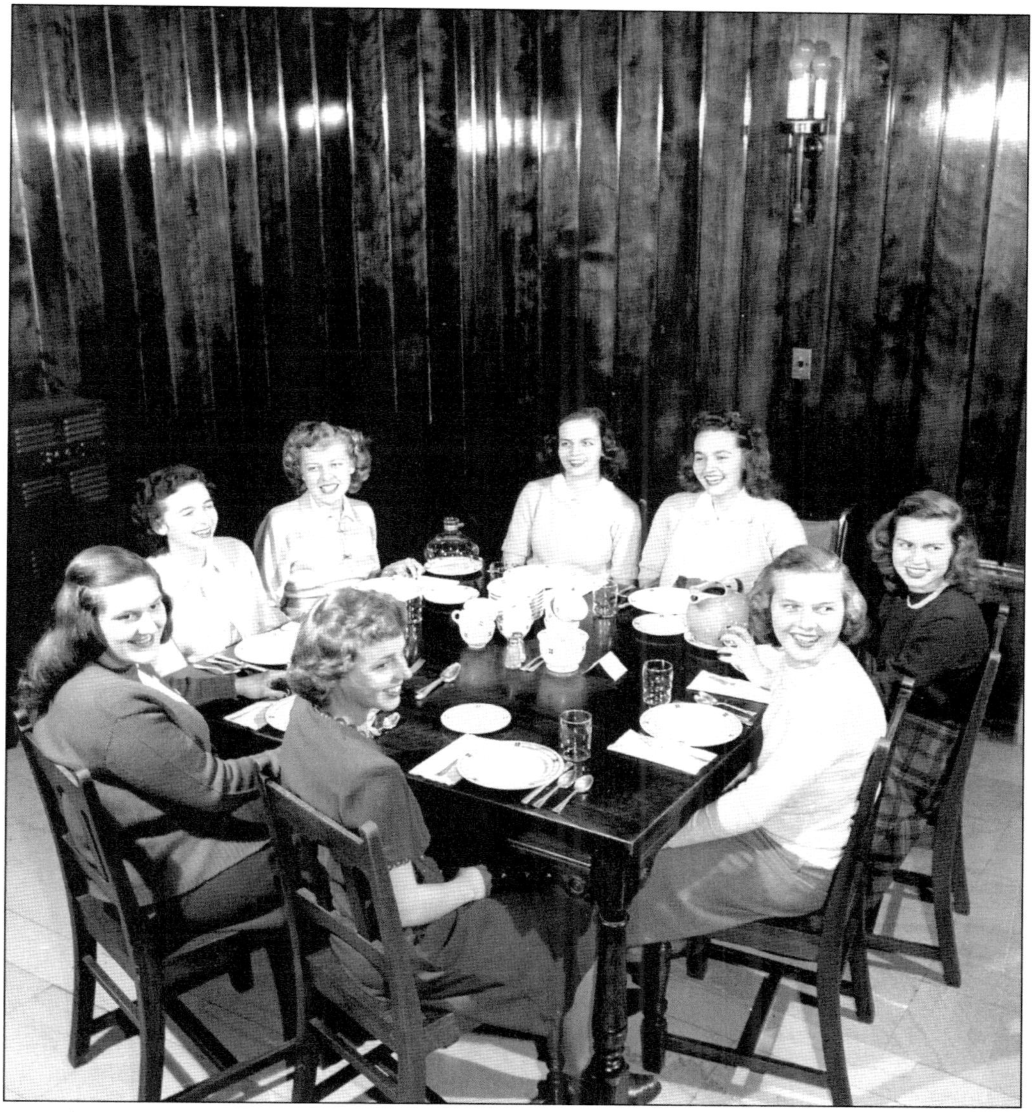

A student council bulletin in the mid-1940s stated that Saint Mary's students were expected to be present at meals unless they were out or excused by the Dean of Women. As a matter of courtesy, they were expected to be punctual. Students were assigned to a table. Everyone stood at her place until grace was said. The Angelus, recited before grace, was offered for world needs, men in service, and peace. The Sister or student at the head of the table acted as hostess. She looked after what you wanted as she replenished your dish. No girl sat in her place in her absence. The girl at the right of the hostess' position substituted from her own place.

The first bell after meals is for silence. Remain seated. At the second signal, rise silently for grace. At breakfast and luncheon, leave by table groups only, not one by one. After dinner, member of the Faculty leave the dining hall first; then upper classmen leave. Freshmen remain at their tables until the sophomores have all left their places. It is juvenile, to say the least, to carry food from the dining hall. You are welcome to stay longer than the others if you wish, but finish your meal at the table.

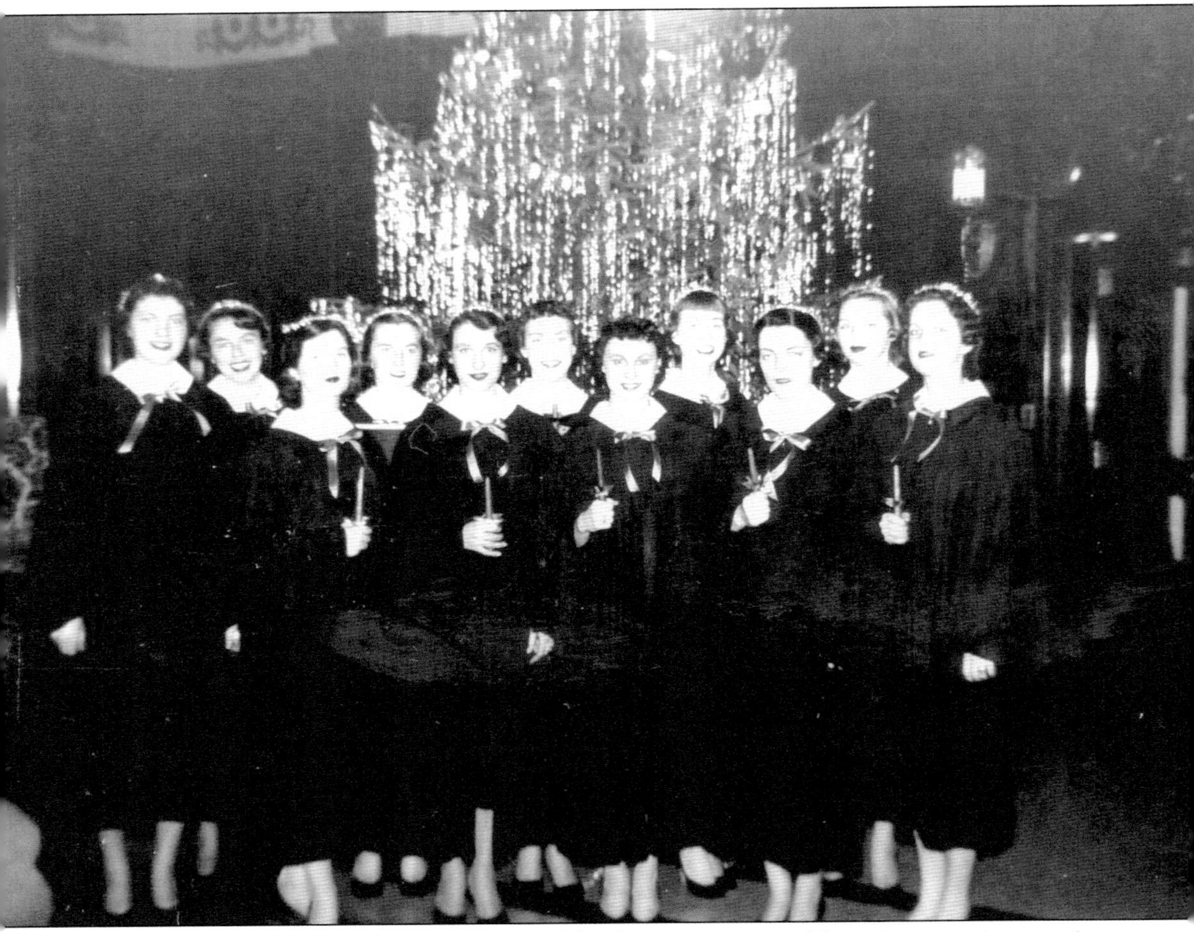

We were called 'staffers' and resided on fifth floor Le Mans and fourth annex. Accepted to a scholarship program that involved full time work through the food service, we could easily be recognized on campus, as we often wore our white uniforms while running between dining hall and class. I'm very proud of my Saint Mary's degree (1966) and the lasting friendships forged there.

When I arrived, Marion McCandless, Alumnae Association founder, lived in Le Mans. Sr. Madeleva was still in residence. My sister, Lillian, was in the novitiate nearby, though by convent rules, we were not allowed to speak even if we met one another on campus. We were limited to three meetings per year in their austere parlor.

Lunch and dinner were served family style, with the President at head table and each table of students with a hostess. Le Mans dining room was elegant: marble floor, wooden columns, surrounded by windows. Christmas banquet was especially beautiful, with fire in the fireplace, lights dimmed as the juniors (in borrowed graduation robes wearing tinsel or holly wreaths on alternating years) came singing into the room. The same juniors went caroling through all the dorms early the last morning before Christmas vacation, passing all the stuffed animals marching down the middle of the hall toward the chapel, reminiscent of the animals in the stable at Bethlehem.

—Camille Ann Sullivan Yost '66

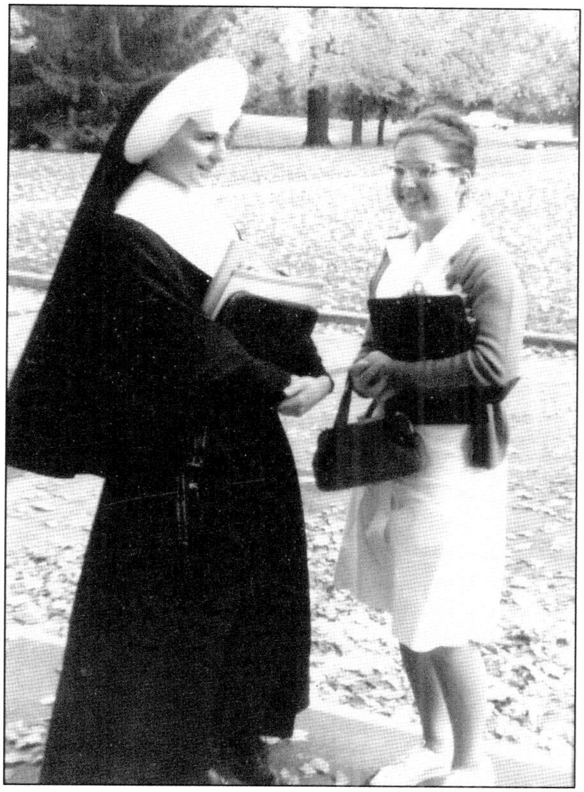

Pictured here are Sr. M. Robert Anita (Lillian Sullivan) and Camille Ann Sullivan.

We staffers had many traditions. One was a long tease for the new freshmen: the first week on campus they were told of the Christmas banquet where they would be required to serve in formals! The fiction was repeated until the last week before the meal. Staffers were known for having great parties in the old Clubhouse, such as Halloween with really crazy costumes just among ourselves, as well as date parties.

Our academic records had to be solid to get accepted to the program, and we earned the respect of our classmates, including some who couldn't quite figure why "the help" was taking classes. When time permitted, we participated in extracurricular activities. I remember working on the Notre Dame mock convention; my roommate traveled to the south for voter registration.

There were about forty in the program at a time; we elected officers among ourselves who arranged work schedules around class schedules. We sang as we worked setup and cleanup; I still recall our unique verses to "My Favorite Things" or "The Boy That I Marry." Everyone was required to report early Saturday mornings for general cleaning: scrubbing sideboards, refilling shakers, polishing silver. We learned to do it VERY fast on home football weekends; I never missed a kickoff. Our dates referred to our gait as "the staff-girl trot" because we were always in a hurry.

My Saint Mary's experience led to fifteen years employment with Saga Food Service. With the exception of 25 year reunion, I hadn't returned to Saint Mary's until recently. I was thrilled when my daughter Liesl chose 'my' college and I've enjoyed seeing her on stage and having her show me 'her' Saint Mary's. It is amusing that she can go to class in pajamas when we weren't 'allowed' below first floor in pants! When Liesl graduates in May, we'll bring a crowd to cheer her continuation of the legacy.

—Camille Ann Sullivan Yost '66

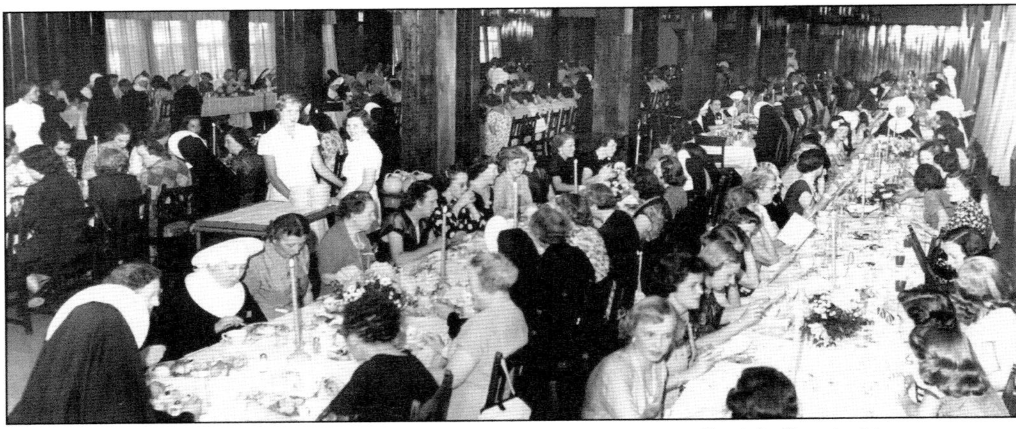

At the college, I was a Staff Student and lived in Le Mans Hall (5th floor). My roommate, Cathy Carter Petzak, was from Idaho. What I remember most, was how loving the sisters were, especially Sister Pieta. She was the Staff Student Advisor.

In 1958–59, the big things I remember are the news about the Second Vatican Council and Sister Madeleva reading poetry at noon (sometimes even reading some "Winnie the Pooh.") Staff Students served in the dining room three times a day, as well as serving receptions for visiting guests and performers. Our class load was about 13 hours. We wore white uniforms while working and were not obligated to wear SMC uniforms. The Staff Student program was phased out sometime in the 80s and the program went through many transformations after I left the college.

—Mary E. Eschelbach, student 1958–1959

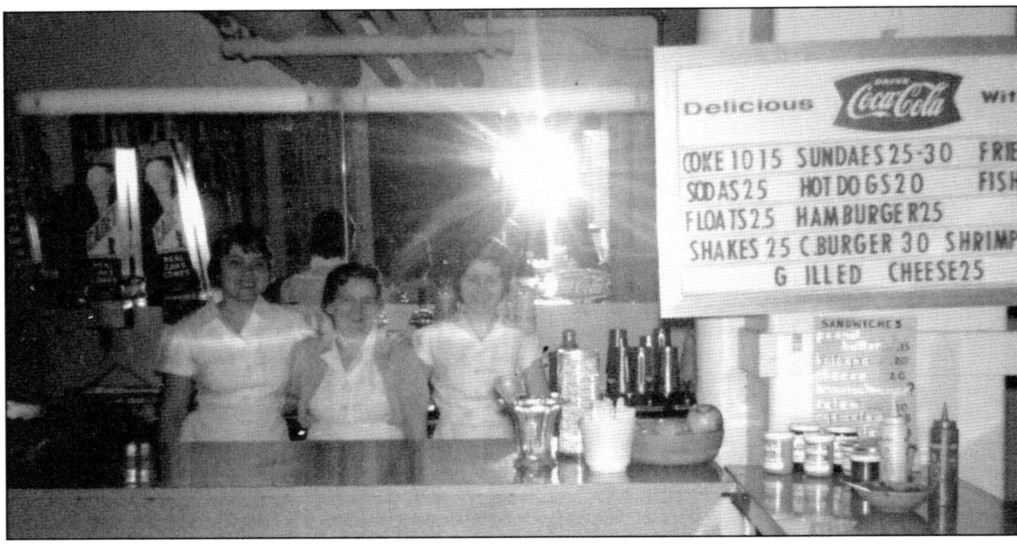

This photograph was taken by Eileen's Fitzgerald's mother in the "Oriole" in February 1964.

Seen here, from left to right, are Eileen Fitzgerald, local worker, Virginia Holdmann. See what cheap prices we had in the "Oriole" snack bar in 1964! I used to make milkshakes with extra ice cream, which made them really thick! I got in trouble with the Saga Food Service boss, Mr. Patrick Finn. He said I used up too much ice cream. Sadly, on November 22, 1963, I was dipping ice cream when word came that President Kennedy was shot. I thought, "No, it can't be true," and kept on dipping strawberry ice cream.

—Eileen Fitzgerald Harris '65

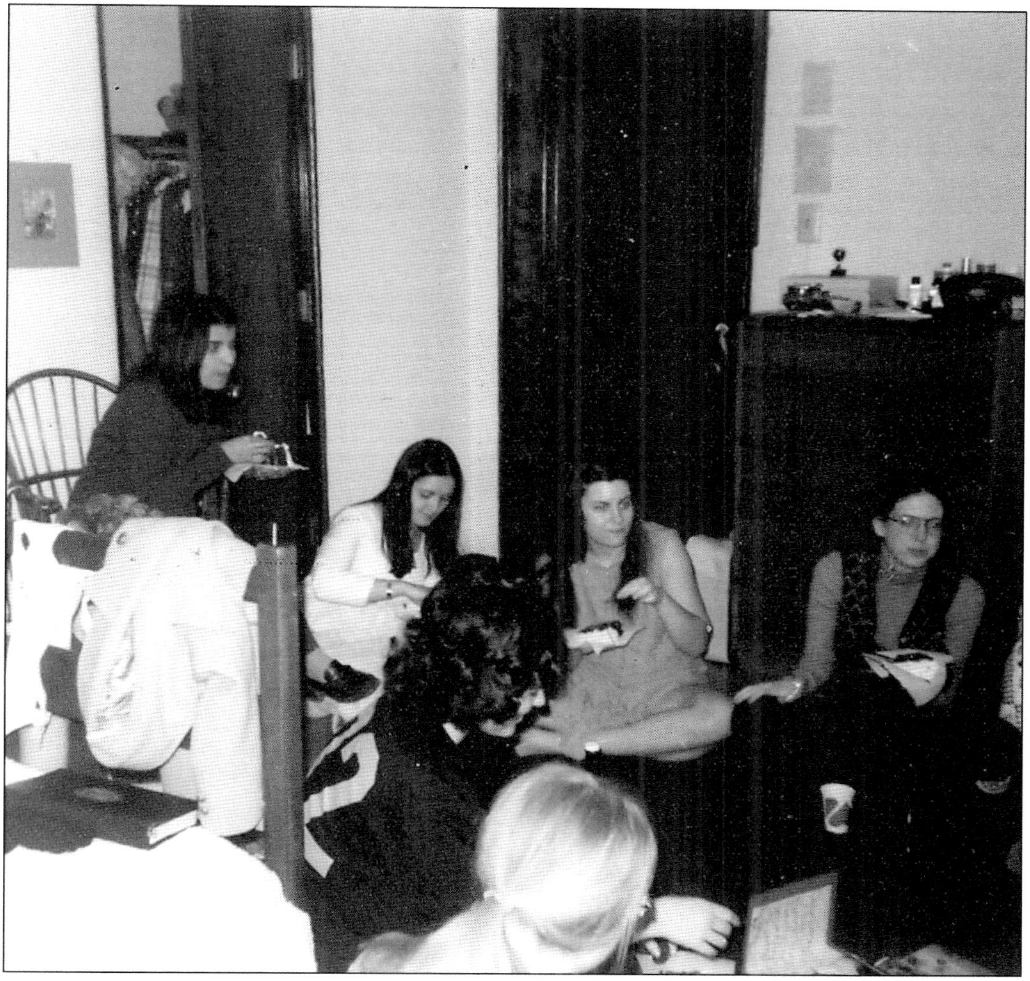

Seen here, from left to right, are the following: Jackie Schimizzi, Judie Moore, Gay Kaschewski, Anne Lechner, Dianne Gibbons and Mary Pensabene, as they enjoy a Dainty Maid cake in Le Mans in April of 1973.

By the time junior year rolled around, we had matured. We were even old enough to vote in the 1972 presidential election, thanks to the 26th Amendment. We took up residence in Le Mans, in more desirable rooms than we were assigned freshman year. Meanwhile, in the wake of the un-merger, many of our friends moved into Badin Hall, as members now of the ND Class of '74. It's funny, though. Almost to a person, those new Domers continued wearing their Saint Mary's rings. Transferring wasn't really an attempt to divorce themselves from their SMC roots. For most, it was simply a "business" decision. Our home bases were separated by 31, but our friendships weren't. We were mature juniors, after all.

—Natalie Dwyer-Haller '74

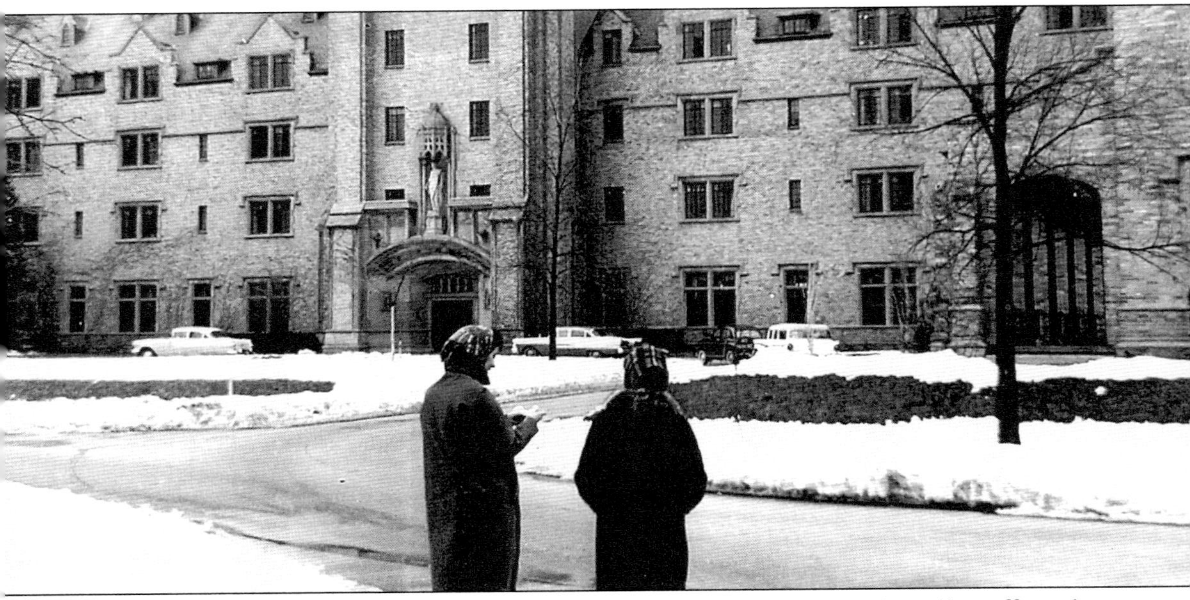

The decision had been made. But no one had discussed it with us. After all, it affected our futures, our lives. Argumentation would become the prevailing form of discussion. I remember it was very cold. And, eerily, it was very quiet.

It was winter 1972. It was the end of the merger. It seemed like the end of the world. Ann Shoemaker, Greta Anderson, and Cathy Hicks hoped for a more intimate meeting with the Superior of the Congregation of the Holy Cross and a personal note was sent to her via the sister at the door. Those three were patient and persistent and I joined them at the stoop. We waited, hoping for an audience. Hoping to get answers. The Sisters were aware that we had waited patiently outside in the cold, and were impressed by our respect toward them. The Superior came to see us.

I remember writing and together we carefully worded the Holy Cross response. This gentle and powerful sister entrusted us to relay the reasons for the merger breakdown to our friends and fellow classmates at Saint Mary's and Notre Dame.

More than any other students that night, we four came to more fully understand and appreciate the position from which the Congregation of the Holy Cross had determined the future of Saint Mary's. To understand was to know that if Saint Mary's were to merge, the principals would have had to ignore that history, those lives, that pride. They would have had to deny her separateness, her individuality, her importance.

Many did not recognize it as Saint Mary's moment of rebirth, but it was. Many did not recognize it as her moment of strength, but it was. Many did not recognize it as THE defining moment of empowerment for Saint Mary's, but it was. It was that definitive moment, that decision to stand up for all that the original group of CSC had envisioned as Saint Mary's; all that Mother Angela had dreamed for young women and had fought for against seemingly insurmountable obstacles here and abroad; that one choice to survive alone; which gave Saint Mary's the strength to become what she is today, a truly respected and exemplary institution of learning. That one decisive moment has allowed her daughters to celebrate this Sesquicentennial.

That February began a time of reassessment, a time of renewal, a time to rebuild on a strengthened foundation. It gave us the right and privilege to believe in ourselves—as the College and as the Women of Saint Mary's. From the rebirth of Saint Mary's came empowerment, hers and ours. It was the right decision.

—Regina Ivory Lupo '73, "The Empowerment"

Four

The Finest Tradition

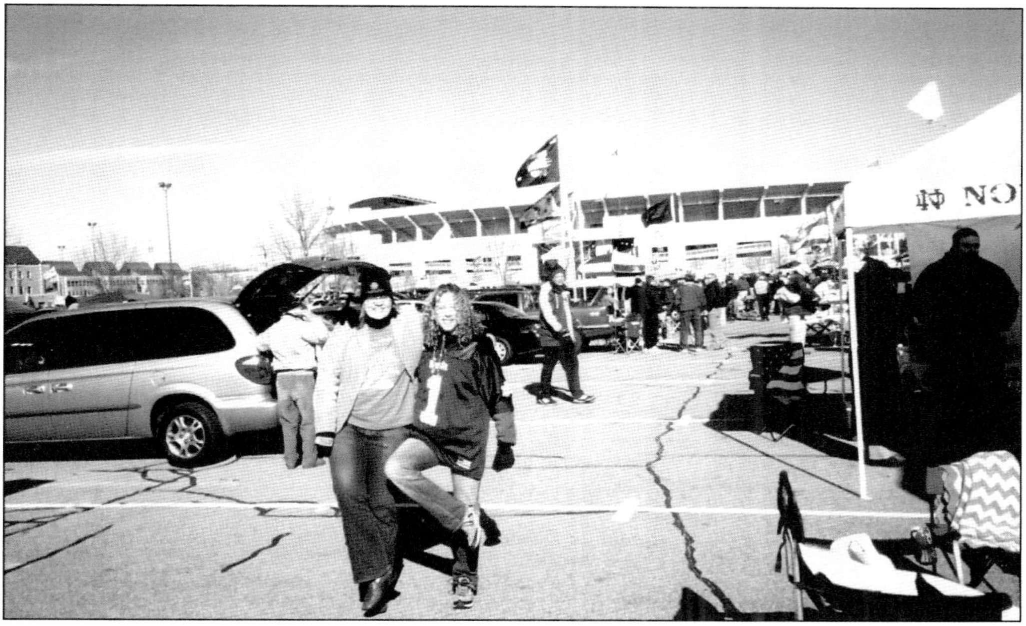

September 1941...green, homesick, freshmen...Big Sisters make us feel at home...With peanuts, pompons, pennants and palpitating hearts-witnessing our first N.D. football game...anticipation of our first Victory Dance, blind dates and all...unforgettable first Friday night at Rosie's with its "cosmopolitan" air...impressive Madonna Night sealing the bond between us and Saint Mary's...Eagerly awaiting the Sunday tea dances...Freshman Formal...The ending of our year with the memorable vision of ourselves heavily laden with books as we transferred them to the new library.

—*St. Mary's Static*, May 1945

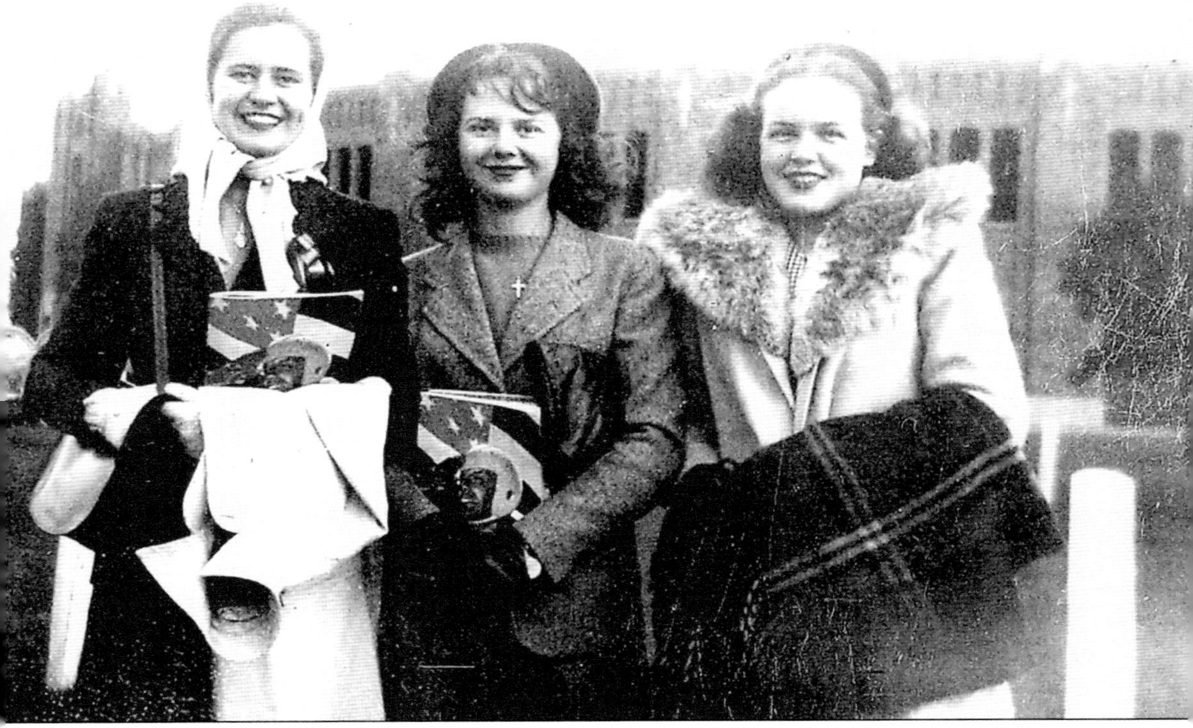

In the fall, we really looked forward to the Notre Dame football games. No matter how cold it was, we had to walk over to the stadium. Only once, for the Iowa game in 1962, were we allowed to wear slacks, and then there was snow on the ground and it was probably 0 degrees! All other times, we had to wear skirts or dresses. But, we always went, always cheered—win or lose, and had a good time. Of course, we were in the end zone, so our view of the game was kind of limited, but it was still fun. And, always at the end, the Notre Dame men would pull out their handkerchiefs and wave them in our direction and chant..."Go back, Go back, Go back across the road". A little nasty, when I think of it now...but, we had to get back there, so they could come and pick us up for our dates with them!

—Sheila Flynn Boone '65

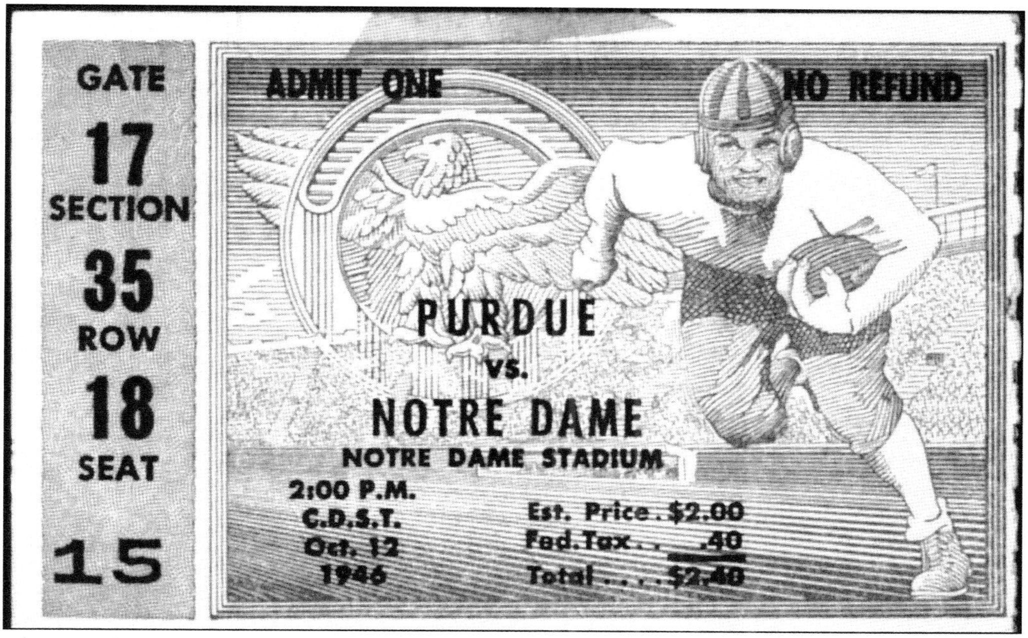

The SMC football tickets were behind the North goal posts. We sat there together as a group. I don't know where this tradition started, but at some point in the game we all took out white handerkerchiefs and waved them at the ND boys sitting in the section next to us on the right. How innocent we all were! Seems corny now doesn't it?

—Nancy Brozovich Lucey '57

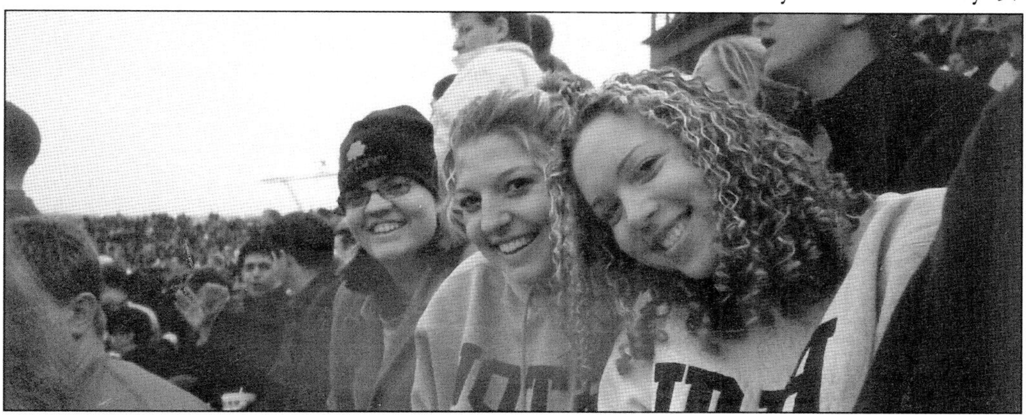

It was one of the main reasons I came back to campus in the fall. This was the year the Irish were going to reign as National Champions. So this dream never became a reality while I was a Saint Mary's student, but Coach Willingham's first year sufficed. I remember my first ND tailgate as a freshman in the soccer fields with the guys to the annual Dunlap tailgate in the library lot as a first-year alumna. Amid the burnt brats and amaretto hot chocolate, it seems like yesterday that we received the call at a Saturday morning tailgate that our ND alum would be watching the games from above from that day forward. We made our way back and forth amid the sea of green from the student section to the alumni section. Would our day ever come where we could sit for an entire game? That day has finally arrived and I wish Harrison, EJD, and I were once again balancing on wooden row 44 in section 28.

—Kymberly Dunlap '04

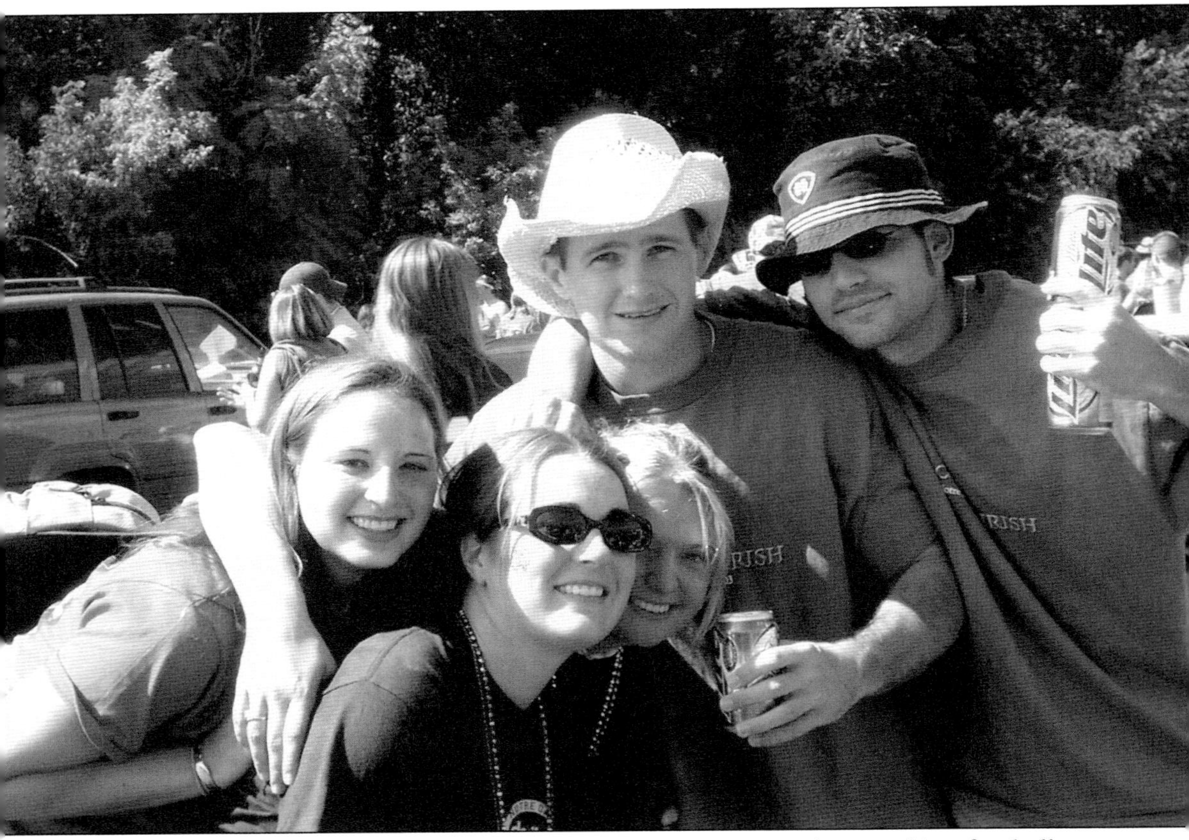

Ah football, the finest tradition of good ol' Notre Dame. But what good is a football game with out a tailgate? We knew college would be an adjustment but tailgating was like learning to ride a bike. College was something you did and then reflected on it later. And tailgating stands as the best mistakes of my life's lessons that I would never ever do differently.

Freshman year we learned that as women we had the right to do as we pleased. So we played hard when it came to the weekends, but shortly learned that it was difficult to go tailgating when you were still drunk. So sophomore year we decided Friday should be our day of rest. We would get up at six in the morning, and drive over to the soccer fields. We paid ten bucks and began drinking at seven and found ourselves drunk dialing our own parents, and sometimes even friend's parents by eleven o'clock.

—Becca Doll '04

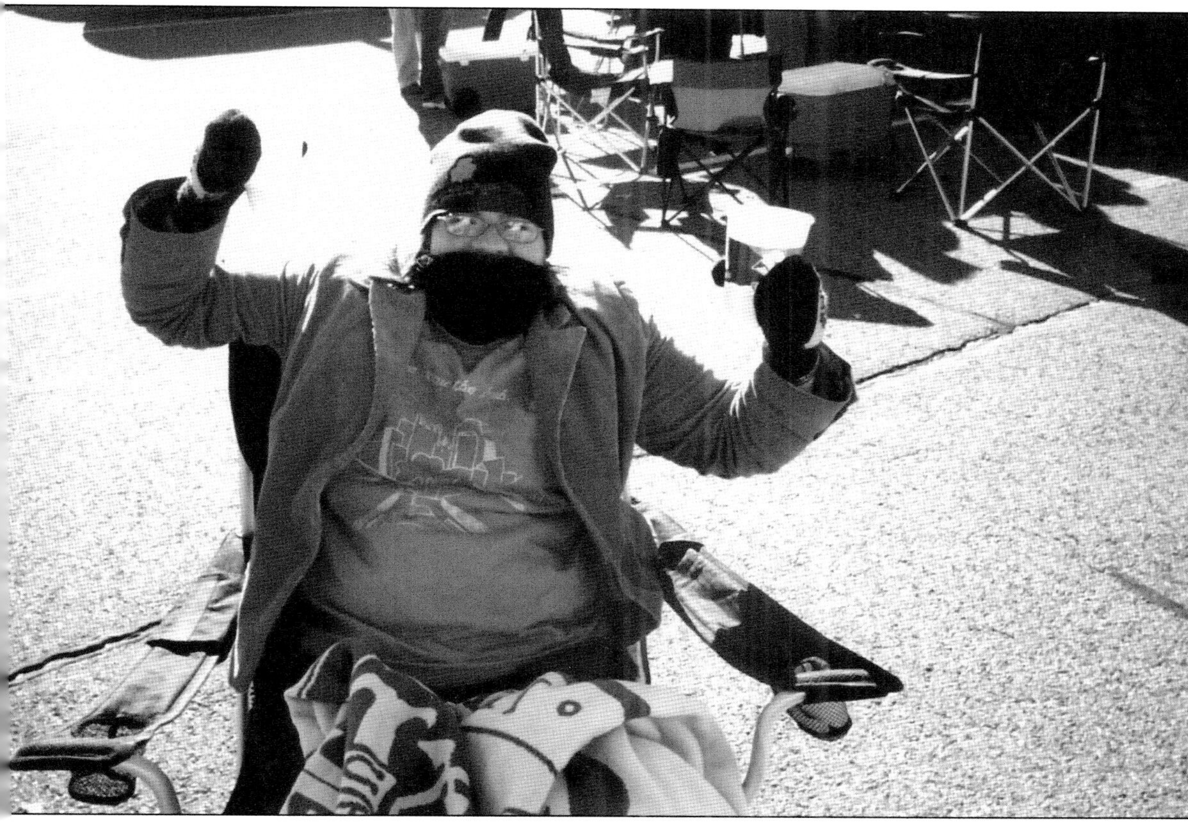

Junior year was the year The Bend saw many new bar names. Finnegan's became The Library and The Boat Club had underage drinkers begging judges for forgiveness, only to eat their words when they were pinched in the next bust. The term "boaters" was coined for these very devoted drinkers. But all of this was a little hiccup in our lives of tailgating because it all came together senior year. By now we were all legal and we did as we pleased. We had no intention of making it to a football game. Over the past three years we had gone from mediocre to a desperate team.

But tailgating was an art that everyone mastered. Tailgating was how we met friends, how we met boys and where you could meet up with parents who would feed you and all of your friends. As a recent graduate we all miss tailgating. And now going back to visit is cause for a reunion. We will be near the beer pong table painted like a mini football field, still trying to learn life's lessons like a college student.

—Becca Doll '04

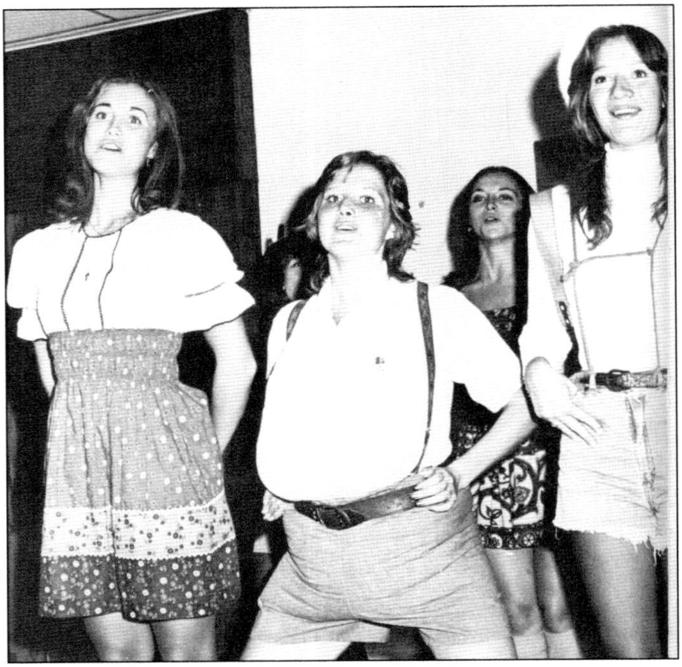

These seniors, from left to right, are as follows: Kim Lynch, Kathy Korhumel, Anne Creedon (in background) and Bard Groskoph. They entertain Oktoberfest attendees with rousing song and dance in McCandless Hall. The organization of Oktoberfest was a monumental effort on the part of Saint Mary's seniors. Their effort paid off with great attendance and a fantastic reception from both the Saint Mary's and Notre Dame communities.
—Trish O'Loughlin Erickson '75

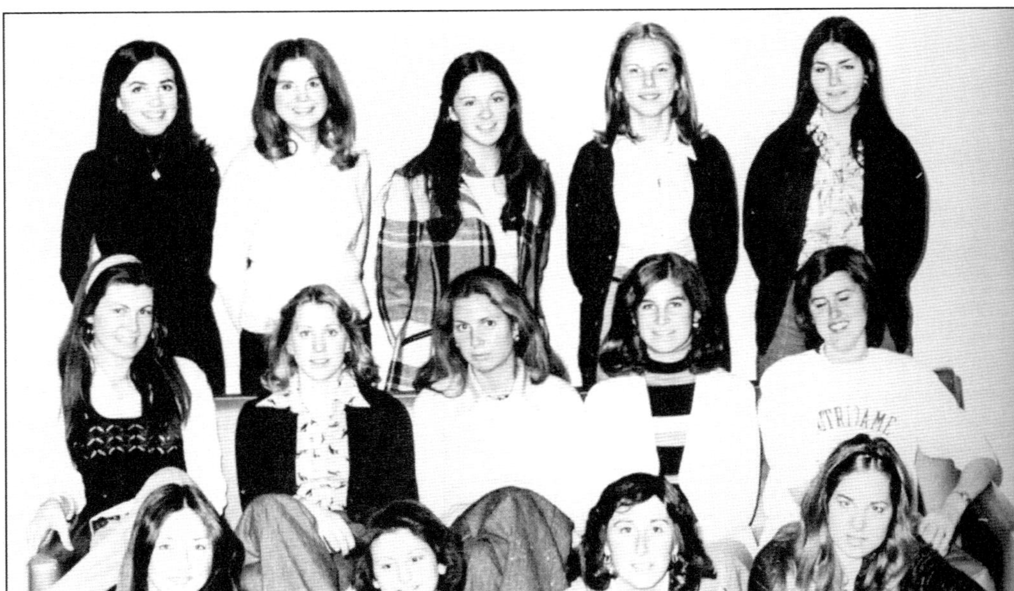

The 1974–75 SMC Social Commission delivered the first ever SMC Oktoberfest. Great organizational skills, enthusiasm and lots of contacts contributed to the success of the event. Oktoberfest provided an outstanding fall social event that attracted Notre Dame students to the SMC campus—a previous void—and provided an outstanding campus diversion.
—Trish O'Loughlin Erickson '75

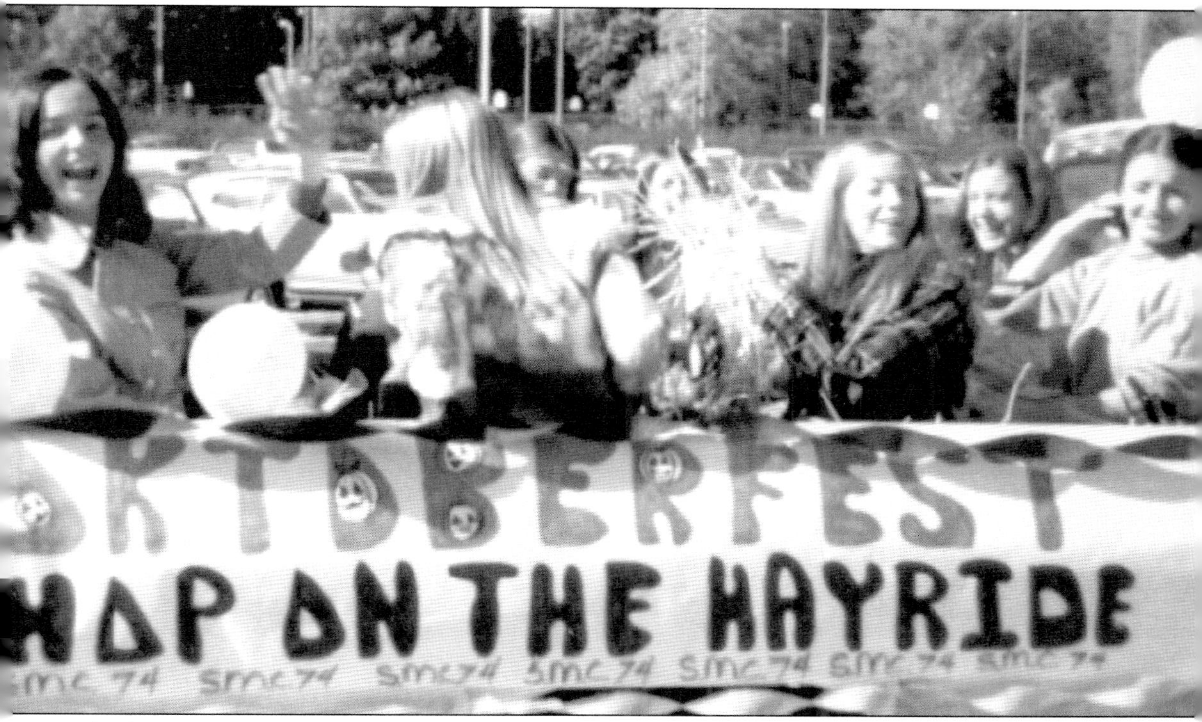

The first Saint Mary's Oktoberfest was held during the fall of 1974. The two day fest featured a German dinner, apple dunking, balloon toss, corn eating contest and a German Beer Garden with keg beer. The site was at McCandless Hall since the event was primarily attended by senior students. A live band and hayride were among the first attractions.

Oktoberfest was the brainchild of my junior year roommate, Margie Fuchs who was serving on the Saint Mary's Social Commission as Social Commissioner. The idea of creating a festival that could be shared with students from both campuses came out of hours of late night brainstorming…something Margie and I did often! Margie was a wonderful roommate and just the right person to take the concept to the school administration. She convincingly obtained permission to launch the event and so the SMC Oktoberfest was born.

As an art major I worked on a 20 foot long banner that hung at the entrance of the Saint Mary's campus. The banner especially was a real labor of love since it involved dying and cutting fabric to create letters that I then sewed onto to the 20 foot background piece of fabric. Hanging the banner was also an enormous task but it was made easier by the recruitment of Notre Dame friends who literally scaled trees to hang the banner across the entry drive.

—Trish O'Loughlin Erickson '75

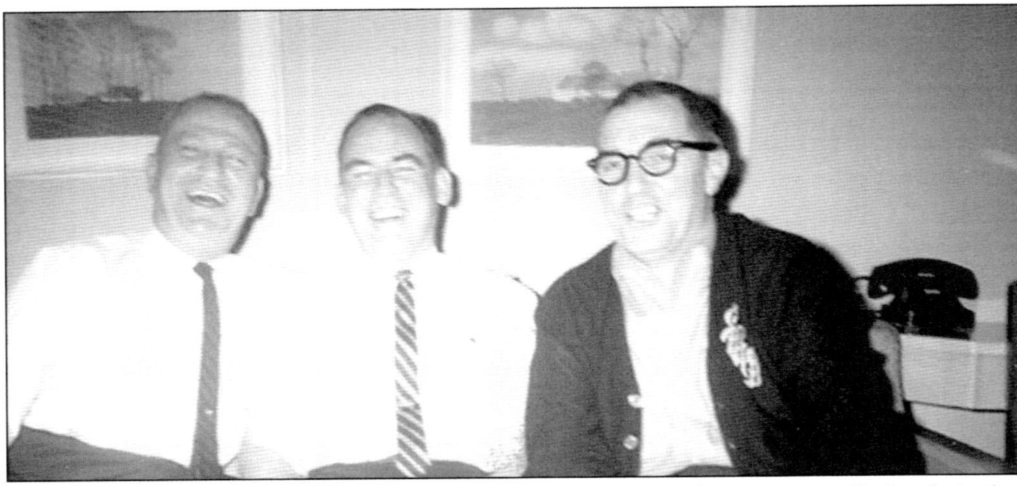

Liz Rice Kaminsky's father, Sheila Flynn Boone's father, and Pat Devine McCarthy's dad are all pictured here.

I hope they still have this junior year tradition, Junior Parents Weekend, it was wonderful. There were lots of school sponsored activities going on, but what I remember most fondly, was just sitting around at dinner or in someone's room at the Morris Inn with all the parents. I didn't appreciate then how nice it was for us to get to know all the parents of our good friends, and for them to get to know one another.

—Sheila Flynn Boone '65

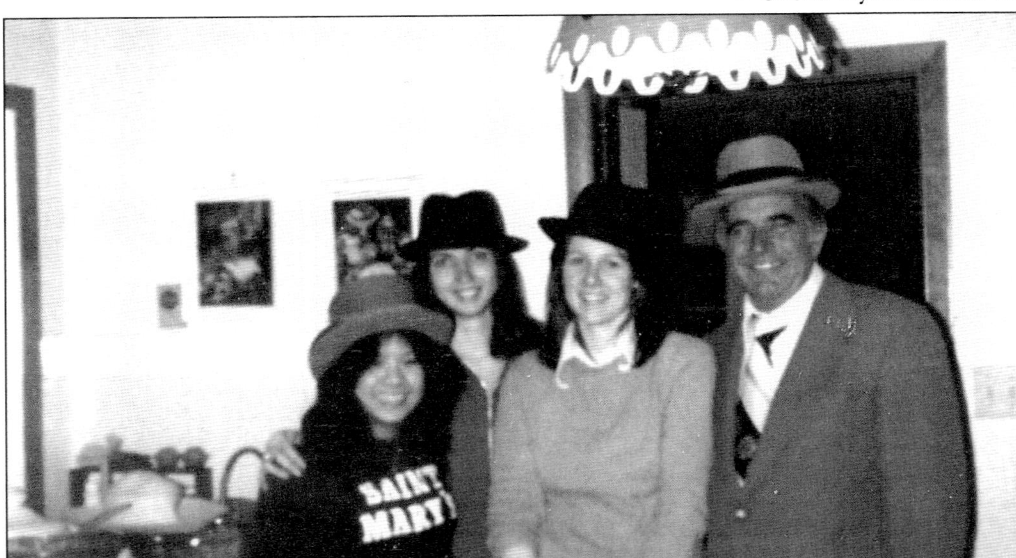

Occasionally a few of my Saint Mary's friends would come home to Streator, Illinois with me for the weekend and my parents would also come to Saint Mary's to visit me. We shared meals, good conversation, and in this picture, we are just having fun trying on my father's hats. My Saint Mary's friends were the kind of young women who valued family relationships and reached out to others. One of those friends, Mary Anne Poinsatte, still keeps in contact with my parents and my parents have visited her in Tennessee. My experience at Saint Mary's was greatly enriched by sharing it with my parents and my friends.

—Mary Beth Higgins '79

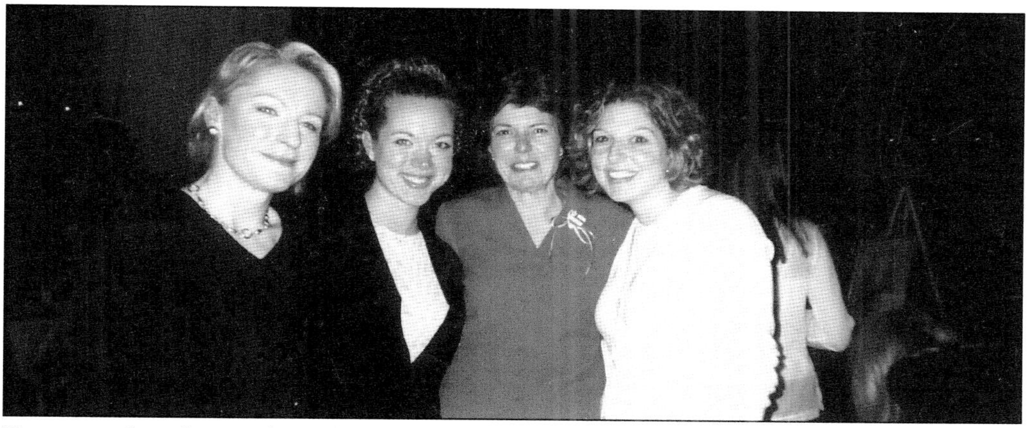

Two annual traditions that allow Saint Mary's women to say thank-you to their parents are Junior Mom's and Senior Dad's Weekend. It's such a wonderful time to see how much each daughter looks like or doesn't look like each parent. It becomes clearer why our friends behave and act the way they do.

Junior Mom's Weekend started off with a wine and cheese taste in Stapleton Lounge and concluded with a sit-down dinner at the Century Center. The Notre Dame Undertones were a highlight as moms and even daughters fell in love with their singing. A silent auction was the main fundraiser on Saturday night. Elizabeth walked away with a gorgeous cedar chest, Kym outbid Mrs. Wojan for a silver framed sympathy card from Mrs. Kennedy, and Kym's mom took home a water colored portrait of the Avenue to hang in the foyer. The partying continued long into the wee morning hours as the juniors and our moms, and even some dads, danced, sang, and drank the night away at Finnegan's and Corby's.

—Kymberly Dunlap '04 and Elizabeth Jablonski-Diehl '04

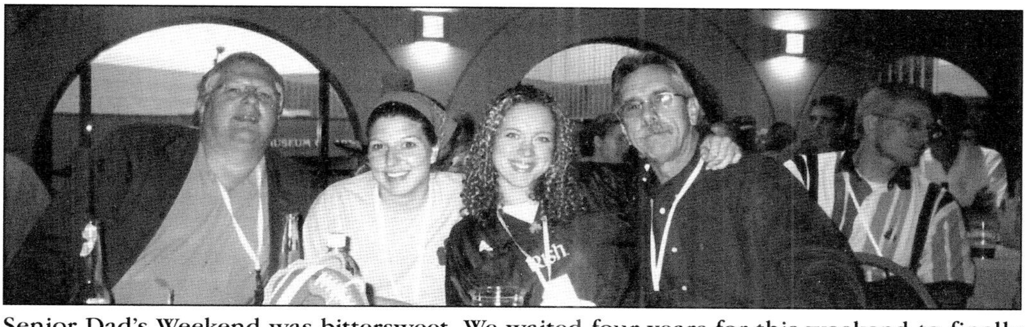

Senior Dad's Weekend was bittersweet. We waited four years for this weekend to finally arrive. We proudly wore the baby pink class t-shirt with "Daddy's Little Girl" across the front. Elizabeth Jablonski-Diehl, Katie Harrison and I, along with our fathers spent a particularly amusing Friday evening at Legends. It's not often that we get to sit with our dads and hear them talk about their college days. Our dads were exchanging stories of their rock n' roll days. In honor of that night we saw "School of Rock" at the movie theater the next day. At the College Football Hall of Fame on Saturday afternoon, we watched as ND surprisingly upset Pittsburgh. I vividly recall the Irish losing streak was at its finest that year. Saturday night the dads and their daughters went to Heartland for casino night. We never thought we would be at that bar together with our dads, but the seniors made it happen. What a perfect weekend.

—Kymberly Dunlap '04 and Elizabeth Jablonski-Diehl '04

CLASS OF SERVICE

This is a full-rate Telegram or Cablegram unless its deferred character is indicated by a suitable symbol above or preceding the address.

WESTERN UNION

1204

JOSEPH L. EGAN
PRESIDENT

SYMBOLS
DL=Day Letter
NL=Night Letter
LC=Deferred Cable
NLT=Cable Night Lette
Ship Radiogram

The filing time shown in the date line on telegrams and day letters is STANDARD TIME at point of origin. Time of receipt is STANDARD TIME at point of destina

199

5H G NL PAID

TOLEDO OHIO DEC 30 1947

MISS CARRIE POWERS

EAGLE RD AT RIVER RD RFD 1 WILLOUGHBY O

HAPPY NEW YEAR CARRIE MANY THANKS FOR XMAS GLOVES COLD HANDS NOW WARM, WARM HEART EVEN WARMER. WINTER CARNIVAL WILL BE A GOOD CHANCE TO DISPLAY BOTH. THANKS FOR THE INVITATION

LOVE

BILL

744A DEC 31

After you're bundled into your snuggies and Sun Valley sweaters, assemble on 2 West where calls will be received from the East Entrance. Use the far west stairway in going to the Rec to meet your date when your call comes. Ice skating will begin at four o'clock and will continue throughout the remainder of the afternoon and evening. Benches will be provided in the portico of the Library for donning skates. If your ankles soon give out, you'll find games being organized on the athletic field behind the school, together with sleds for those who would indulge in a bit of coasting on a snowy slope. You won't want to miss the sleigh ride which will run at regular intervals from four until ten. Be on hand for the coronation of the royal couple at five in front of the library, to be followed by an ice show on Lake Marion. Calls for dinner will be made at 5:45pm. There will be a place for the boys to leave their wraps, but girls are asked to take theirs to their rooms. Informal dancing will run continuously in the Rec for your enjoyment, and smoking will be allowed there.

—Winter Carnival Program, 1946

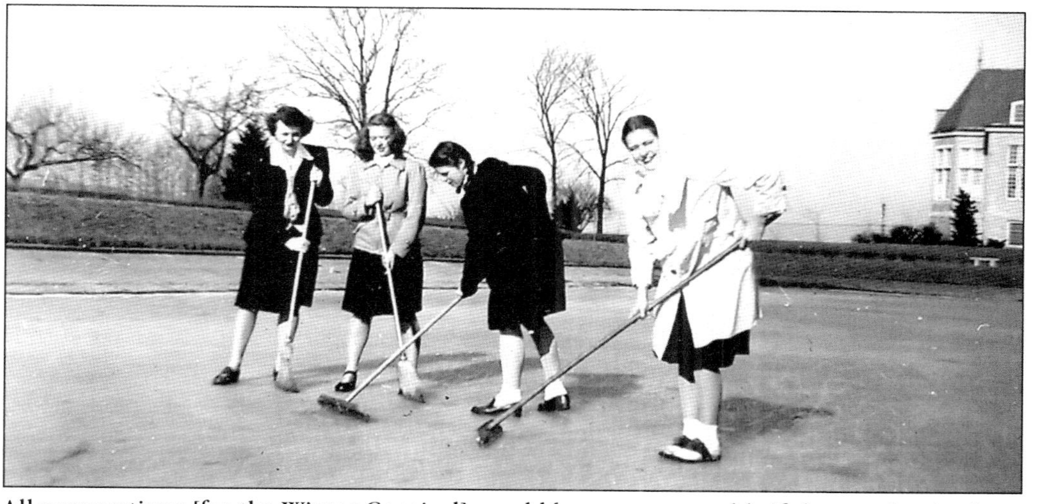

All preparations [for the Winter Carnival] would have run smoothly if the weather in these parts hadn't lived up to its usual reputation of contrariness. The Carnival was preceded by a week of disgustingly sunny weather. Instead of keeping the ice cleared of snow, we donned boots to flood the lake, or else push off a top layer of slush.

—Harriet Enneking '48, *St. Mary's Static*, January–February 1946

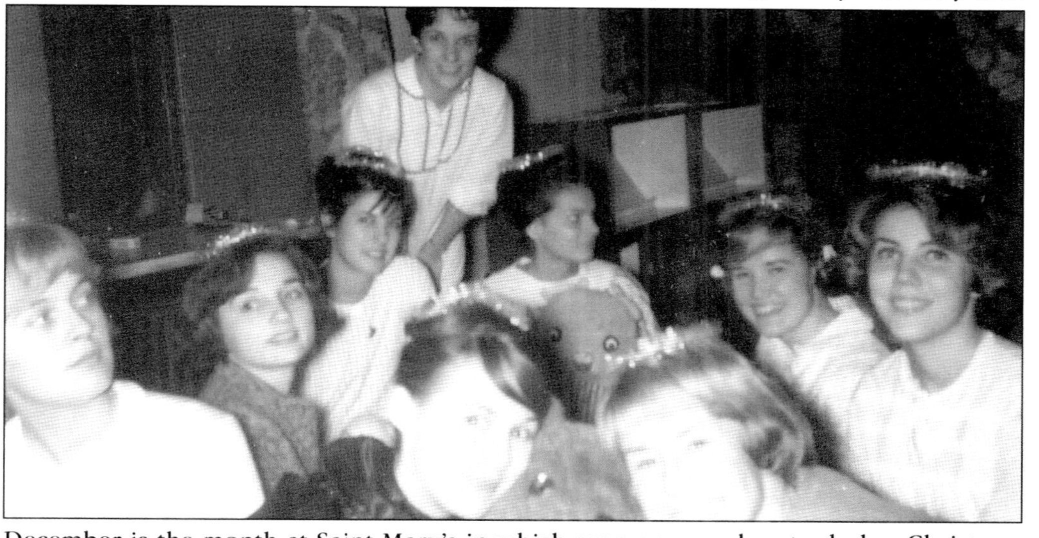

December is the month at Saint Mary's in which everyone resolves to do her Christmas shopping early, but, of course, doesn't. So everyone spends her three days at home before Christmas in a frenzy. This is also the month of convos, it seems.

The spirit of Christmas has been in full swing at Saint Mary's for several weeks. Christmas trees grace every hall, and decorations, every door. Dodo Ritter even has her Christmas tree, complete with lights, popcorn, and cranberries.

Christmas for Mim Botts will be especially wonderful this year, with her newly received Notre Dame miniature. Best wishes, Mim.

Now that trains are running for sure, we are all certain we can make it home for Christmas. That is, if we can find the taxis to catch the trains. So, assuming we do, "May God bless all friends here with a merry, merry Christmas and a happy New Year."

—Harriet Enneking '48, *St. Mary's Static*, December 1946

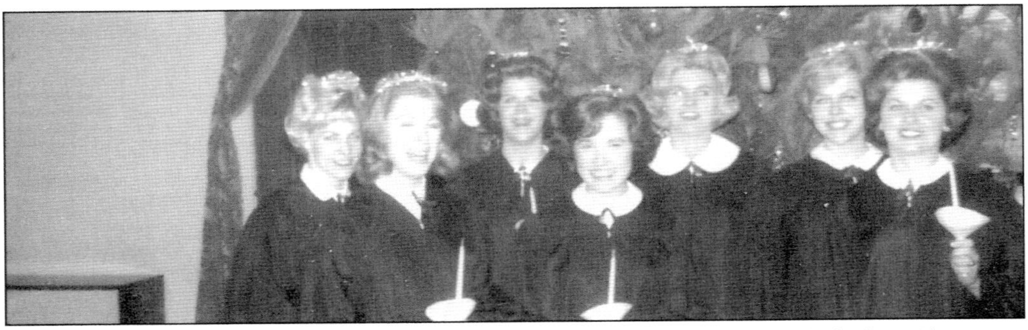

One of my favorite memories was the Christmas season especially the night before Christmas vacation. Many of the hallways and social rooms were decorated. Huge trees were placed in the gorgeous main entrance halls in Holy Cross and Le Mans. The Christmas dinner was held in the west dining hall of Le Mans. No one went off campus this evening. The dinner was traditionally sponsored by the junior class, who wore academic gowns, red bows and tinsel halos. Juniors sung carols in the hallway as they greeted students, faculty, and guests who entered the dining area. The dining room remained dark until the light of the new liturgical fire from the Le Mans Chapel was carried into the room in a lamp. A candle at each table was then lit by this lamp. The dinner concluded as the junior class president hung a holly wreath in the Great Hall. Juniors would then go caroling through each of the residence halls. The procession began with carols sung before the Christmas tree in the entrance of Le Mans Hall with Sr. Madeleva sitting on the couch surrounded by nuns and students. It was such a 'magical' night for all of us.

—Nancy Brozovich Lucey '57

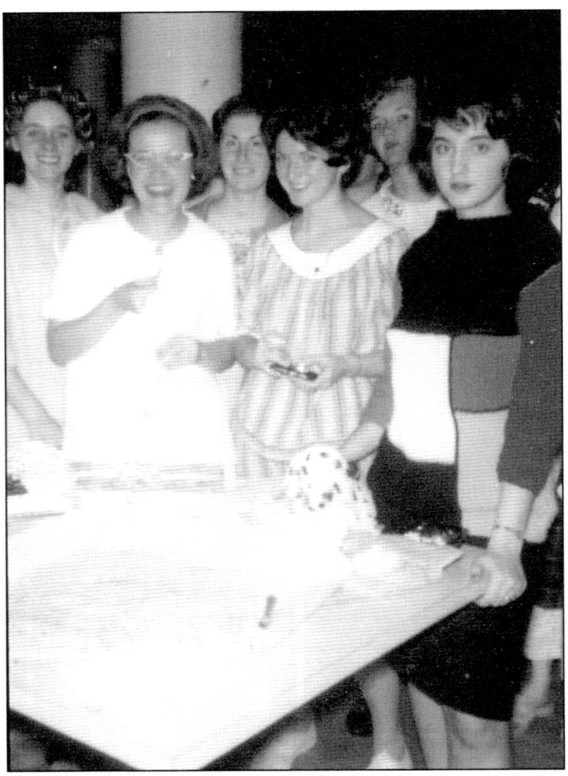

Seen here, from left to right, are Pam White, Sheila Kelly, E. J. Caluwaert, Sandy Miller, Carolyn Fleming and Joan Blila celebrating Sheila Kelly Ames's birthday party, junior year in October 1963.

Celebrating birthdays was always a big deal. As I recall, they were "surprise parties"...but, I'm sure they were really expected. I guess the surprise was "when" and "where" the party would happen. We would always order a cake from Dainty Maid Bakery in South Bend—they surely made a fortune from us.

—Sheila Ames '65

Pat Devine McCarthy, Sheila Flynn Boone, and Michael Pruitt pose for this photograph in May 1964.

Come nice weather we could hardly wait for the weekend, and trips to the Dunes. I think getting there was probably about an hour trip. I don't remember that many cars around, most of the time, but the Notre Dame men had them for the dunes trips! We didn't go in the water—it was much too cold. We played football, and volleyball, and just sat around on the beach. I guess the attraction was being off campus. But, it was sure fun!

—Sheila Boone '65

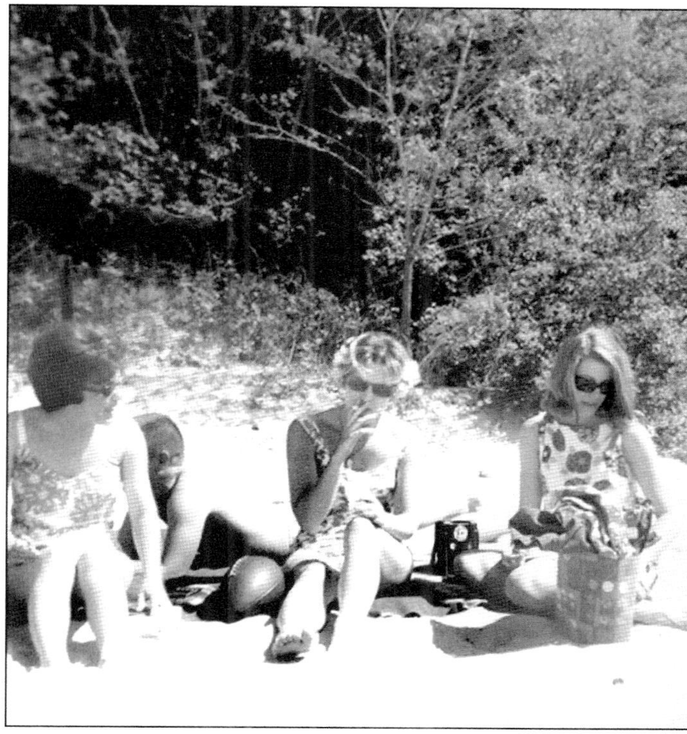

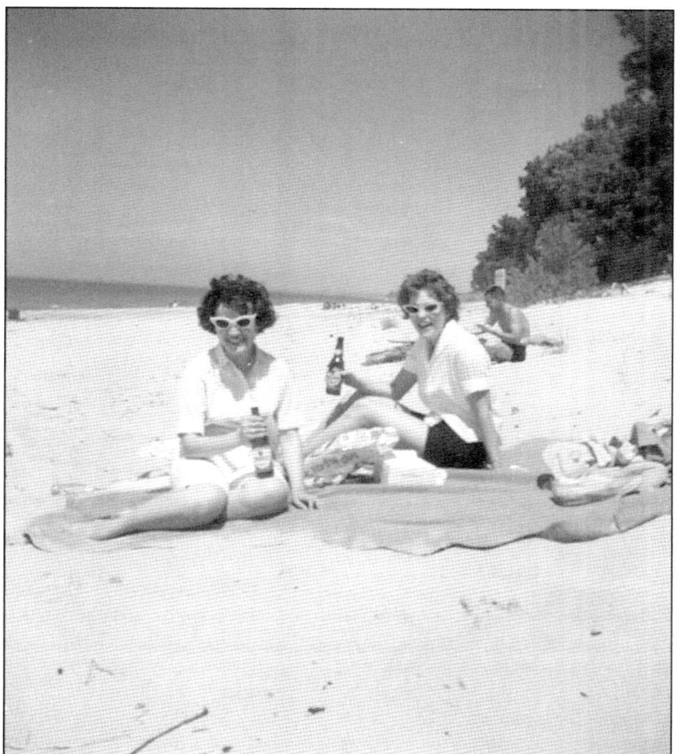

Sheila Kelly Ames and Sheila Flynn Boone are seen in May 1964.

Heading to the Dunes in my red convertible in May of senior year. I was only supposed to use the car for student teaching, but the Dunes beckoned. The car was overloaded with friends, the top was down and we passed right by Sr. Basil Anthony. She never said a thing. In my mind I thank her still.

—Sheila Ames '65

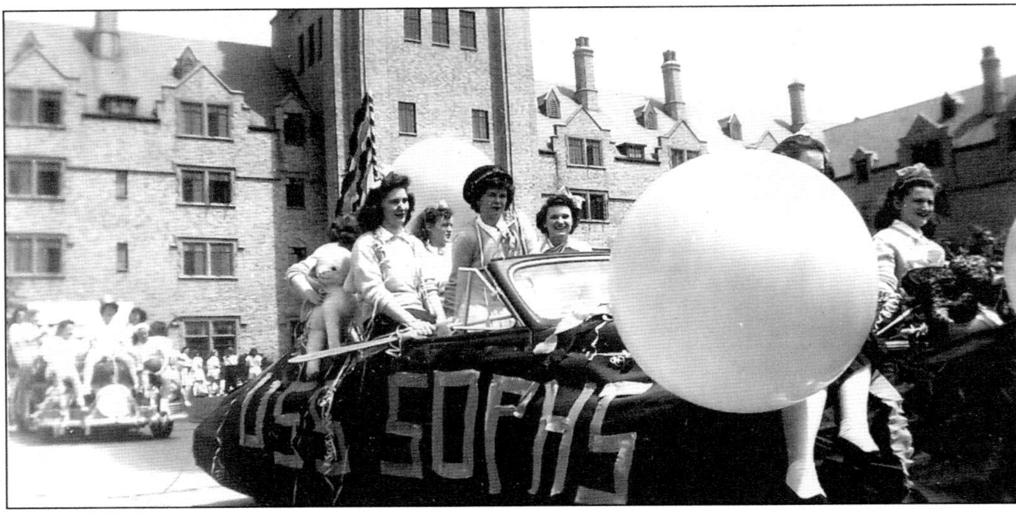

The W.A.A. Sports Day Program in May, 1946 began with the entrance of the sports queen, attendants, floats, and horses at 11:15am. A luncheon was served in the North court at noon, which was followed immediately by a volleyball game between lay-faculty and students. At 1:15pm the doubles tennis finals took place and a half an hour later the volleyball match-ups featuring seniors and sophomores versus juniors and freshmen. The track events, singles tennis, softball, canoe class, and tug-o-war finals were concluded at 5pm with a presentation of awards at the tennis courts.

—Carrie Powers Powell '48

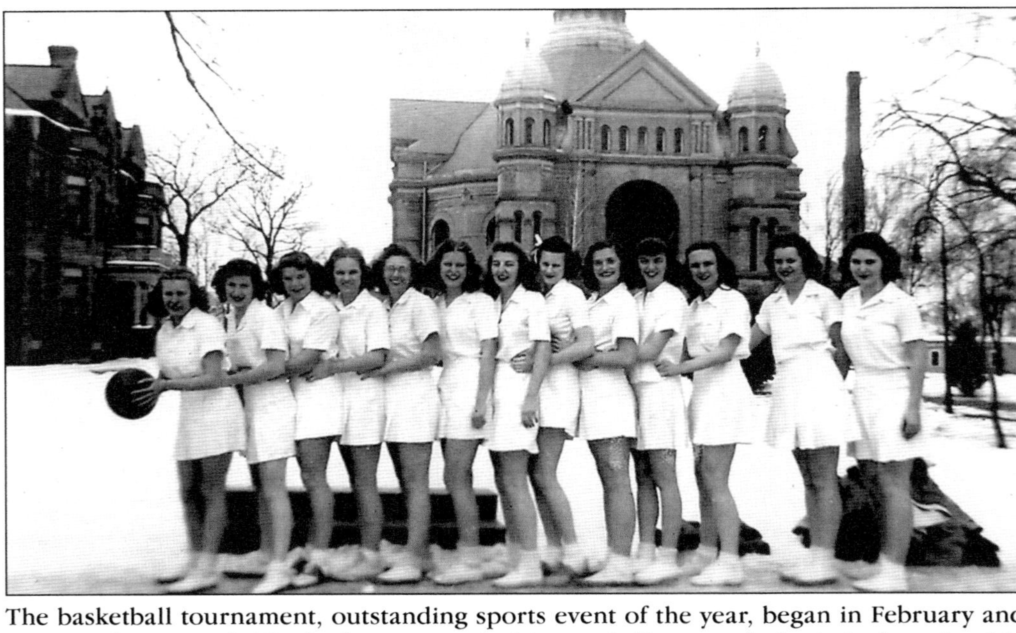

The basketball tournament, outstanding sports event of the year, began in February and continued into March. The freshmen were the biggest challenge to the junior's championship in 1945. The freshman lost to their big sisters by three points in the last game, 33-30. Here is a picture of the freshman team who later celebrated their team party "with bells on" at The LaSalle Hotel on March 18.

—Carrie Powers Powell '48

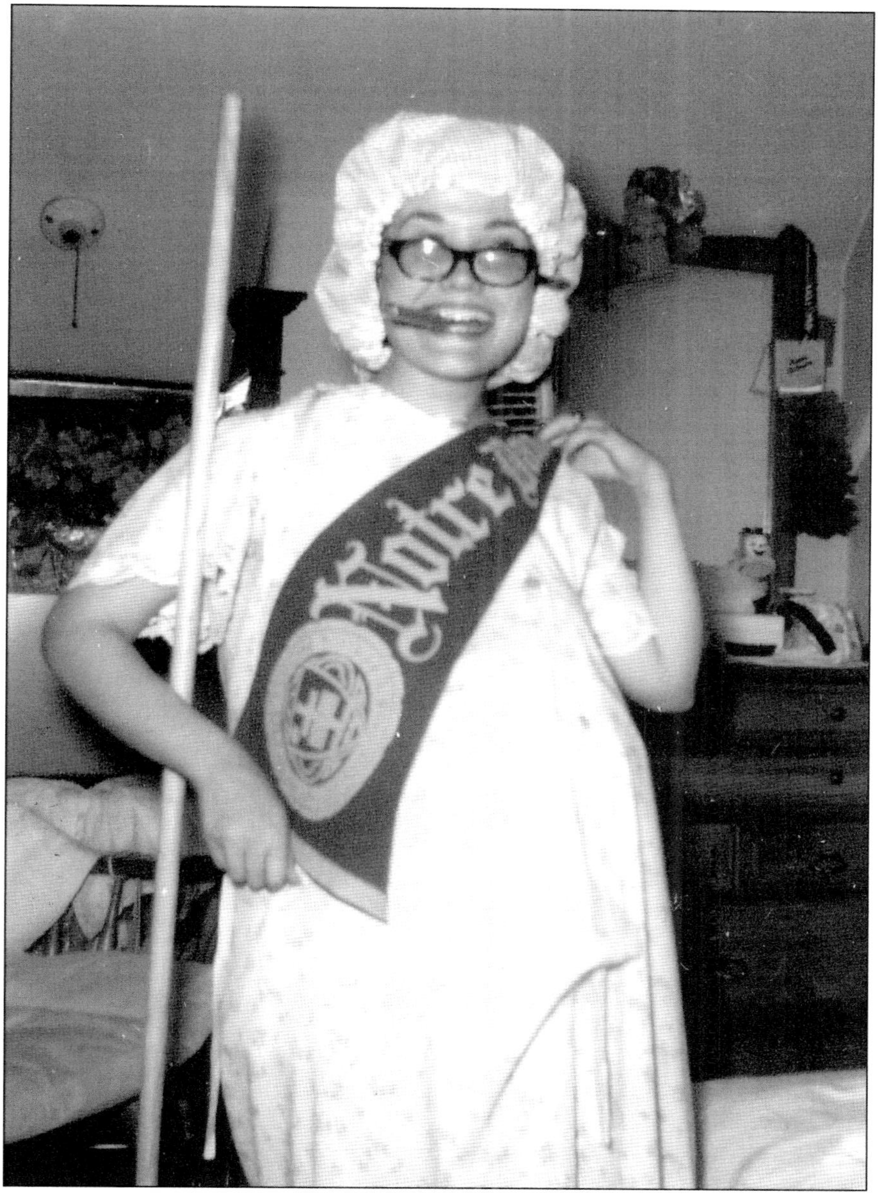

Suddenly spring brought the "panty raids". Now, they were really something. A very large throng of fellows (remember, it was all male at ND then) would come running over, yelling as they ran. They would then go into the halls and rooms (unlocked, you know), or find the laundry, and steal our undies. Of course, we had our names sewn in them, so then we'd get a call telling us that if we wanted our things back, we would have to go out on a date with them. (I don't recall that anyone ever did.)

Sophomore year I opened my door and my younger brother from N.D. was standing outside of it. He was as surprised as I was. A bunch of the boys somehow infiltrated Miss Marion McCandless' rooms in Le Mans and filched her corset that they ran up the flagpole. The raids didn't last long, but they sure were fun.

—Sheila Kelly Ames '65 as "the Whole Woman"

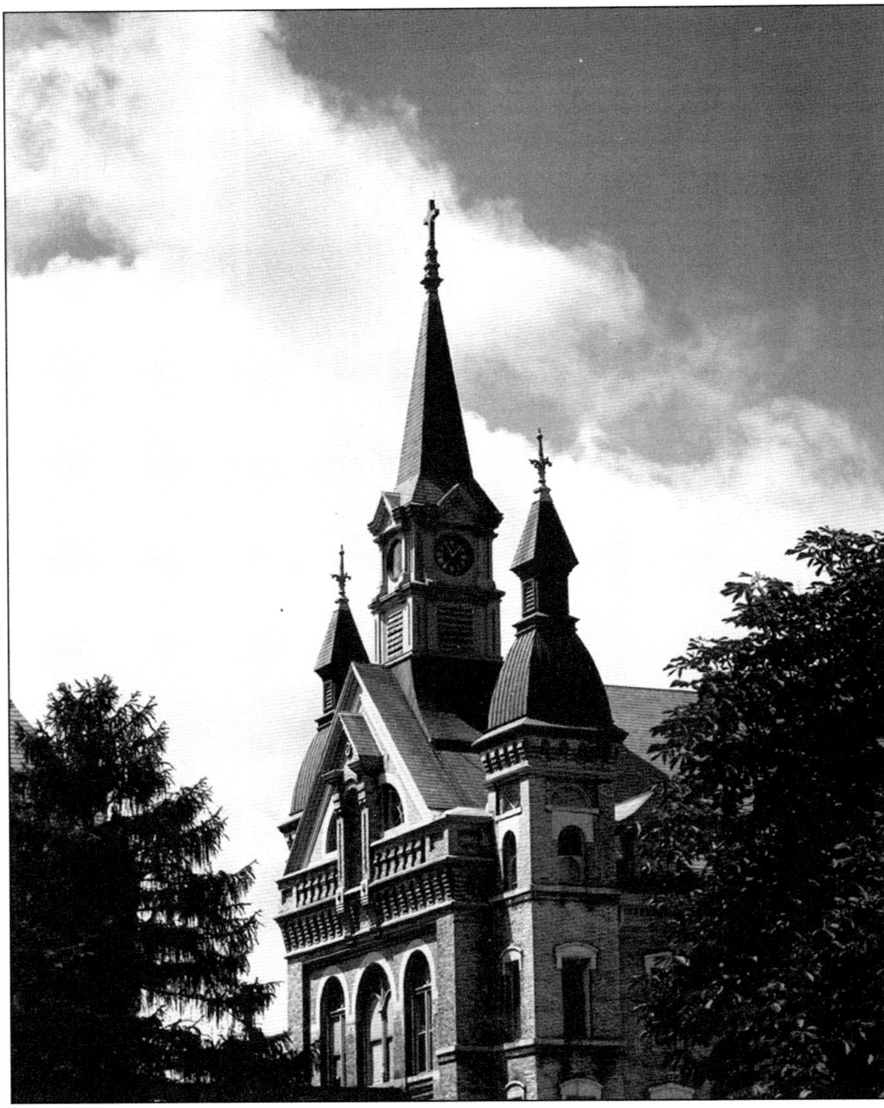

The sound of the large bell on campus, which is heard throughout the day, may have become so familiar to students as to go unnoticed. The ringing at 5:30 every morning means that another hour of sleep, and during the day, it is "just a bell."

This bell was sent from France to America by Father Moreau in 1884 and was used at Notre Dame almost a half century before it was placed in the tower at Saint Mary's.

The 5:30 rising bell is sounded 33 times in memory of the years of our Lord's life on earth. To call the Sisters to a religious exercise, the five-minute bell is rung fifteen times in honor of the mysteries of the Rosary, while the second bell sounds five times in memory of the Five Great Wounds which Christ received. Each hour in the day is marked by a sevenfold peal commemorating the Seven Dolors of the Blessed Mother.

When a Sister dies, the bell tolls once every minute for a quarter of an hour, and then there is a full peal for another fifteen minutes. The same procedure is followed at the hour of burial.

—*St. Mary's Static,* May 1945

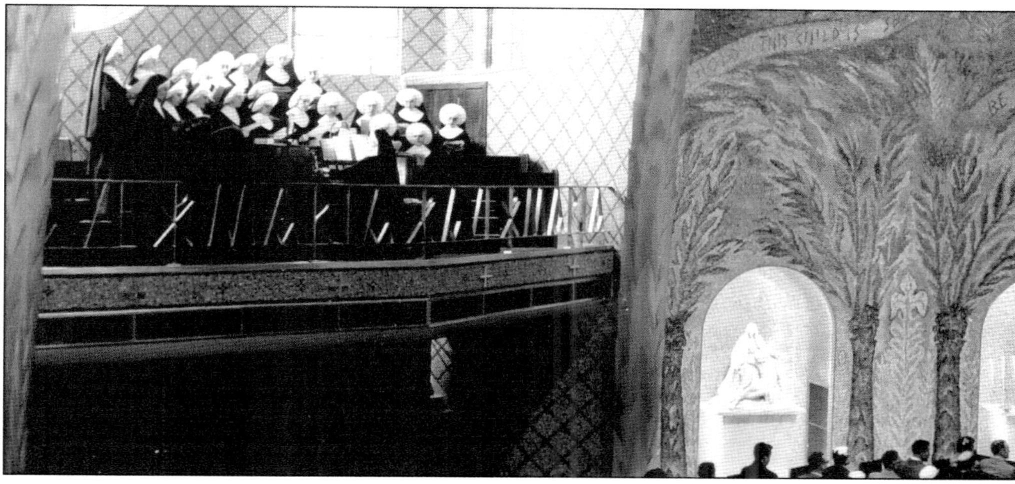

My most poignant memory of Holy Cross Hall is the night that we saw the novices in their black and white habits out in the moon light either playing child games or dancing in a circle. It was breathtakingly beautiful or the night we sat at our desks, studying, and the convent death knell began to toll. I cannot give you the exact, final number, but the deceased sister had to be in her 90s, and the tolling went over 70. At first we may not have realized we were counting, but when we passed 50, we began to look up and count aloud. At 75 or 80 we opened our doors and stared at each other. When it was over, we went back in, went to work and studied. What could we say that the bell had not said?

—Catherine Opper '54

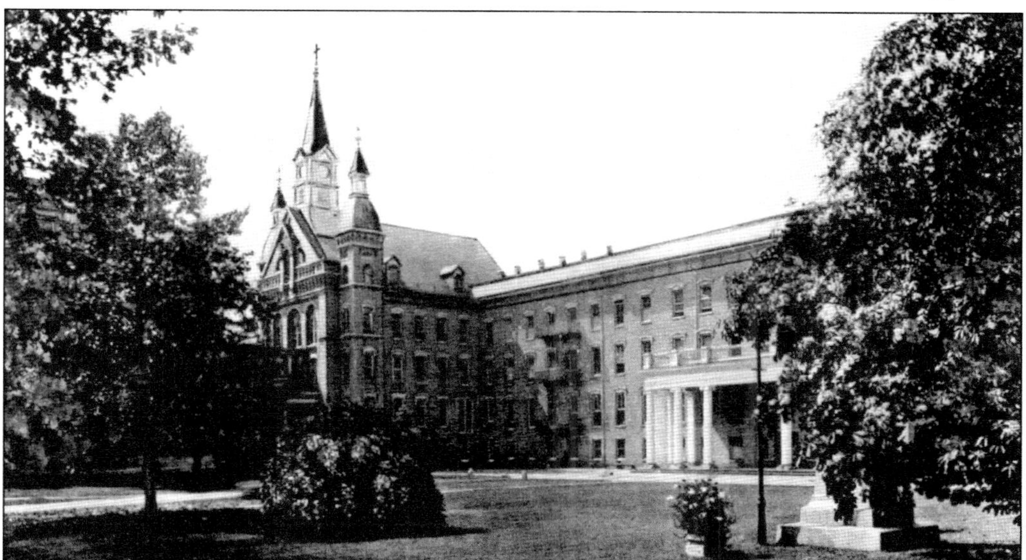

Without our knowing, a nun in the convent behind Holy Cross had passed away that first week of orientation. Tradition apparently dictated that the bells were to start ringing at 5AM in the convent chapel for a number of days. There was a "dong" every 5 minutes for quite a while after the initial peal. Carolyn and I thought that this was the daily norm, and that we would probably never sleep soundly again for 4 years.

—Sheila Kelly Ames '65

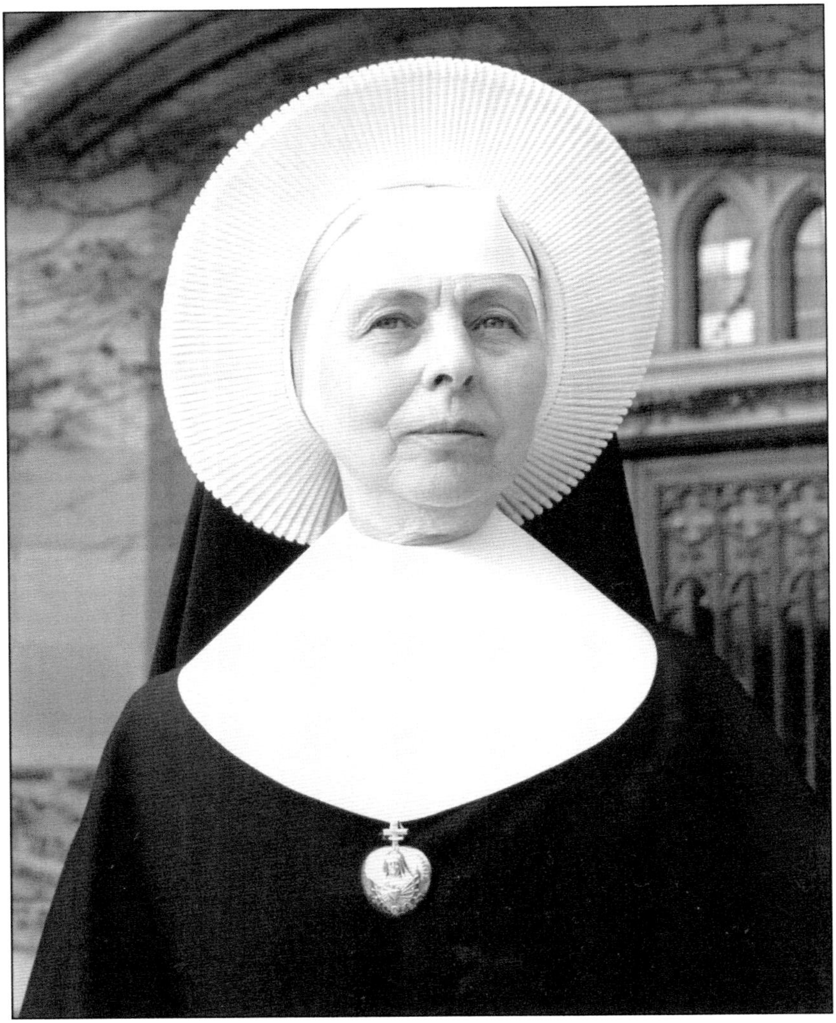

Fall, South Bend, 1941, I walked with Sister Monica Marie (my piano teacher and chair of the Music Department of Saint Mary's College). We strolled behind Le Mans Hall. At the other end Sister Madeleva said "Are you a good girl?" I quickly responded, "Not very, Sister". That was the beginning of a real relationship that I treasure. She and the Holy Cross Sisters took me under their wing. They gave me the most any child can imagine: private harmony, private lessons. I played with the Saint Mary's Orchestra (my debut) at 12 playing Beethoven Concerto #1. Summers they employed me in the library or switchboard as I aged. I was employed as an accompanist for Saint Mary's-Notre Dame Choir—all this for a little Jewish town girl from South Bend. I was a great fan of her poetry at 13.

In 1954 Sister Madeleva came to a school below San Mateo and arranged for me to visit her. It was a great joy for me to see my dear friend of 12 years. She spoke of the great achievements of higher education in the U.S., only deploring our worship of "the golden calf of the Ph.D."

In parting she recounted our first meeting 14 years before in every detail. How fortunate to have had 2 grandmothers, my Lithuanian Jewish one and Sister Madeleva, distinguished President of Saint Mary's.

—In memory of Laurette Goldberg (January 16, 1932–April 3, 2005)

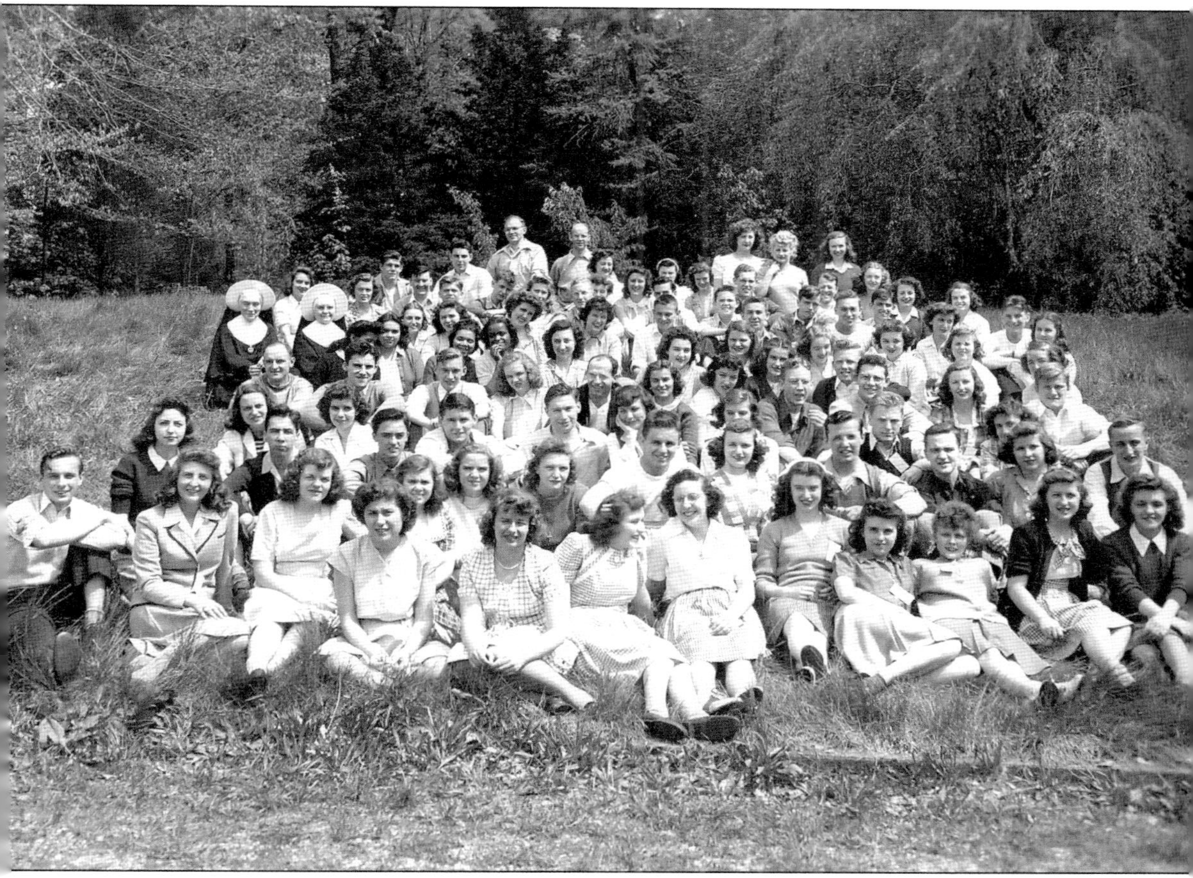

On May 17, 1945 we honored the Home Coming of Our Sisters Olivette and Caecilius after three years of internment in Manila. We made a living avenue of columns from the Avenue's front gate to the Church of Our Lady of Loretto. The order of procession included the College seniors in cap and gown led by Sisters M. Judith and Maria Renata from the gate. The first two seniors carried the Papal and American Flags and the next two seniors carried banners of the Sacred Heart and Our Blessed Lady. The seniors were followed by college students in uniforms and white veils, lay faculty in academic regalia, secular guests, Academy seniors in cap and gown led by Sisters M. Louise Irene and Amadeus. The first two Academy seniors carried sodality banners, who led the Academy students in uniforms and white veils, Junior school students led by Sisters M. Joanna and Good Counsel, guest sisters, postulants, white veil novices, scholastics, and professed Sisters in rank led by Sisters Maria Luisa and Agnes Claudia, with the oldest Sisters near the Church door.

—Carrie Powers Powell '48

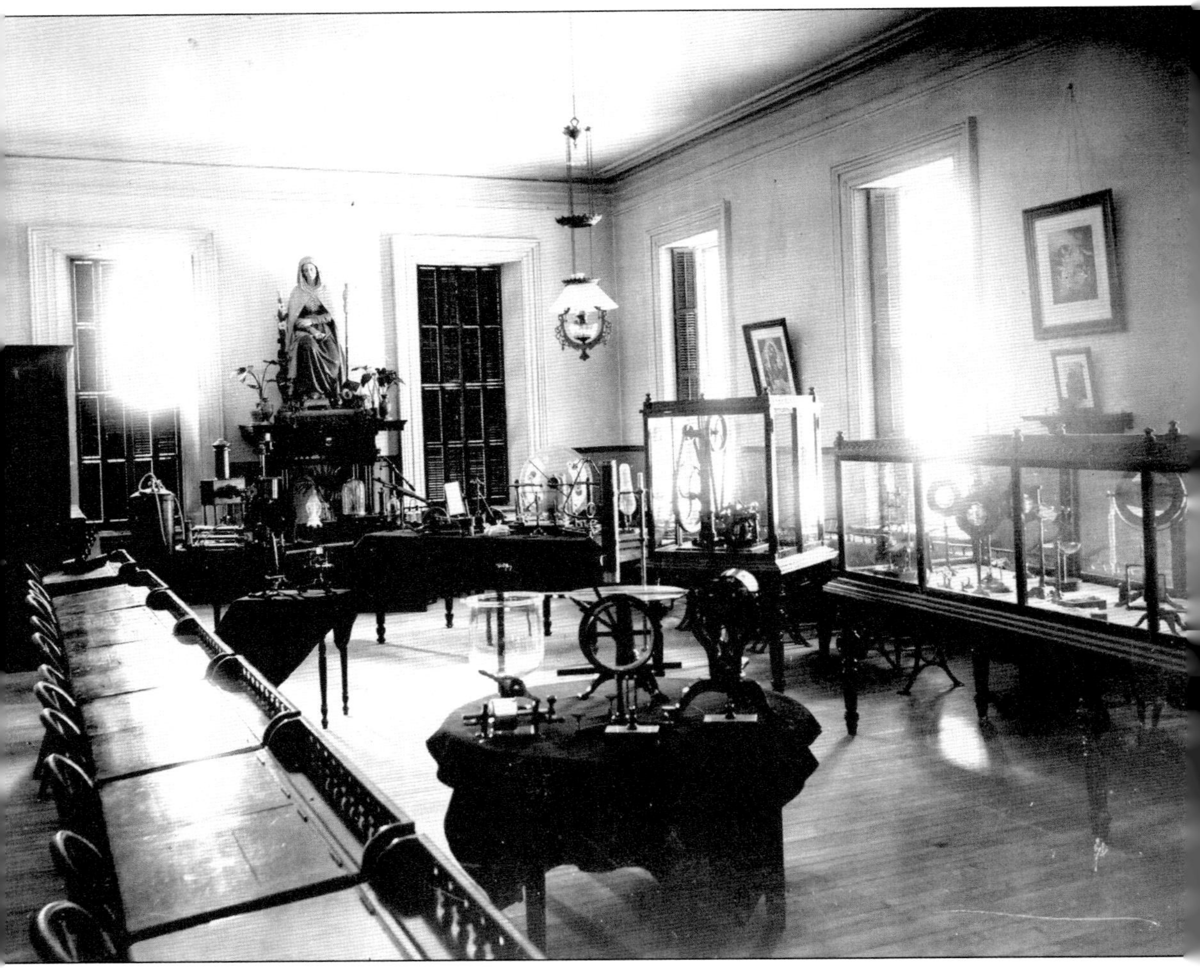

Wednesday, November 13, 1907:
The Juniors took their annual ride today. There were thirteen in the party and on the thirteenth day of the month. No wonder they had bad luck. They took the Saint Mary's car to the Bend and there they missed the car for Elkhart, or rather let it go by them without knowing it. They did their shopping in the Bend and finally went on to Elkhart where they spent an hour with the Sisters, getting back around 6:30PM.

Louise and I worked in the laboratory this afternoon from 2 till 4:30 making gelatin. We came very near spoiling it too but finally got it safely in our test tubes. Louise broke a beaker trying to break up an egg. After I had trotted down to Sister Uticius after another beaker and we had the precious mixture on the bare flame, we nearly burned the whole business up.

—Excerpt from the diary of Cora Miller '08

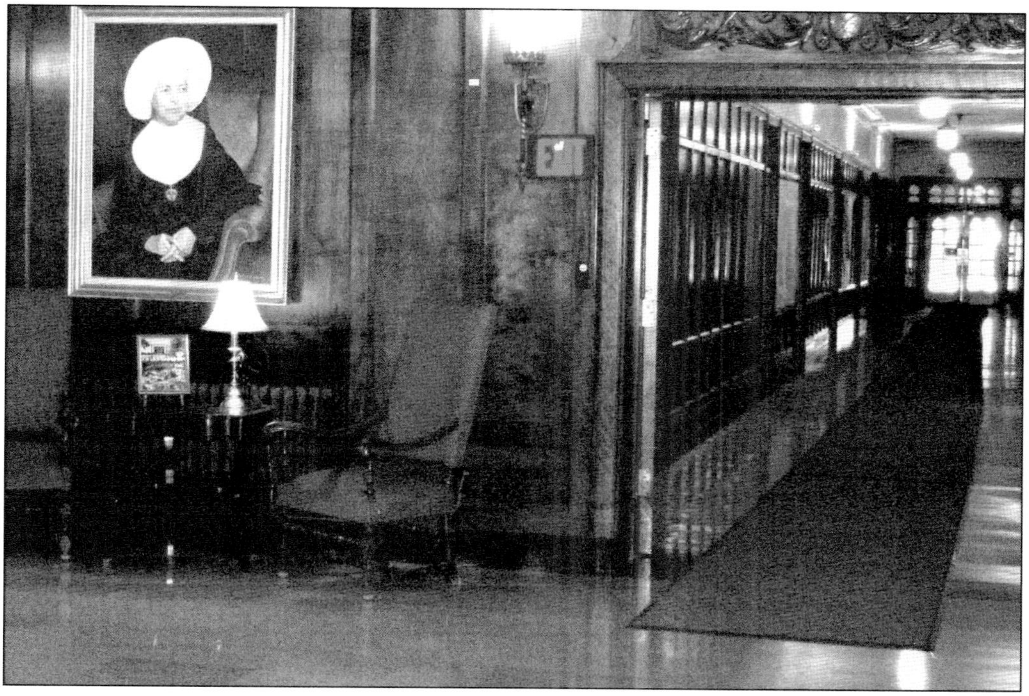

One of my fondest traditions began in the fall of my senior year. After an eventful evening out, I was walking down the main hallway of Le Mans and realized all of the overhead lights were still on despite the late hour. As I walked past the light switch I outstretched my hand to flick off the lights. I went all the way down the hall as I shut off the lights, swiped my card, and made my way up the stairwell to 2 library.

Some nights later, two of my closest friends, Harrison and EJD, joined my ritual of turning off the lights. Right before we clicked the lights off in the Great Hall we said goodnight to Sister Madeleva's personal portrait and turned to our right Mother Angela and did the same. We turned off the remaining lights and walked up to 2 library. Almost every night up until our graduation no matter what time it was or how inebriated we were, the three of us always remembered to say goodnight to Sister Madeleva and Mother Angela.

—Kymberly Dunlap '04

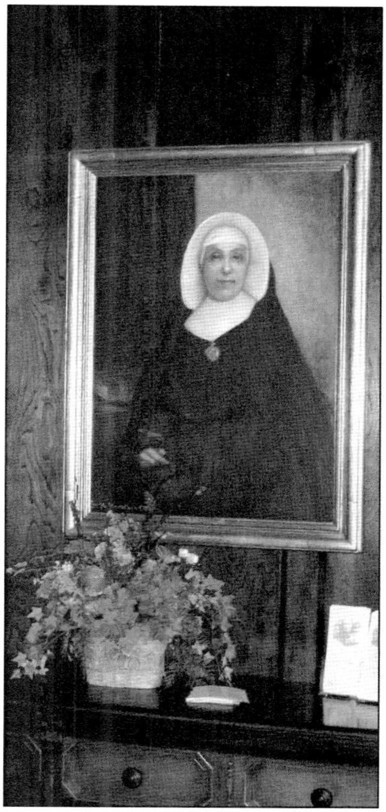

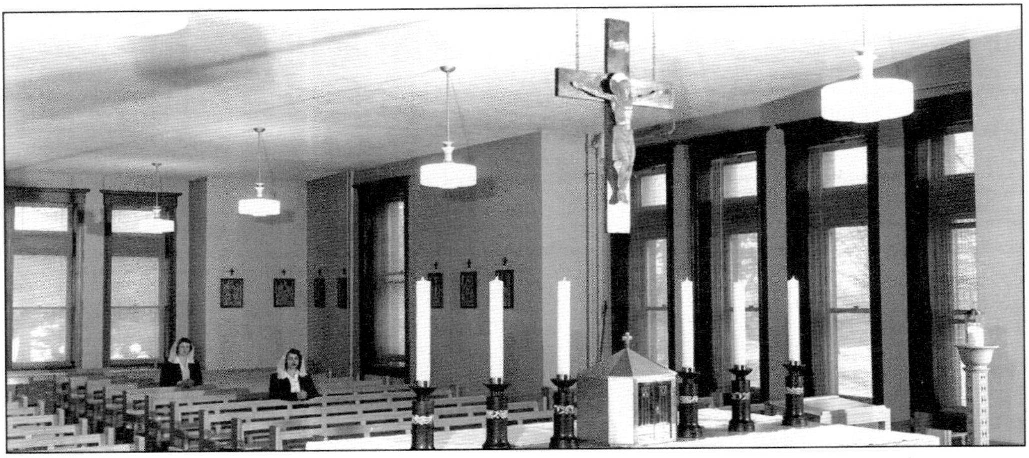

We were on the first floor in Holy Cross and our door opened directly into the front guest hall. The nuns lived behind us in a connected building. One day we heard moaning from the hallway. Sister Borremero and another nun were inching down the hall. It seemed they had taken her father's boat out into the lake wearing bathing suits. Her father then proceeded to entertain a guest on the dock for several hours at midday. They were fried before they could come back in and were trying to avoid having their scratchy habits touch their flesh.

Our second year we lived in a quad above the chapel. We were learning the Charleston and were being rather active when a knock came at the door. It seems a nun had been trying to pray below us and all the lights in the chapel were shaking.

—Sandy Bartlett '61

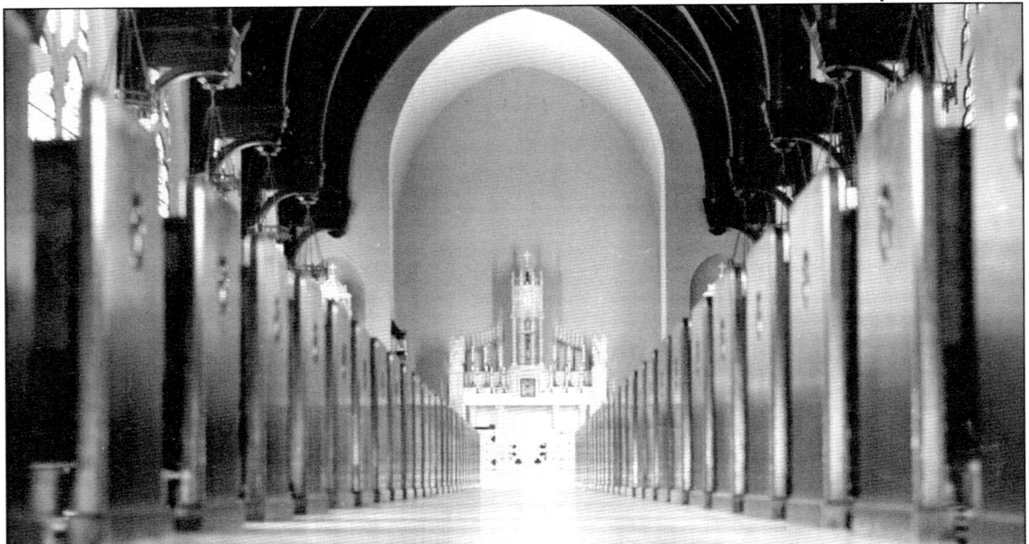

I lived with Lee Iserson, Marge Quinn and Pat Gregoire in Le Mans on the 4th floor in the big room opposite the chapel choir. I loved it there. I used to like getting ready for bed and then going over to the choir loft to say prayers. The chapel would be mostly dark and it was a lovely feeling. Another nice thing about that room was that we had a big round table in the middle of the room, with cards always waiting for bridge. Sister Rebecca, who was often a sort of hall monitor, came in and played with us once. That was an experience.

—Mary "Mudd" McHale '50

DOW

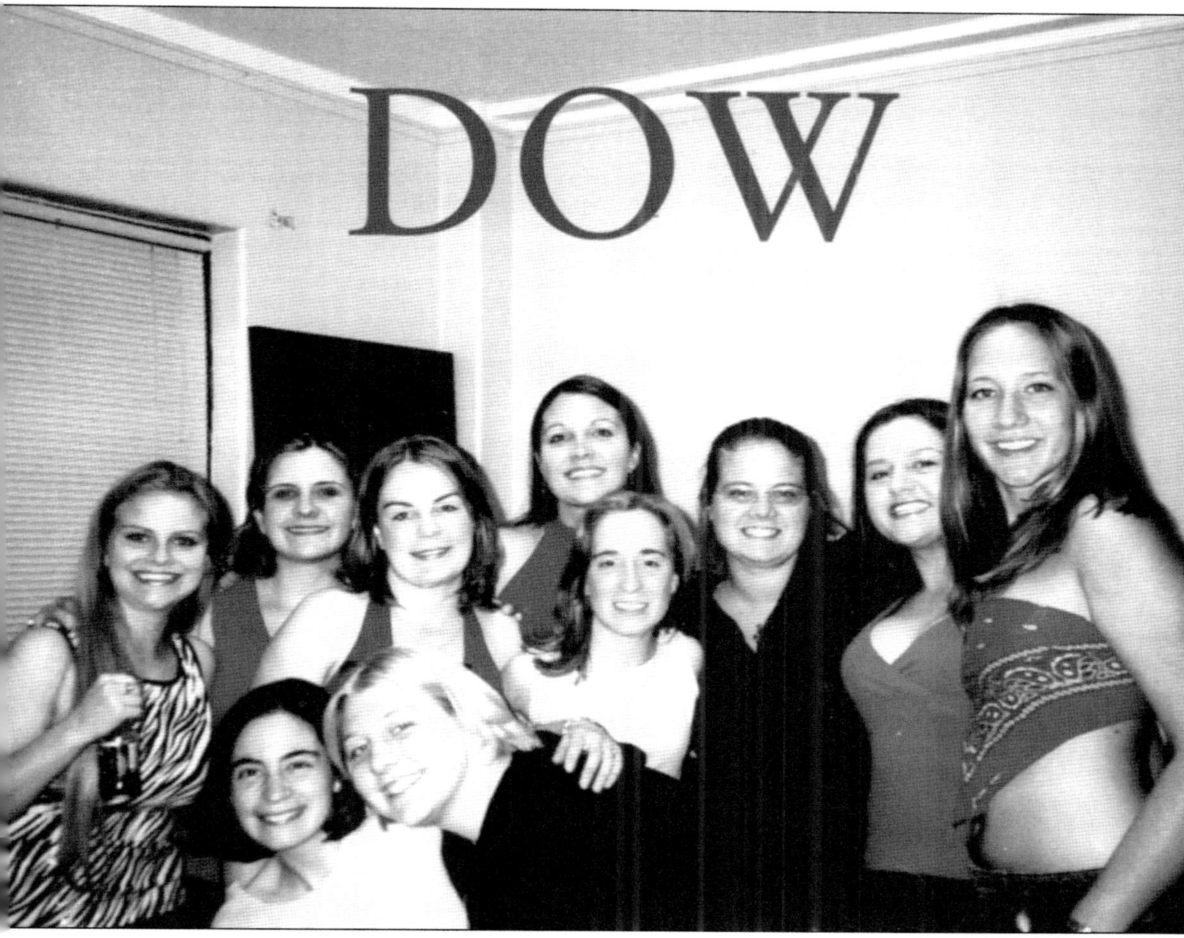

Whenever I reach for my Saint Mary's ring, I find myself saying aloud to no one in particular, "I need my girls with me today." The ring is a touchstone; I call it my 'power ring' for good reason. It brings to me the good fortune I had while attending Saint Mary's College and meeting the best group of friends a woman could ever hope for.

We all lived in LeMans Hall our junior and senior years and started a weekly ritual. Every Sunday night, we gathered in one of ten girls' rooms and hosted a "Drink of the Week" (DOW) night. More important than any crazy concoction we created are the deep friendships that resulted. We were silly together (hallway Olympics) and solemn together (September 11, 2001). We adopted each other's families for Junior Moms, Senior Dads and graduation weekend. We planned outrageously-detailed spring breaks to Florida, riding in style in the Heavenly Ham van all the way. We even went so far as to have matching DOW bags and T-shirts!

Despite the many miles among us, the DOW is still very much alive. Our circle has grown to include friends, significant others, husbands and babies. We have truly become a DOW family.

The 10 original DOW members include: Bonnie Arends, Sarah Hoshaw, Amanda (Spica) Listen, Megan McCoy, Tessie (Howland) Pollock, Katie Rzepka, Sunny (O'Brien) Shaw, Lori Sichtermann, Therese Svarovsky and Margaret Zeh. One of the DOW dads created a wooden bar for our DOW nights. At graduation, we all signed the bar and passed it to the next graduating class in hopes the DOW tradition would continue.

—Katie Rzepka '02

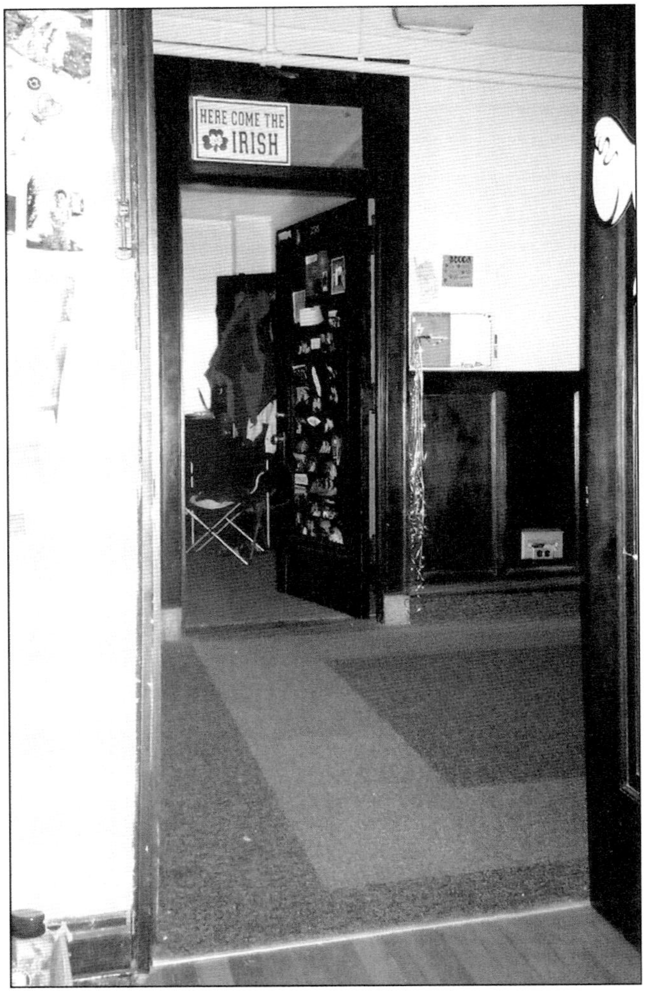

When Spring arrives each year, it brings not only showers and flowers but a special Saint Mary's custom—sometimes properly called an ordeal: signing for next year's room.

Along with deciding on a new room, you must show your present one to all comers. They may arrive at any hour of the day or night, but they usually wait until you're taking a nap, hurrying to dress to catch the bus, or the day before the maid cleans and you've been rushed all day and haven't made your bed or put away the books strewn all over your room.

They sometimes come alone, but more often they travel in large groups. The week after they've finally claimed your abode as their own, you have more company than you've had all semester.

Your sales-talk immediately gets all their attention, as you explain how happy you've been here all year. "Only one window?" You brush off this critical question, with advantages like a good view of the East Parlor traffic and the inspiration of the Golden Dome all winter.

But when the last has gone and the new owner has chosen, you sit and look around and feel a certain sense of loyalty. Now you wish you could unsay all the things you've said all year about the poor thing.

As you pack the last golfer in the trunk and get ready to leave, you think, "This really wasn't such a bad little room after all."

—Kay Hardesty, May 6, 1956

Five

And So I Say Goodbye

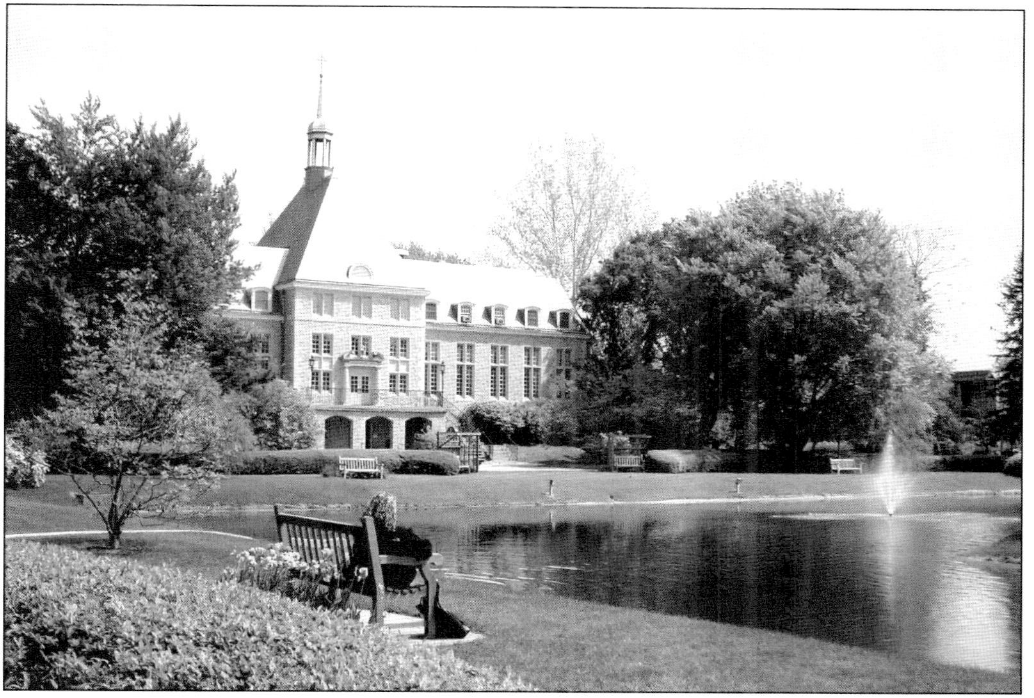

April's a nice month at Saint Mary's College—it's only three weeks long, for one thing. Besides, there were the K. of C. Ball and our own Spring Formal, and oh, yes, the seniors preparing for comps. Everyone's affected by them in one way or another. There's the senior who goes around muttering things about ologies and isms; the freshman who sees her and doesn't know what it's all about; the sophomore who looks, pities, and shrugs her shoulders, thinking that why should she worry two years too early; and then there's the junior who looks, pities, and shudders, thinking that in only twelve months.

—Harriet Enneking '48, *St. Mary's Static*, April 1947

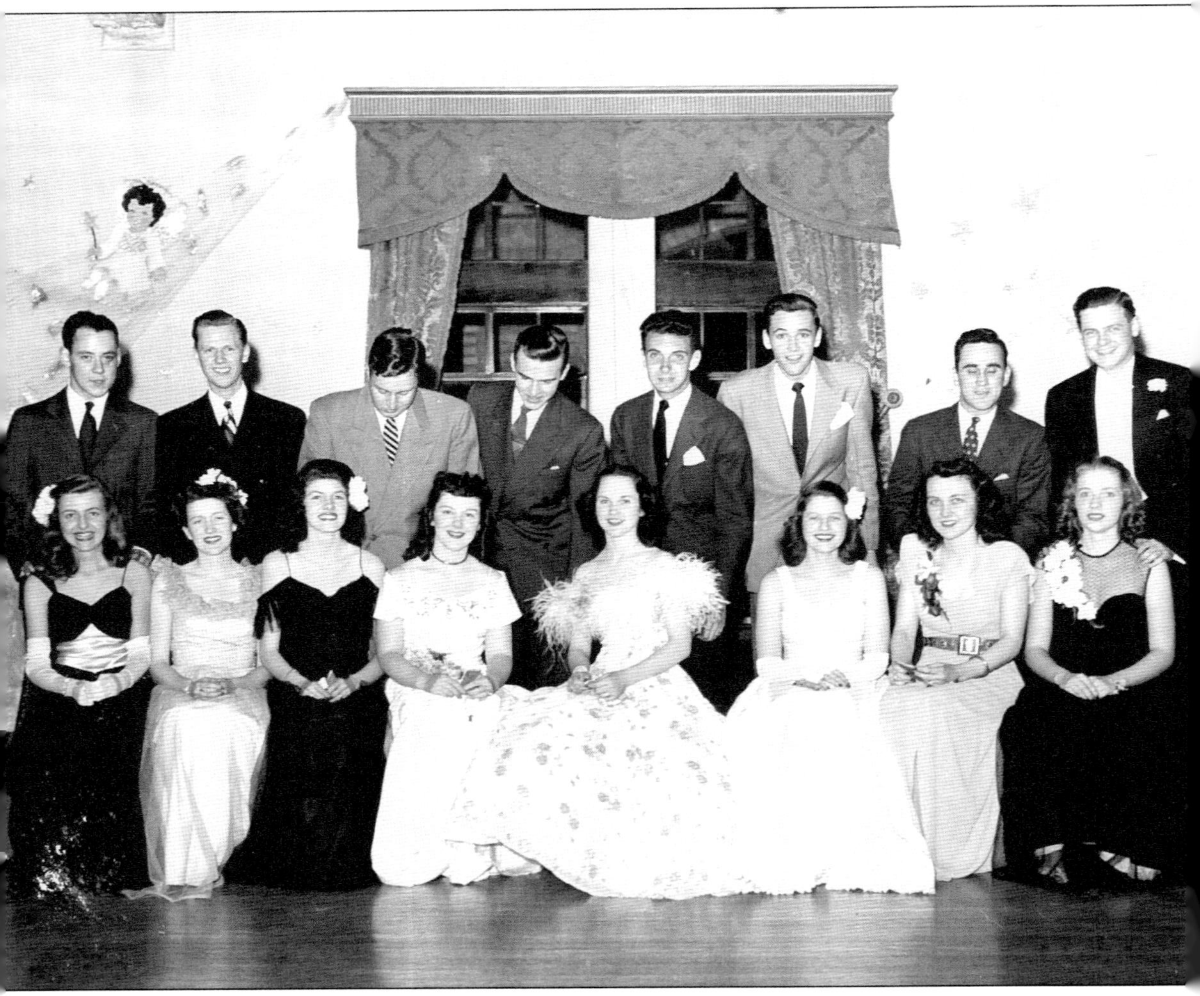

Seeing the freshmen when we returned this fall gave us pause: they thought we were old! The "last times" began—our final football season. Never had any of us seen a mass migration like that after the Oklahoma game. We "discovered" South Bend when we student taught and decided the town had more appeal that we'd thought. The snowiest Winter Carnival of all joined October Jubilee on our calendars as "Great Fun" times. Many of us acquired "commitments" during the September to Christmas stretch and sported diamonds, miniatures and pins. We took semester exams for the last time and got in more skating than we ever had before. Then comp study became accelerated as we compared notes in the Rec while peeling the remnants of a Florida tan. Nineteen days, we said at Monday morning breakfast. The AAUW tea, like the earlier Alumnae breakfast, made us feel as if we were already graduated. Senior Ball in O'Laughlin meant almost as much as the Mass and Communion breakfast the next morning.

The seniors look back...We anticipate happiness; we believe we now understand what happiness is. Remembering the days at Saint Mary's, we leave knowing that it is right to go, that we are prepared for whatever comes, but somehow wishing that it hadn't flown so fast. Self-ashamed of our own sentimentality we look back, and wipe a few tears.

—Paula Lawton '58

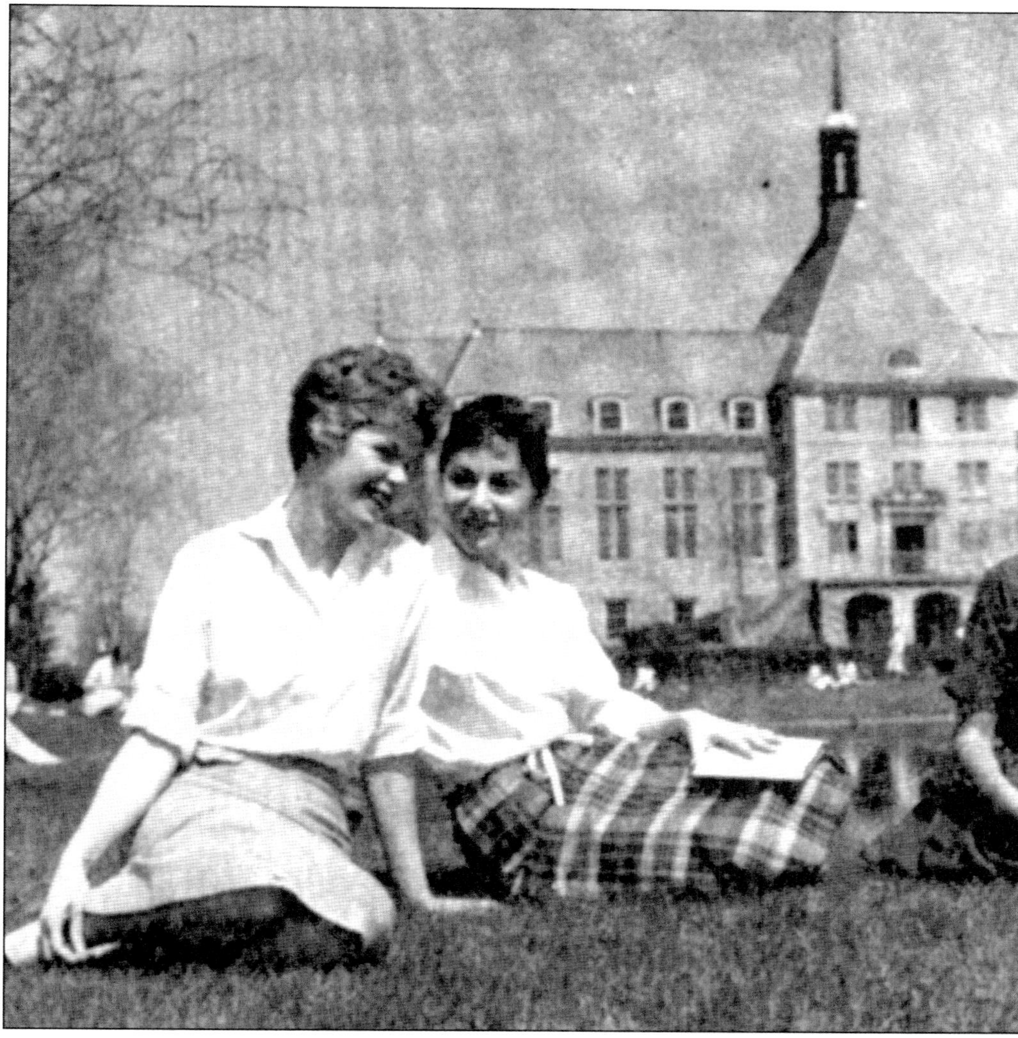

It can be easily said that May is the most enjoyable month at Saint Mary's. Dances, picnics, that weren't cancelled by rain, walks to Roseland, tennis, and all of this topped by a wonderful last week of exams, packing and shipping. You do all your exam studying under the willow tree, and of course expect sad results. As spring progresses there are more rings and pins coming SMC-ward. There's Rita Wilson with an N.D. ring; Mary Ann Fellinger, Mary Kay Liebmann and Rita McCann with miniatures; and Mary Lou Malone with an N.D. pin.

Seniors gladly cast off their caps and gowns and accept a brand new degree instead. Juniors gladly take the cast-off caps and gowns, eagerly accepting their new status. Good luck, seniors.

—Harriet Enneking '48, *St. Mary's Static*, April 1947

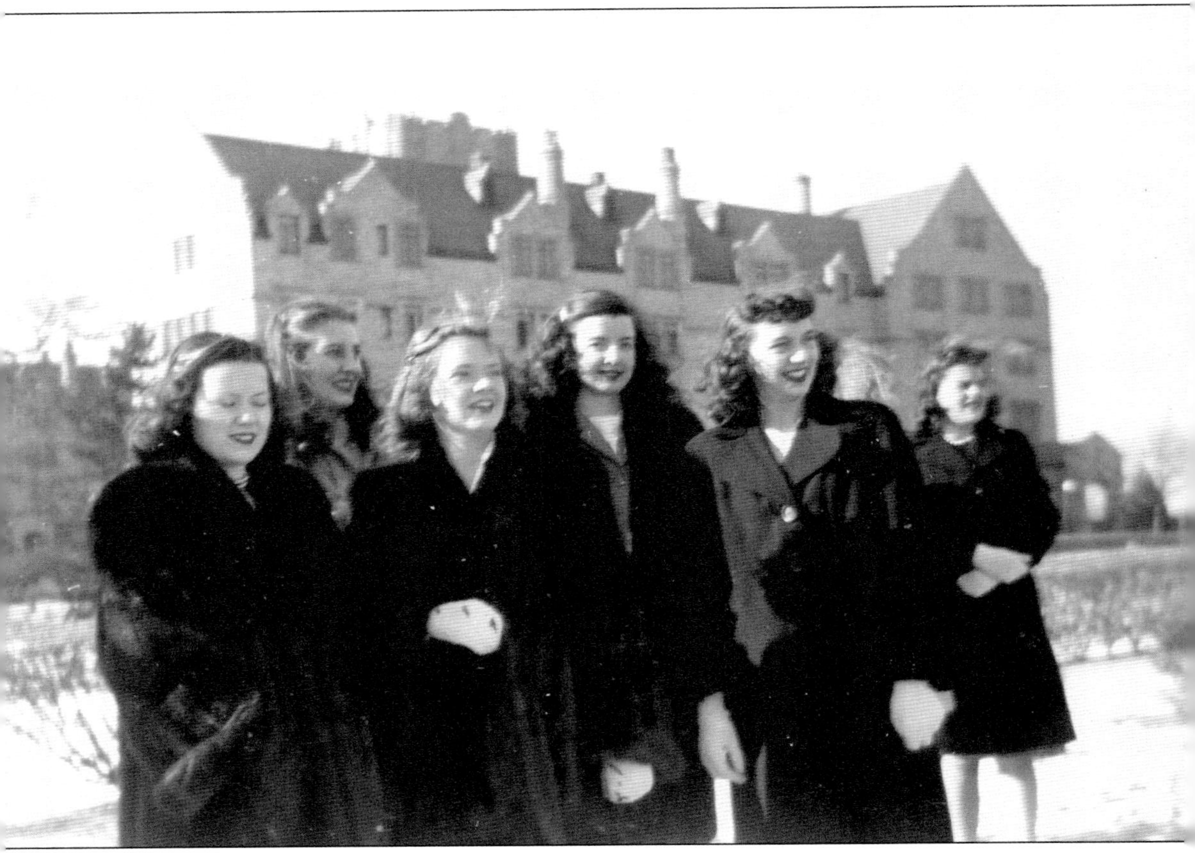

Blizzards, Charity Ball, Notre Dame dances, campused "pink slippers", snowball fights on the avenue, ice on Lake Marion, early winter twilight dulling the famous Gold Dome, terrific assignments, the formal Christmas dinner, tulle and velvet, silver tinsel and scarlet poinsettias, and finally, hastily packed suitcases and packed trains—that's December, our favorite month, all three weeks of it.

Of the "men in our lives" the fathers are usually overlooked in favor of the others, but you've never seen anyone happier than Louise Brady when her father stopped in to see her. Colonel Brady has been overseas since Lou was a sophomore in high school.

Knitting socks, mittens, and sweaters must seem too prosaic to that freshman we spied in the Kell last week. She was very energetically knitting a THING which appeared to be about six inches wide, and four or five feet long. In the knitting line, Rosie Reuss leads the school. She's knitting all her Christmas presents, brave girl.

—Clare Kessell '46, *St. Mary's Static*, December 1945

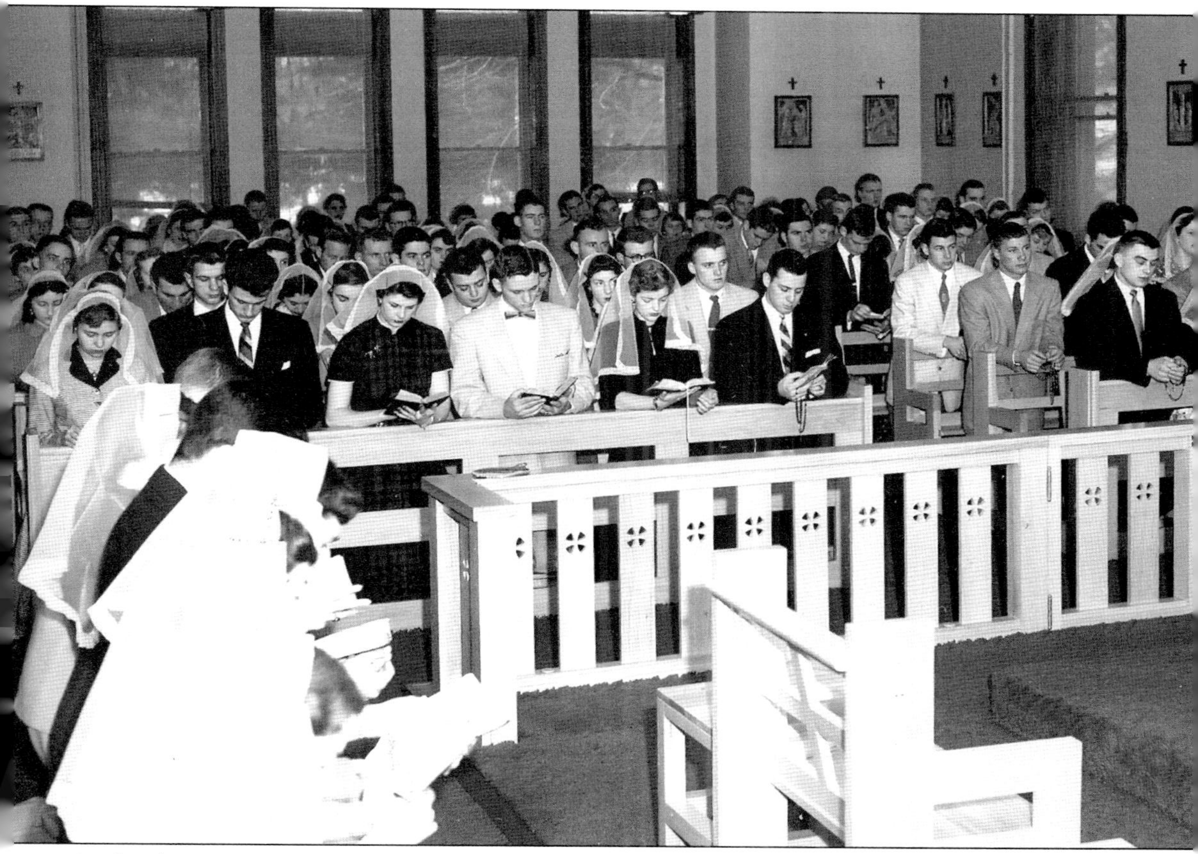

As the departing magnolias and the budding lilacs erase the recollections of the monsoon season, the seniors develop a mass case of nostalgia, complicated by spring fever. Memories of other springs on the campus make this May especially cherishable. "Rec" chatter is punctuated by the "remember this" and "will you ever forget that" as the seniors look back.

When we were freshmen, ten-thirties meant a Friday night permission. Quarterlies terrified us and our first Christmas dinner charmed us. We rolled our hose and wished we could wear sox.

Sophomore year meant a move to Le Mans, except for the fortunate forty still in HC. Four annex got Arctic cold. We ran the Winter Carnival that year, with the help of our very understanding and "young-of-heart" Sister Rose Loreto. We underwent the agony of declaring majors, changed our minds, resigned and sometimes changed again. Christian culture and medical technology majors opened new vistas for us. We said goodbye to many classmates—some left to marry, some to transfer, some to work.

Big sisters ourselves in the fall, we conducted tours around the Notre Dame campus and later got blind dates through our little sisters. The glamour of the opera dazzled us. We got lost a million times in the O'Laughlin labyrinth. The Christmas festivities were ours to manage. Despite drooping eyes and dragging feet, we loved every candlelit minute of the pre-dawn Christmas caroling. Everybody seemed to be tipping the canoe and Sister Gretchen was an angel about shortening that formal for the big ND dance. The time flew and suddenly it was Cap and Gown night. The jokes about tassels in the eye, dipping hems and sleeves that could hide a Webster's Unabridged only masqueraded our new awareness of the inexorable passage of the "best years of our lives."

—Paula Lawton '58

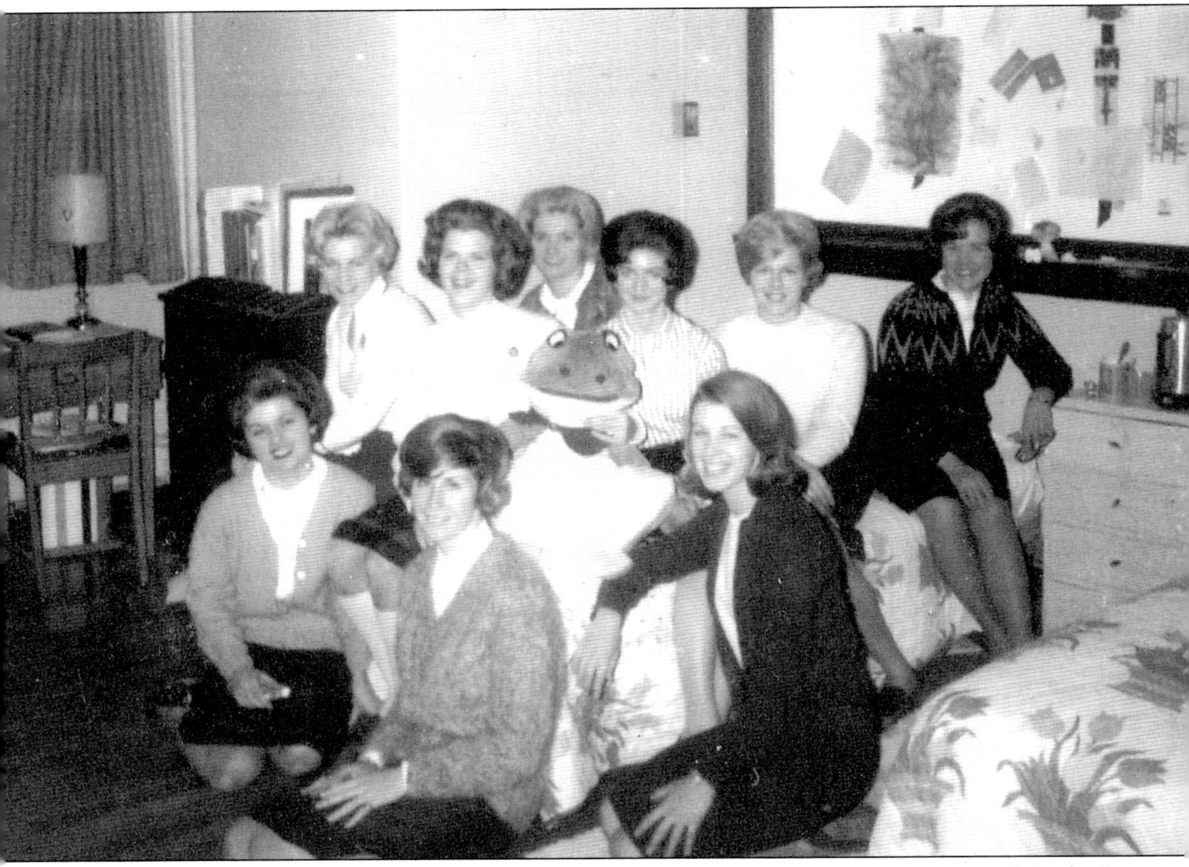

I met so many wonderful women at Saint Mary's College, who are very successful people today. In my four years there, my roommates alone were from all corners of the United States... from Vienna, Virginia to Wanatah, Indiana to Minneapolis, Minnesota to San Diego, California to Houston, Texas...My roommates and I went from Saint Mary's to ...work for a very successful investment fund, become a teacher, become a nurse, continue schooling to a doctorate level, research cures for cancer and become a member and active participant in the commodity futures trading worlds. In addition, most everyone married and has a family. I am from Long Island, New York, and having this diversity of people at Saint Mary's opened doors and windows to the world. I saw a lot of this country, just visiting my roommates and their families. I learned much about myself and about different people. In my junior year I moved off campus to the Campus View Apts., and again met a diverse group of SMC and ND people, who also became close friends, and still are today. I think the diversity of people at Saint Mary's is an important part of the education package. Attending college at Saint Mary's was a wonderful adventure, and people were a big part of that and my own success today.

—Mary E. Pellicane '80

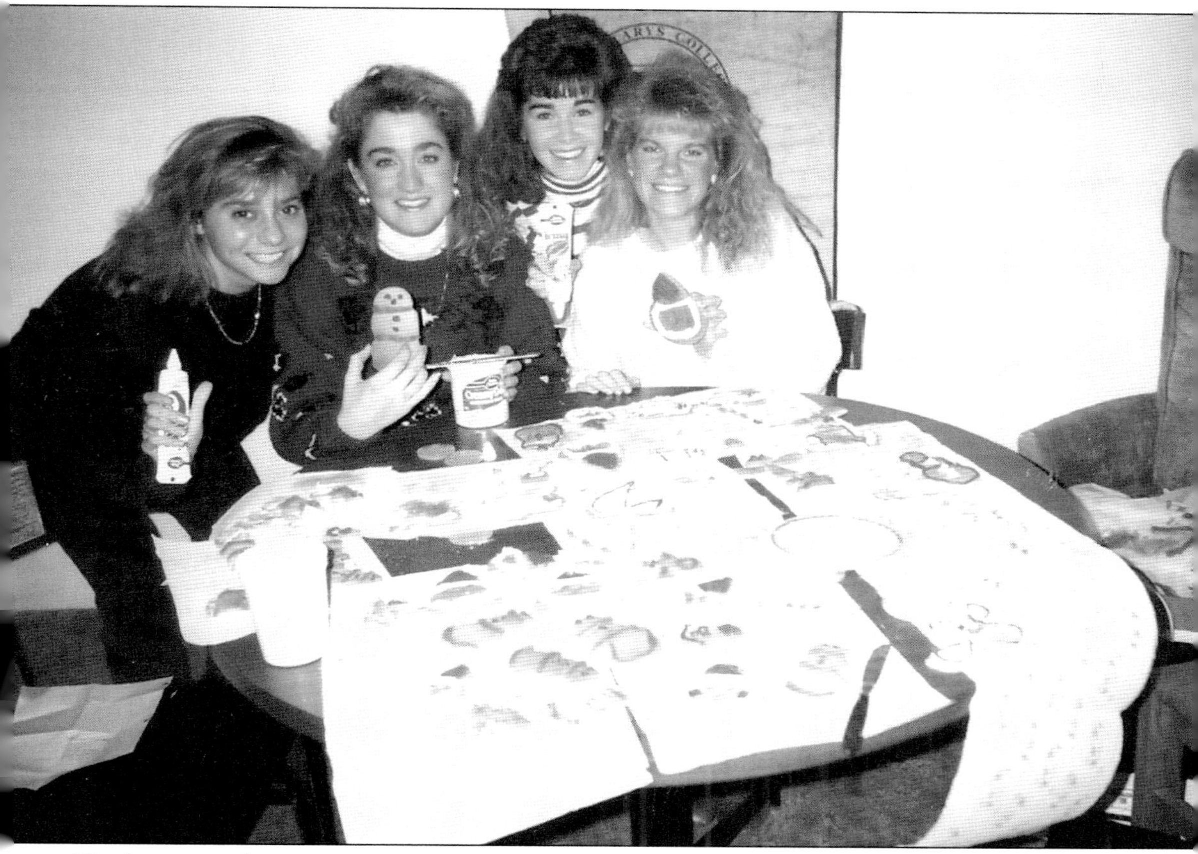

The four years that I spent at Saint Mary's were some of the best in my life. The most important lesson personally that I learned was the value of true friendship. My memories were wonderful because of my roommates and friends. We shared our joys and our disappointments were always made better because you knew there was always someone you could talk to and count on.

Some of my favorite memories with my friends at SMC are: being at Bridget's on Saint Patrick's Day at 7A.M.; road tripping in a very small car to go skiing in Colorado and to New Orleans for Mardi Gras; always ending up at the Commons late at night to have some popcorn (we called it "the buffet"); visiting our home towns together and learning about everyone's childhood; getting ready for and celebrating the holidays together; getting our families together during the weekends for sophomore parents, junior moms and senior dads; playing bookstore basketball; all the SYR's and Senior Formal in Chicago.

The memories and friendships that I have from Saint Mary's are life long and I could not have wished for a better college experience.

—Katy Calsin-Keffler '91

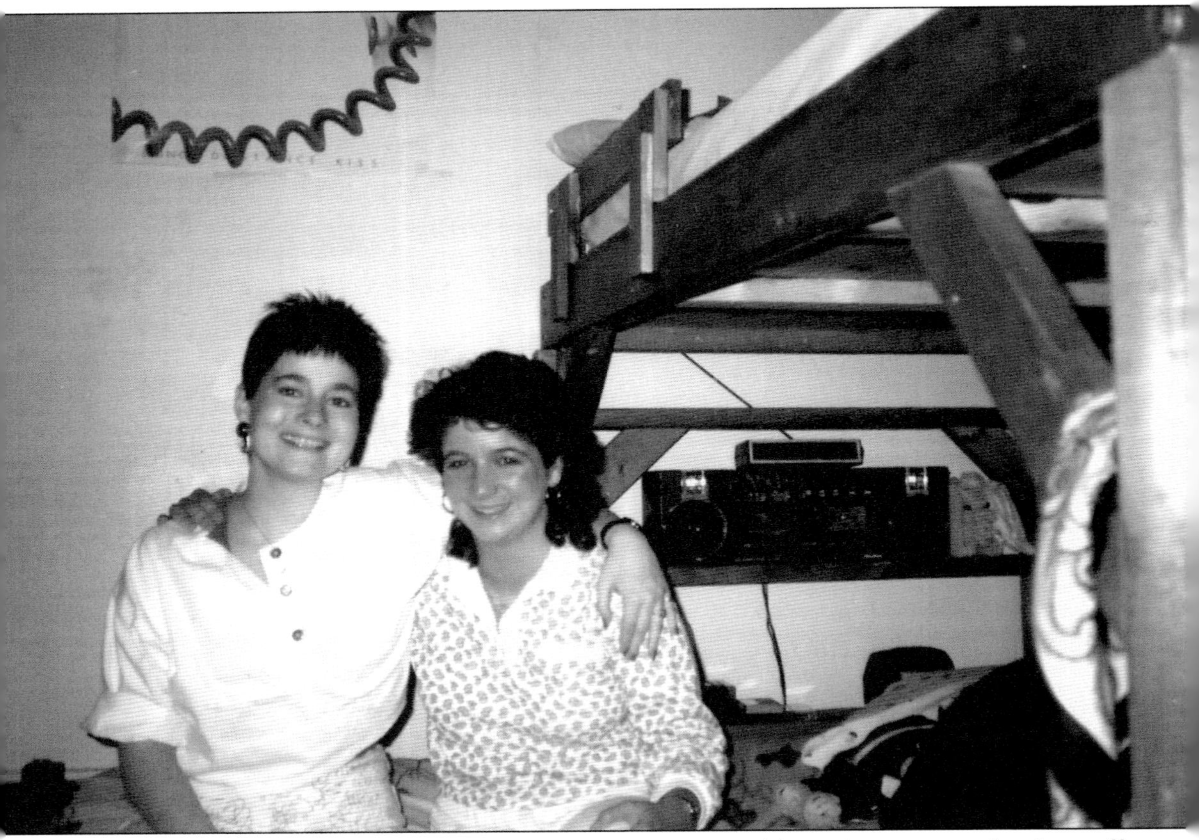

My most memorable experience was the compassion and love shown to me by the staff and teachers to fulfill a dream and make one student feel special.

I was diagnosed with Systemic Lupus Erythematosus when I was sixteen years old and told that I would probably not live to be twenty. Chemotherapy left me weak and frail. Although I made it to my fifth year, the workload and energy required to make it to graduation seemed impossible.

It is because of these staff members and teachers that I was able to come to realize that it's the little things that truly make an impact on one's life. They took the time to show me—one student—the compassion and attention I desperately needed. The cafeteria workers would send over my favorite foods to get me to eat, since they knew that I needed the energy to get to my many tests. The teachers, like Professor Shannon, convinced the other teachers to give this determined student a chance to try and graduate.

Because of the help, encouragement, and dedication from all of these amazing people, I proudly graduated with my class in 1988 with a Bachelor of Business Administration with a minor in Chemistry.

The lessons you learn in college are vast. You learn about who you are and who you want to be, but the most important lesson for me was to be compassionate to all who cross my path in this life journey. You'll never know when it will come back to you tenfold. You'll never realize the impact it has on someone's life. Your education doesn't just come from the books and lectures, but from the people around you throughout your life. Thank you to all the staff of Saint Mary's College, you have made a difference in my life and made me feel special.

—Jennifer Glunz Faulk '88

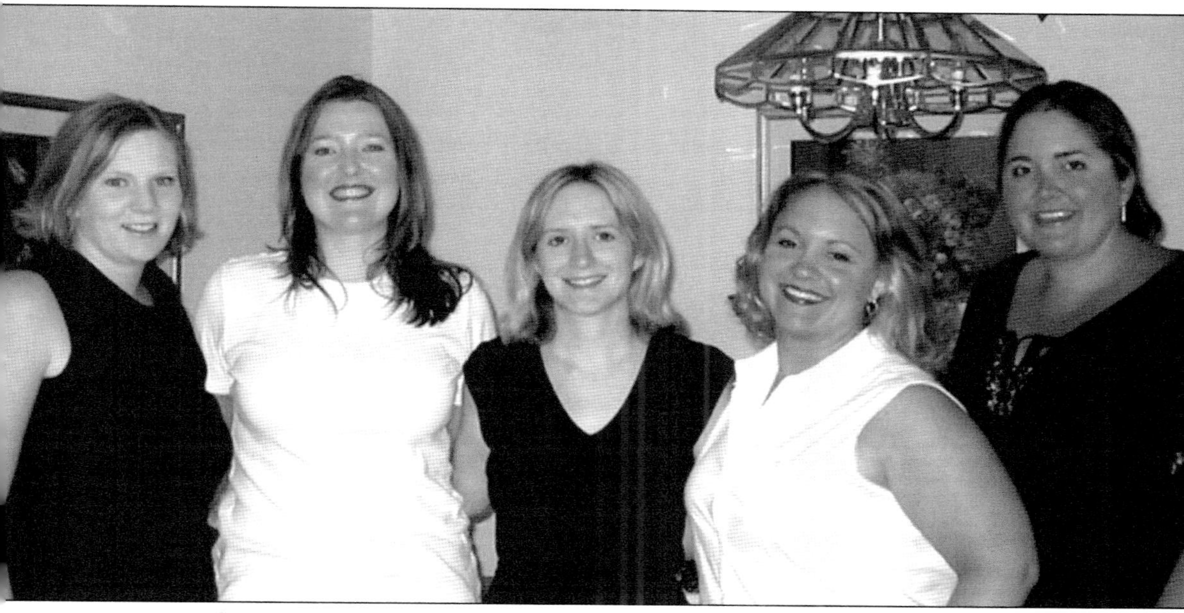

As I prepare for graduation, I remember that I might not have been here; I might not have gotten to wear my cap and gown and I might not have been able to receive my diploma. Without my four guardian angels, I may not have been able to experience any of these things.

It was a quiet Sunday morning here at Saint Mary's College or, at least, that is what my roommates and I thought. My roommates Kathy Kasmer and Lindsay Richardson and I were preparing to go to brunch in the dining hall. This day was supposed to be a day preparing for finals. I was sitting on the couch in our room when the right side of my body went numb. I could not move and I could not talk. My two roommates watched me go from slightly coherent to totally oblivious but they kept their cool and phoned for help. When security arrived in our room, they tried to get me to stand up. I stood there, no feeling, grasping my roommate for dear life.

I was rushed to the emergency room. My roommates stayed while countless tests were conducted. Shortly, our friend Colleen Kross came to my bedside as well. They tried to entertain me even though they knew I was in pain.

When I was released, my friends made sure I was under constant supervision. One of the tests I had at the hospital was a spinal tap, a very painful procedure where spinal fluid was taken from my back to determine if I had a stroke. During this procedure, it was Colleen Kross that stood by my side.

After the procedure, I returned to my bed in Le Mans Hall. Lindsay, Kathy, Colleen, along with our friend Brooke Brumbaugh made the "Shelley Shifts"; this schedule made sure that I was never alone. These four exceptional women unselfishly took time out of their study time in order to be with me. They rearranged their work schedules to get food for me in the dining hall and come and eat with me. Lindsay even delayed going home after her last exam in order to be with me.

Only a few people at Saint Mary's College are even aware of this incident. I can confidently say that without these caring, brave, unselfish and loving women, I would not be here today. During this year's graduation, look around you my four guardian angels may be right next to you!

Thanks Lindsay Richardson, Kathy Kasmer, Colleen Kross and Brooke Brumbaugh. I love you.

—Shelley Raley '00

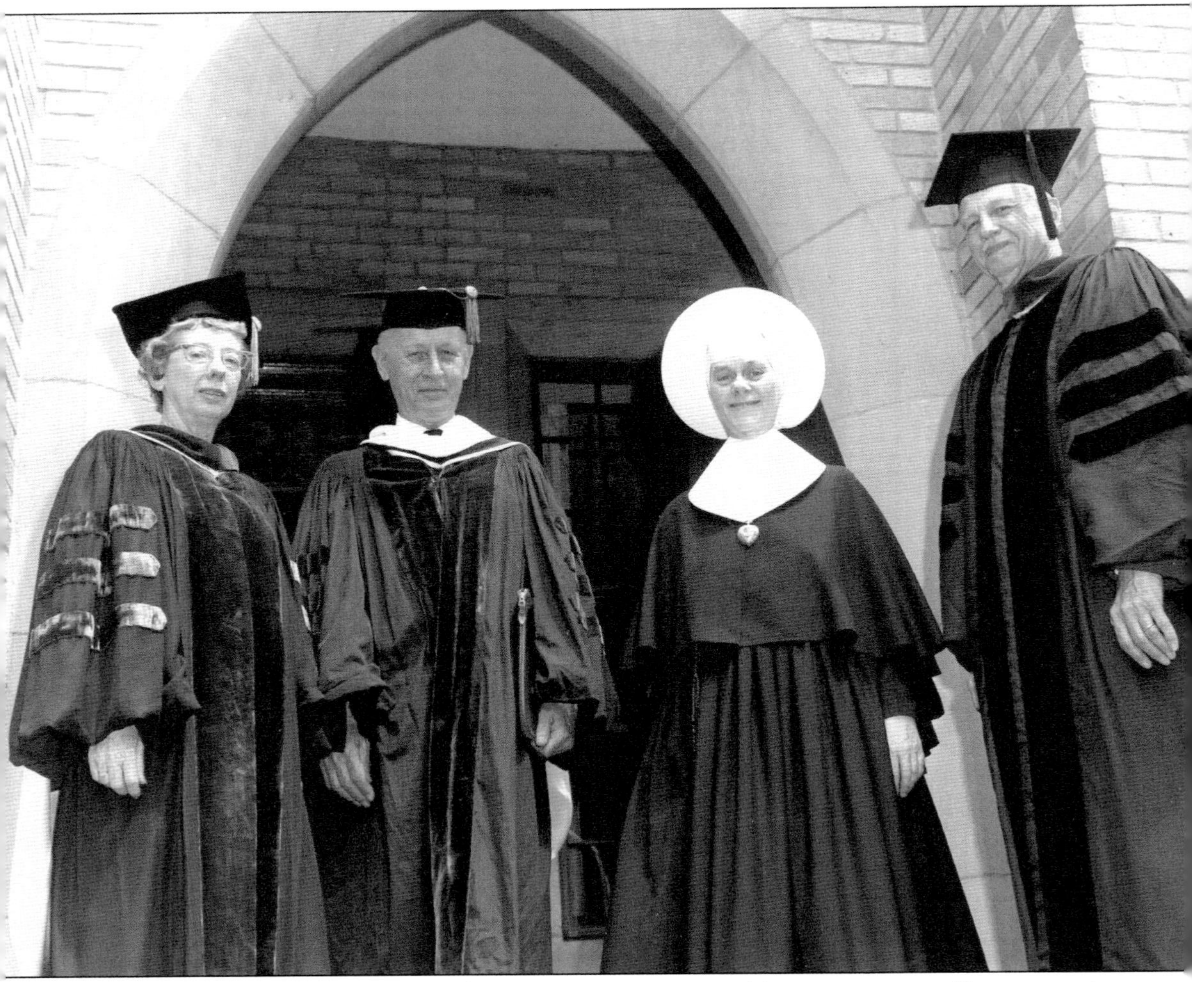

Education at Saint Mary's is not about memorization or writing papers or reading mountains of books, although all of that will be a part of your life here. Education at Saint Mary's is not about graduating with the ability to think clearly about complex problems, or about acquiring the ability to think critically and creatively, or even about developing competence in diverse academic fields, although all of that will be part of what you acquire here. Education at Saint Mary's is about taking a girl from high school and transforming her into a young woman with a keen self-knowledge, a lively imagination, lifelong intellectual and cultural interests, and the ability to make socially responsible choices. Saint Mary's does not simply teach that women have some responsibility to make the world better than we found it. Saint Mary's assumes that women seek quality higher education because we are destined to be educators, philosophers, and leaders.

—Excerpt from address given by Elizabeth Jablonski-Diehl '04, student body president (2003–2004), to accepted students in O'Laughlin Auditorium

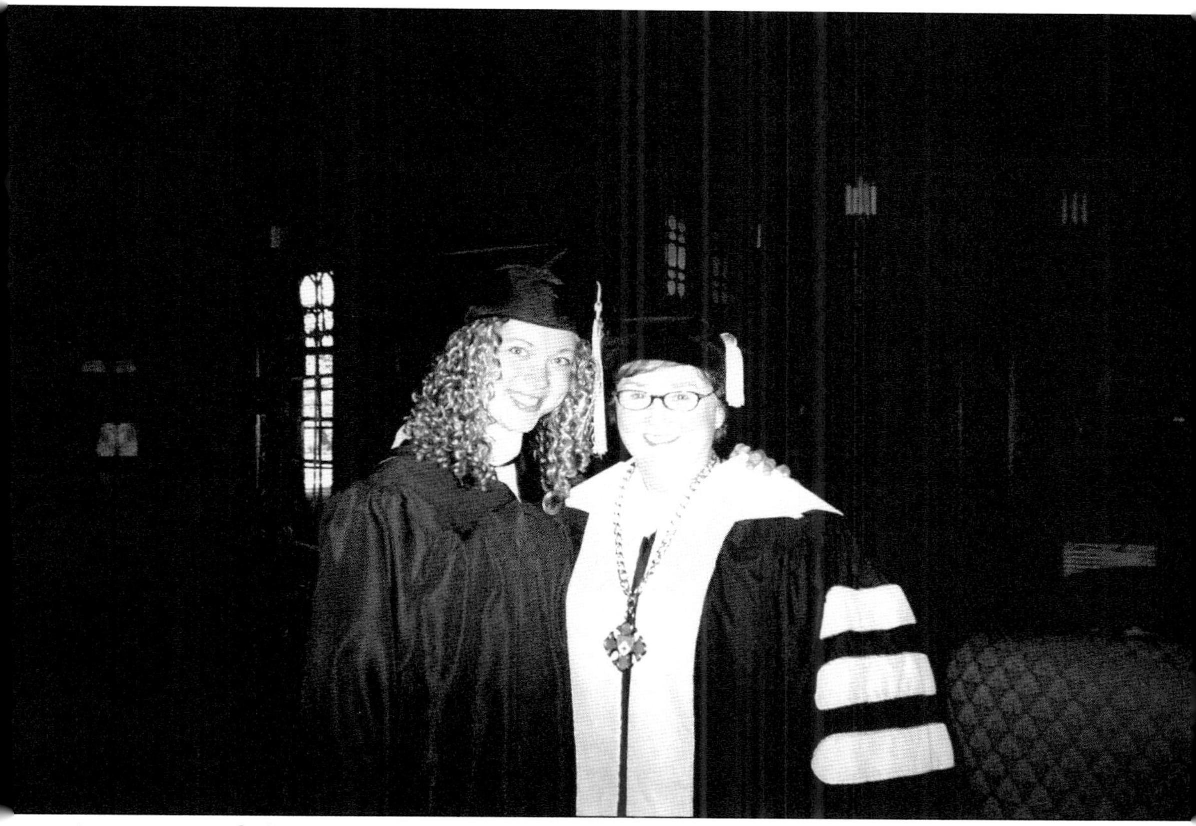

An amazing gift that Saint Mary's College offers is the role models all around you ready to help you achieve your dream. From the College President who serves as a daily reminder of what a dedicated woman can achieve, to women who graduated only a year before but still care enough to help you with living arrangements for your first year out of college. Saint Mary's College women write national best-sellers. Several of them are members of Congress. More than a handful run major corporations. Saint Mary's cannot give you a seat in Congress, but it can teach you to communicate with precision so you can win one. Saint Mary's cannot make you a corporate president, but it can teach you the analytical skills to become one.

—Excerpt from address given by Elizabeth Jablonski-Diehl '04, student body president (2003–2004), to accepted students in O'Laughlin Auditorium

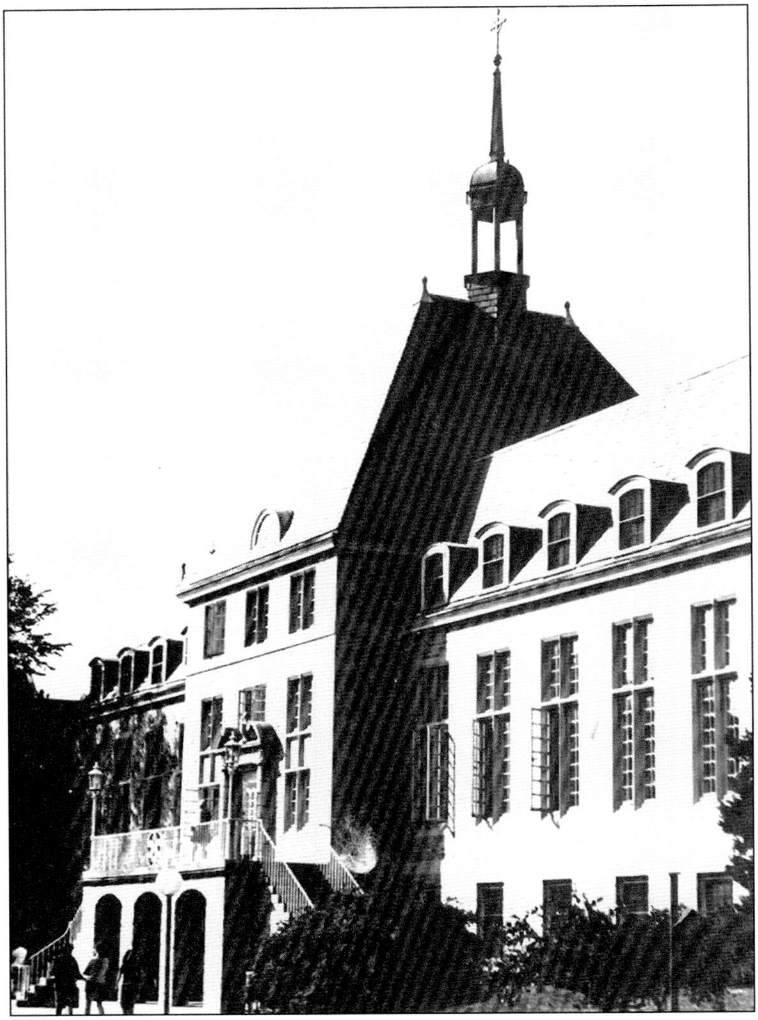

Coming to SMC, in 1964, for freshman year, was an experience. Even the 4 years saw changes. Even to go to the library, you had to sign in/out. Of course, the ND library was a big attraction. Did we really study there? Freshmen had "big sisters" (juniors) and "secret sisters" (sophomores) to help you through your first year.

Panty raids. Loved watching those ND guys coming down the lane. Going off campus. You had to have a written note from the person with whom you would stay. The note would stay in your sign out sheet. Telephone duty. No phones were in the rooms until the end of senior year. You had to sit at the phone in the hall, answer, walk to the room to get the person, and write a message if the person wasn't there. Sign out/in for a date. Sister Immaculata was always at the desk. With a curfew of 10:30 weeknights and 11 or 11:30 weekends, you were afraid to be late.

House mother. Each dorm had one to check that lights were out, all in their beds, and no cooking was going on in the rooms (stuffing towels under the door did not hide the smell of popcorn, or the light while studying in the closet). ND boys taking up your luggage and trunks to your rooms at the beginning of each year. Who could forget the days of Saint Mary's, the friends made, things learned, fond memories, and 4 wonderful years!

—Sally Blackley Clemmer '68

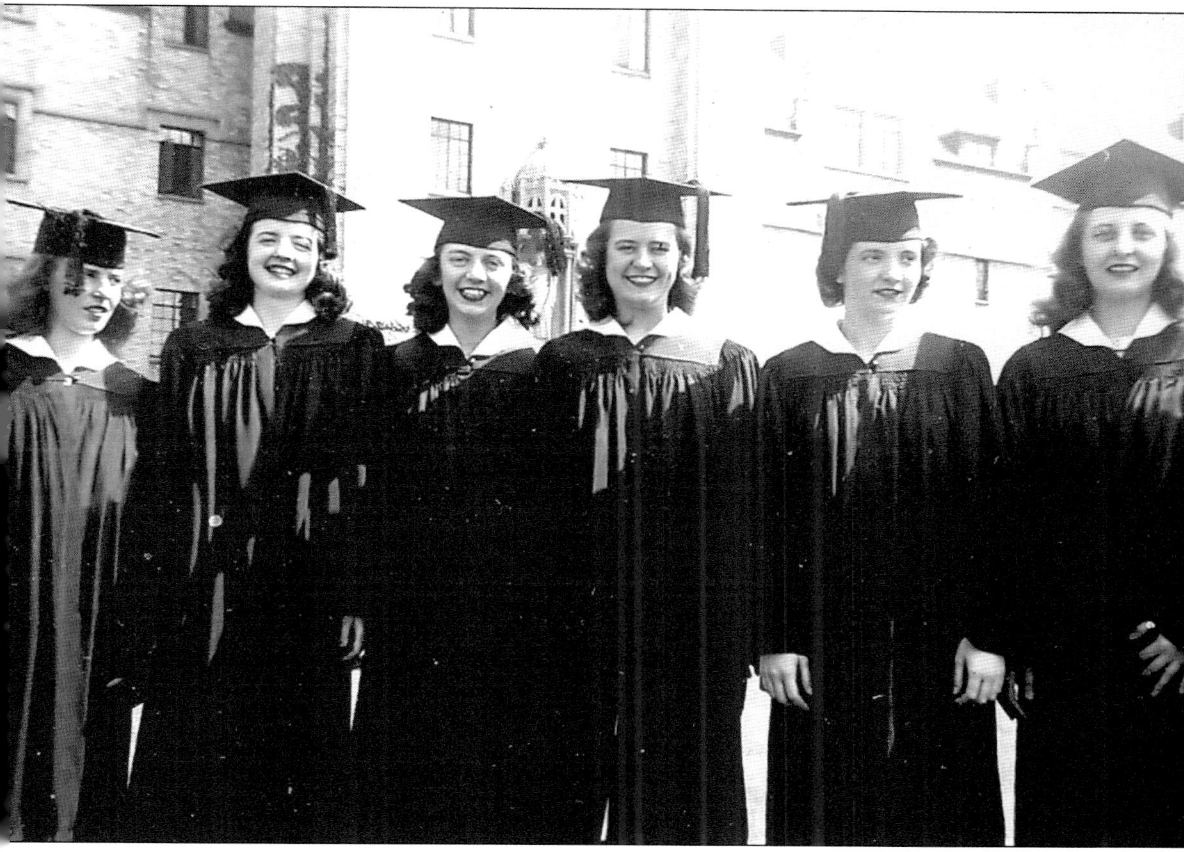

Do I remember? How could I forget: Freshman Week of 1942 and my copy of "Notes on Planning an Attractive Room"...the Oliver Coffee Shop was the place that year...Sister Rebecca and her rascals...Carlos took our pictures and not even our parents recognized us...we met the Trapp family...and so on. That was one year of college as usual, college "in the grand manner."

By September of our Sophomore year the war had caught up with us. It swept away many of the trimmings but discovered to us a college life that we had failed to appreciate fully before. Perhaps we were beginning to come of age. That was the year we functioned as the "utility class"...Notre Dame took the National Football Championship..."The Summons of Sariel" won the play tournament...the era of botany and biology...and the admission to the Friday night movie was by war stamp only.

Junior year we came into our own as Big Sisters...playing hostess at the Christmas party...the unforgettable "I'll Be Seeing You" Junior Prom...winning the basketball championship for the third year...the first time we tried on our caps and gowns.

Senior year came and the byword was "This is our last Charity Ball"...or our last football game or Mardi Gras or Lent at Saint Mary's..."Birthday of the Infanta" won the play tournament... comprehensives and the survival of the fittest...that last Sunday at Mass and the sound of the organ....

—Peggy Kirby, *St. Mary's Static*, May 1946

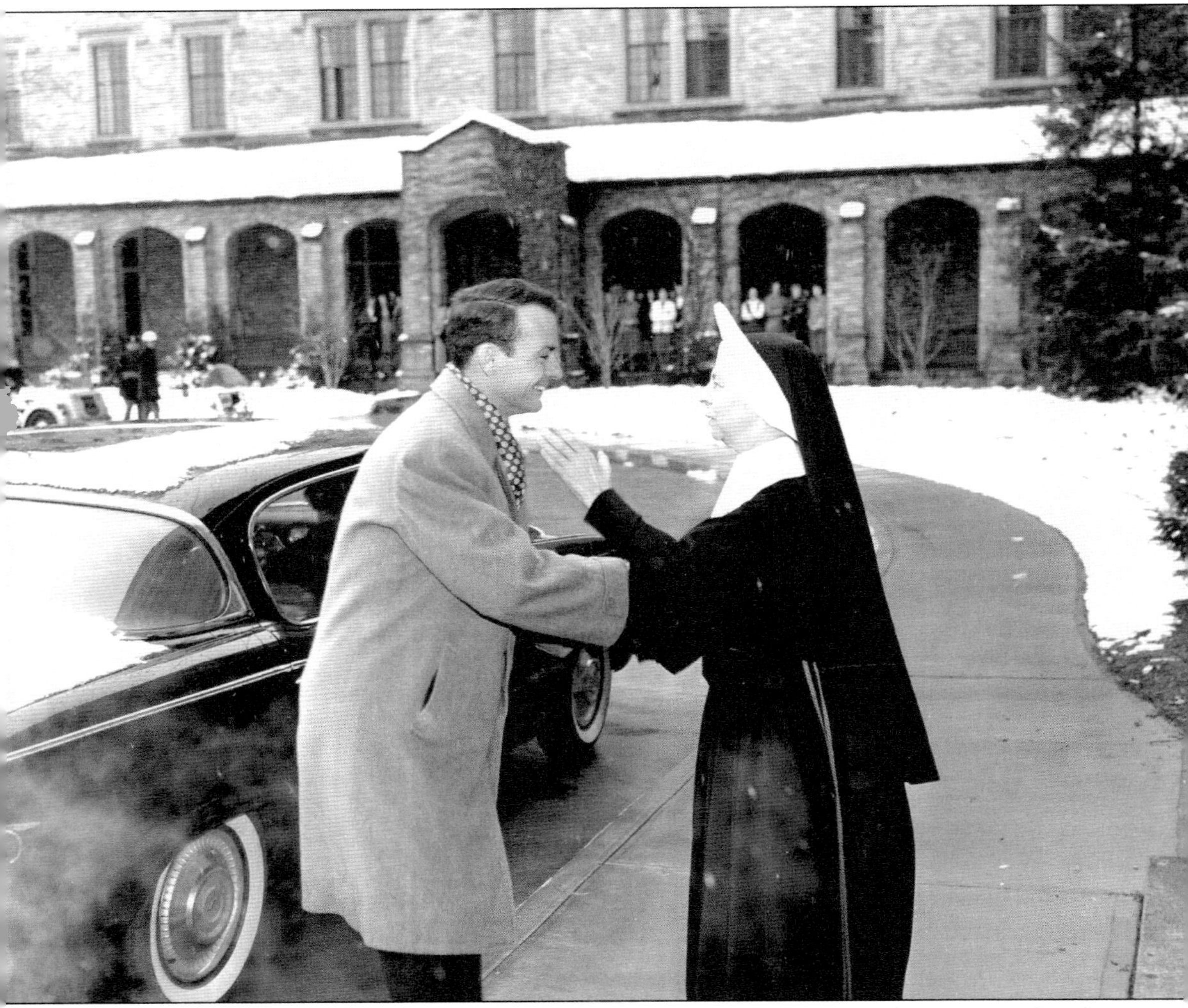

The high point of graduation day 1960 at Saint Mary's was the meeting of my younger brother, David Ryan, who was then age thirteen, with honorary degree recipient Doctor Tom Dooley. Doctor Dooley was a celebrity at the time because he had been ministering as a doctor to the impoverished in Southeast Asia and had written a best-seller about his experiences. I believe that at one time he was being considered for beatification.

David was standing outside the theater after graduation when Doctor Dooley came up to him and asked him to find out (I believe from Sister Madeleva) where he was to turn in his robe. It was a high point of the day for my family.

—Nancy V. Ryan Soller '60

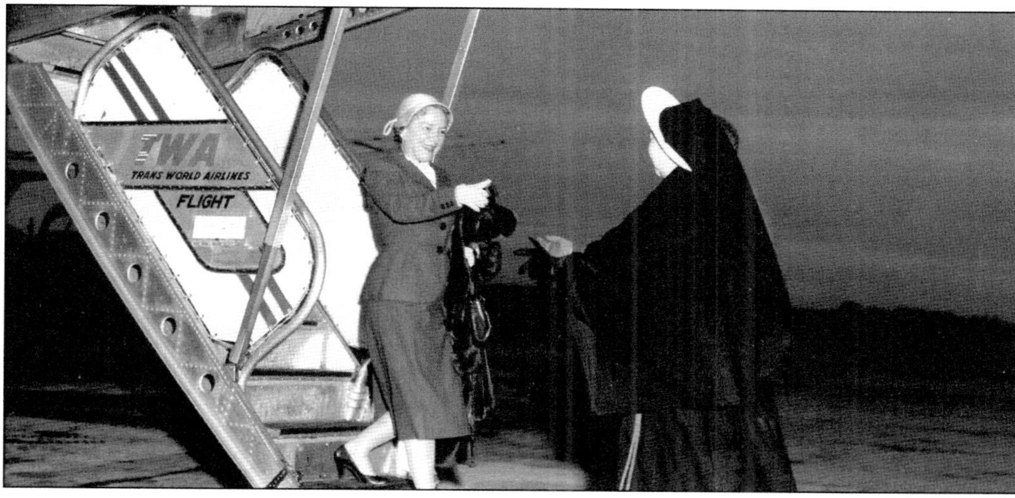

I remember meeting Helen Hayes and helping to unroll some student work to show her when she came to visit the art department many years ago. The work was a mural of the crusades done by Joan Pearson '60 as her senior art comp. I believe that later it was put in the new dining hall as a mural on the wall. Helen Hayes was as sweet, ladylike and gracious in person as she was on screen, TV and in the theater.

It was part of the work of my class too that did the mosaic that I believe is still on the outside wall of Moreau Hall. My part of the project was the right side of the Tree of Jesse.

—Nancy V. Ryan Soller '60

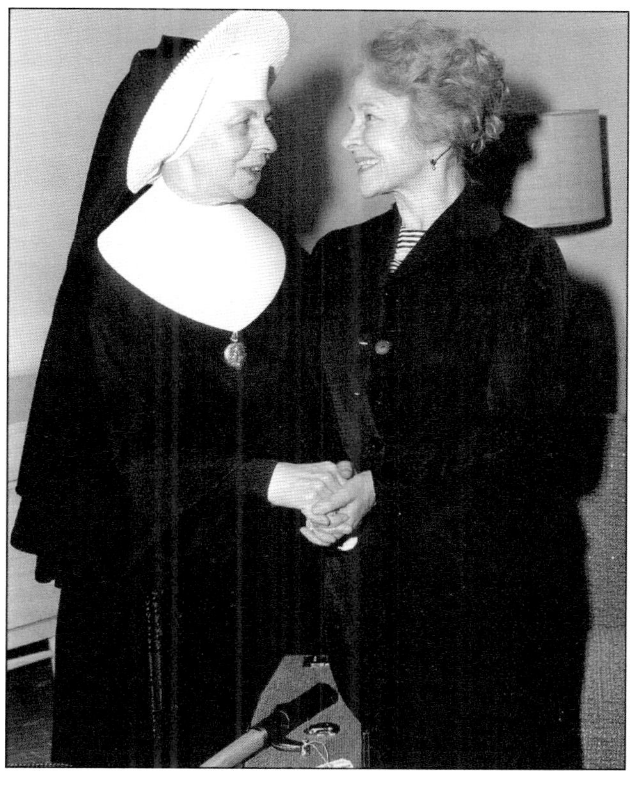

Helen Hayes, first lady of the American theater, laid the cornerstone of O'Laughlin Auditorium and Moreau Hall.
–St. Mary's Static
Senior Week, 1959

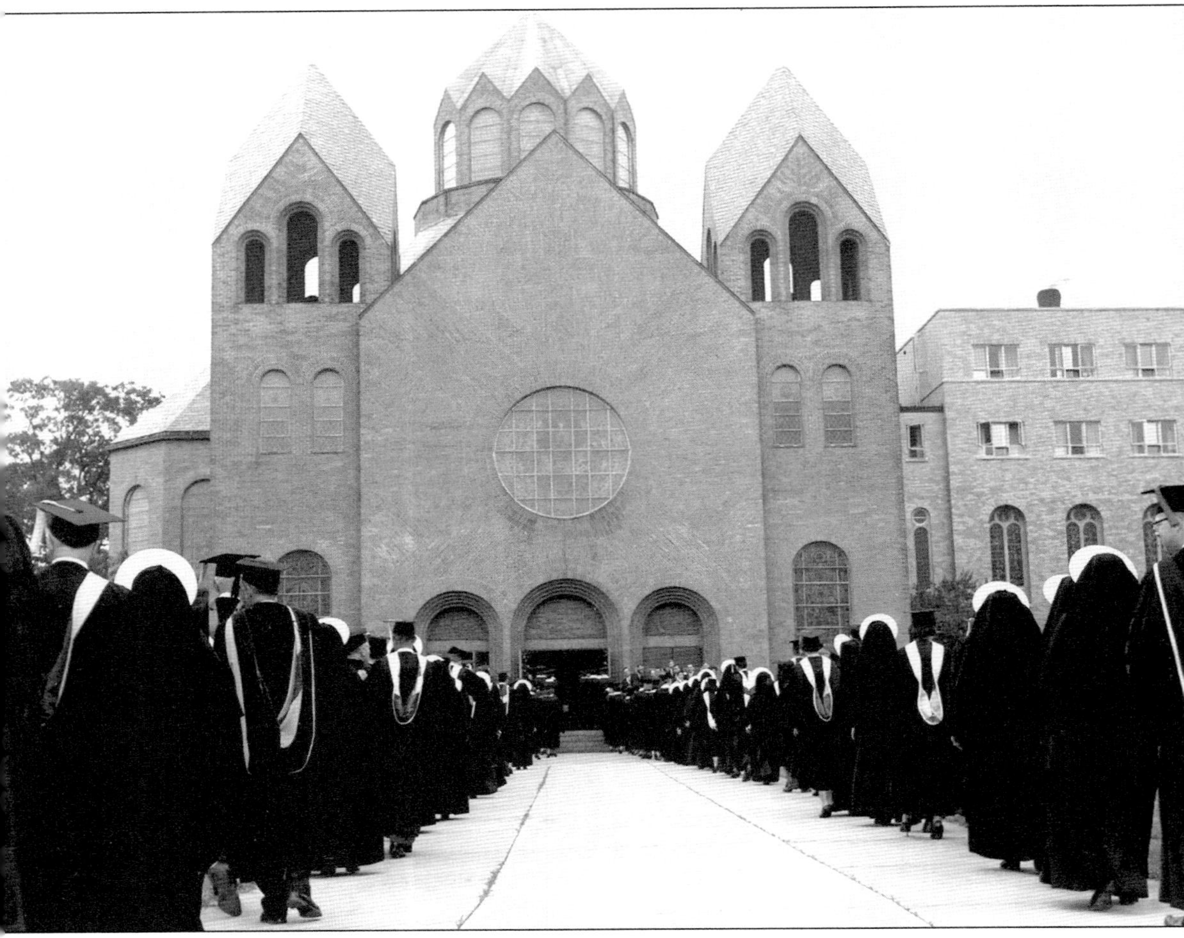

Things I'll miss:

Early morning Mass in Le Mans Chapel...the sun streaming through the open window...the dignity and priestliness of Father Schumacher. The walk to the gate in the spring...The stuffed animal parade leading to the chapel the night before Christmas vacation...Visits to the Chapel of Loreto...the rosary...The accents of girls from all over the world talking...and actually understanding each other....Sister Madeleva's Christmas "Convo" of candle light. Robert Speaight's readings...The real visual change of seasons here...The long walks at night...with the lights out...with someone...Sister Sophia's closing "convo" words:..."God be on your pillow"...Wonderfully thick letters from home....Mrs. Creighton's special thick strawberry shakes...Chocolate marshmallow birthday cakes...Father Hanley's retreat this year...Springtime at Saint Mary's...Those special teachers...the Breton-caps and blue cords of the Holy Cross Sisters...The walk from the Dixie to the Grotto...Memories...and more of a father, dead...and his living love of Notre Dame...The Lady...who protects and binds together into one...the ideals of our two schools...Saint Mary's...Notre Dame...A group of girls...all different yet all individual...A few close friendships...and many friends...Closely guarded important days...The thrill of Notre Dame games...that white handkerchief...Bits of Earth which seem special...because of where they are...traditions...Big sisters...and little scared faces...SPES UNICA on sweatshirts, wastebaskets, stationary...and just about everything...A life we'll never forget...memories we'll always treasure. The class of '59...

—Elaine Freitas, Senior Week 1959

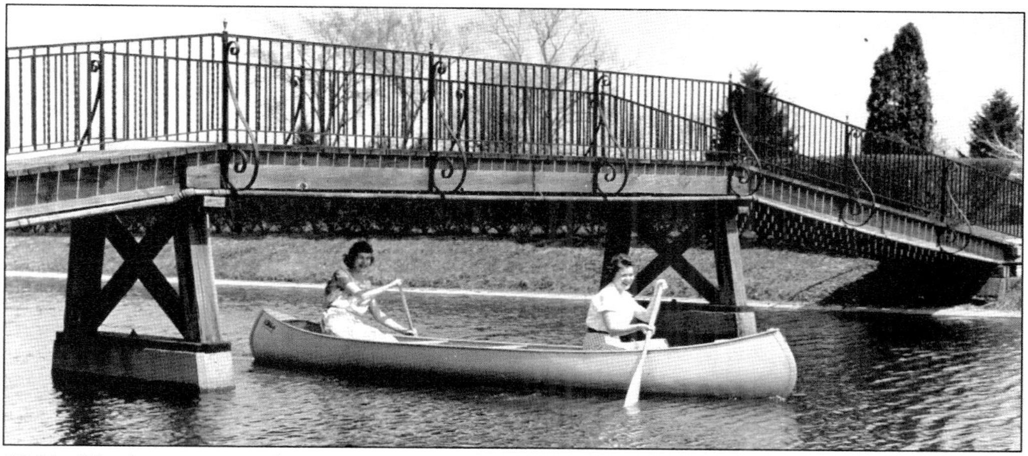

1944...The beginning of the end...Our senior year...Being entertained in the "Rec" by our talented Little Sisters...Our last retreat at Saint Mary's with the profound realization of its significance...Comprehensives climaxing the intellectual development of our college career...our Senior Ball...Wedding showers...refreshing dips in the lake, complete relaxation, carefree-senior week...Presenting the future seniors with their caps and gowns.

Thanks for the memories of Sister Kathryn Marie's "convos," canoeing on Lake Marian, visits to the Chapel of Loretto, Sister Madeleva's talks on poetry, fear of rain on Sports Day, bargaining with Sister Gretchen, 4:45 rush to the Oriole, Friday morning liturgy with Sister Judith. With gratitude not yet fully realized, we close the book of our college life.

—*St. Mary's Static* May 1945

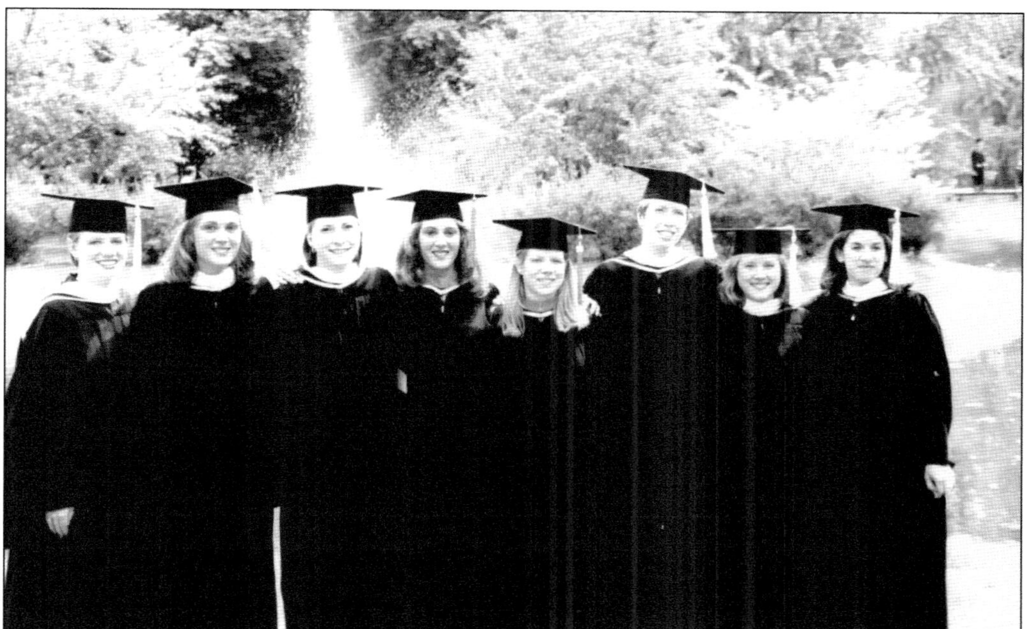

A very happy day, indeed, for all of us. May 16, 1999. Rachel Reynard Prickman, Jaime Sessions Kammerzell, Erin Emig LaCourt, Jennifer Sessions Kramer, Anne Eckert Yearsich, Jen D'Anastasio Prickman, Maureen Gill, and Mary Hubert.

—Erin Emig LaCourt '99

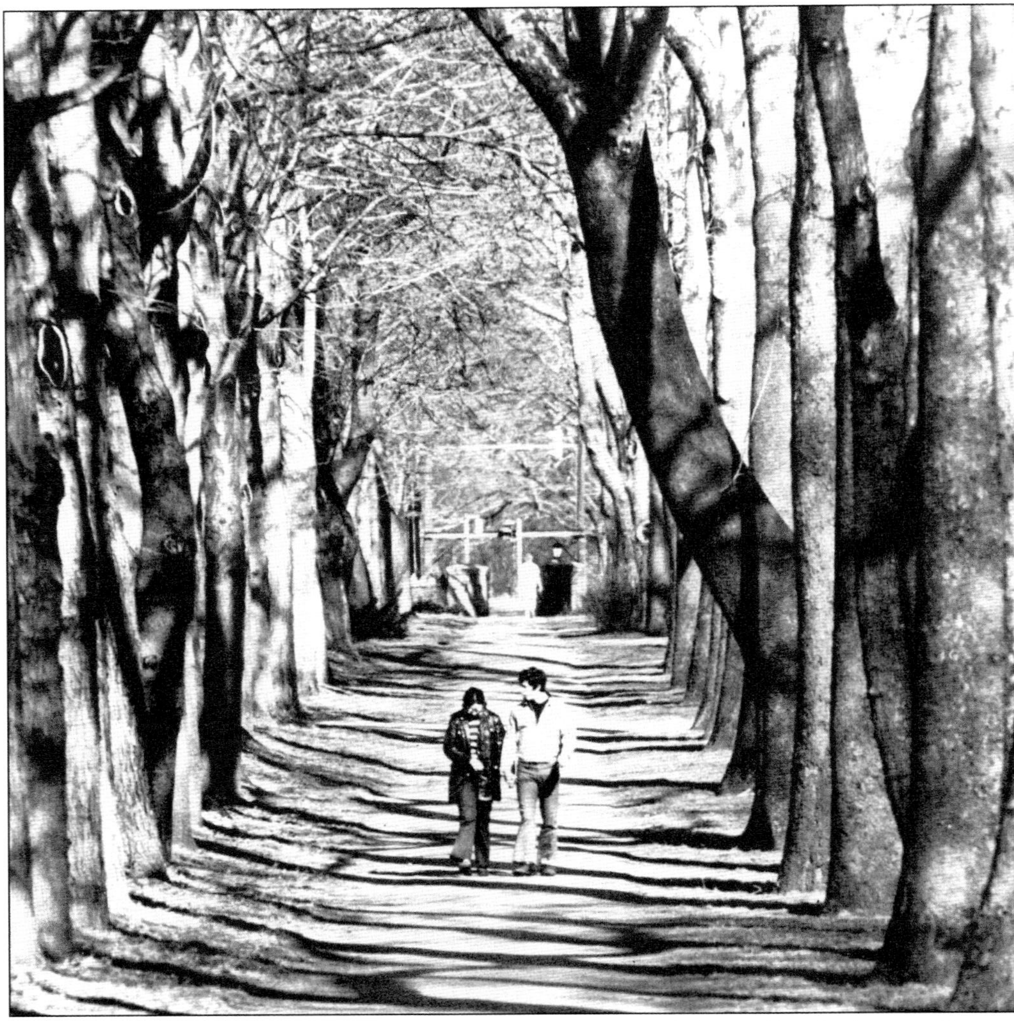

The phones in the halls and having guests in the parlor. And, the walks, the long walks, and my rocking chair and bicycle.

It was all so heavenly, such a wonderful feeling of community.

Sheila, we were blessed that we were able to go to school there. It was my Dad's dream that I went to Saint Mary's. My mother was neutral, because she had gone there. I think she wanted me to do all the things she did. But I rebelled and had my own experience. All those boys and the freedom from my parents expectations to be what they thought I should be.

My years at SMC and the evening I sat with FD, under the trees, and listened to them playing guitars, to me, is what heaven is going to be like.

—Junie Miller Smith '65

SAINT MARY'S COLLEGE
NOTRE DAME
HOLY CROSS, INDIANA

Feast of Our Lady of Mount Carmel
July 16, 1948

My very Dear,

Now that you have become one of our youngest alumnae we shall have to share you and your future wholeheartedly with Marion McCandless. Nevertheless, you will be interested in some bits of summer school news. Here they are.

Ninety students representing twenty-two different religious orders and some very splendid laywomen are enrolled in the School of Sacred Theology. There are two hundred students in regular undergraduate classes. So you see we are about half the size of the regular session and almost twice as busy. Possible?

Our alumnae reunion everyone thought the finest we have ever had. Because of the crucial needs of Catholic education and Catholic hospitals, the alumnae were asked to do all that they can to develop religious vocations, especially to active orders, and quite logically to the Holy Cross.

I am asking you to join in this great project. It is quite possible that you know or will meet someone who wishes to become a sister. Please encourage her. Send her name to me or ask her to write herself. As we told you on Honors Night, Catholic education depends on you and your upbuilding of religious orders. The future of the Church, under God, is your work, the major responsibility of your generation. Be tireless in your generosity and zeal to make it a golden age of Christianity. God has given you your education for this.

It has been delightful to hear from so many of the class of 1948 during the summer. I am sure that you are remembering your morning and night prayers, grace at meals, perhaps even the angelus and our dear sacraments: Confession, Holy Mass, Holy Communion. Know that we keep you in our hearts and prayers constantly. We shall remember you particularly on our Lady's feasts of Mount Carmel and the Assumption.

Yours in the Holy Spirit,

Sister M. Madeleva

SMM:SBM

Sister M. Madeleva, President

A letter from Sister Madeleva to the alumnae class of 1948 requesting their support of religious vocations.

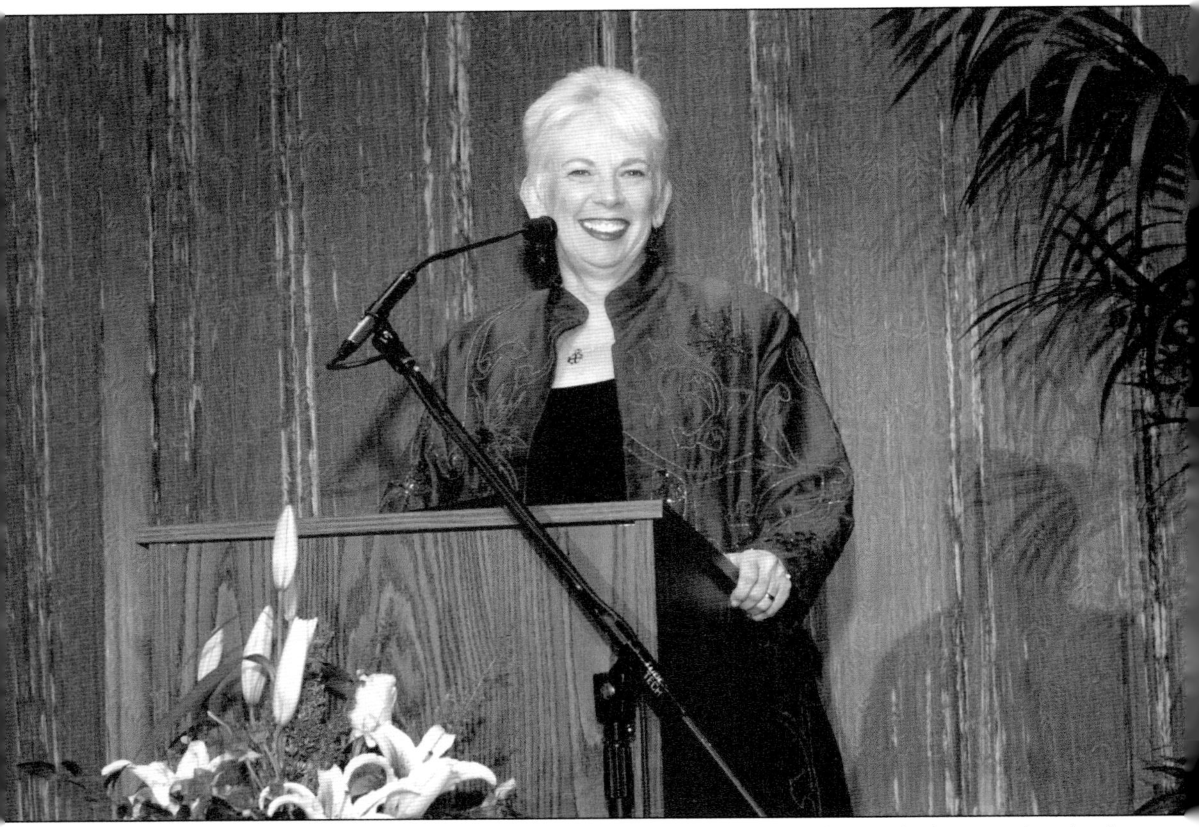

For me and for many other women, Saint Mary's College is a powerful symbol. It is a place built by women for women—not in the last 40 years, when women have talked more about their power—but over the past 160 years. Our students come here seeking a first rate intellectual education and something more. That something more is the support and encouragement of a faith-based community that prepares our graduates to respond 'yes' to the use of their God-given talents. That something more is an education that sensitizes them to see the needs of their communities and their world. That something more is an education that prepares them to take up the challenges they will face during the course of their lifetimes. Something special happens to young women in the course of four years spent at Saint Mary's College and it is a sacred trust to accompany those young women during their time here. It is a sacred trust to play a role in the continuation of the work begun 160 years ago by those 4 brave young Sisters. As I begin my presidency, you have my promise that I will work hard, be faithful to our heritage, and work with all of you to shape its meaning for both today and tomorrow.

—Excerpt from inaugural address given by President Carol Ann Mooney '72, Saturday, January 15, 2005. (Photograph by Heather Gollatz.)

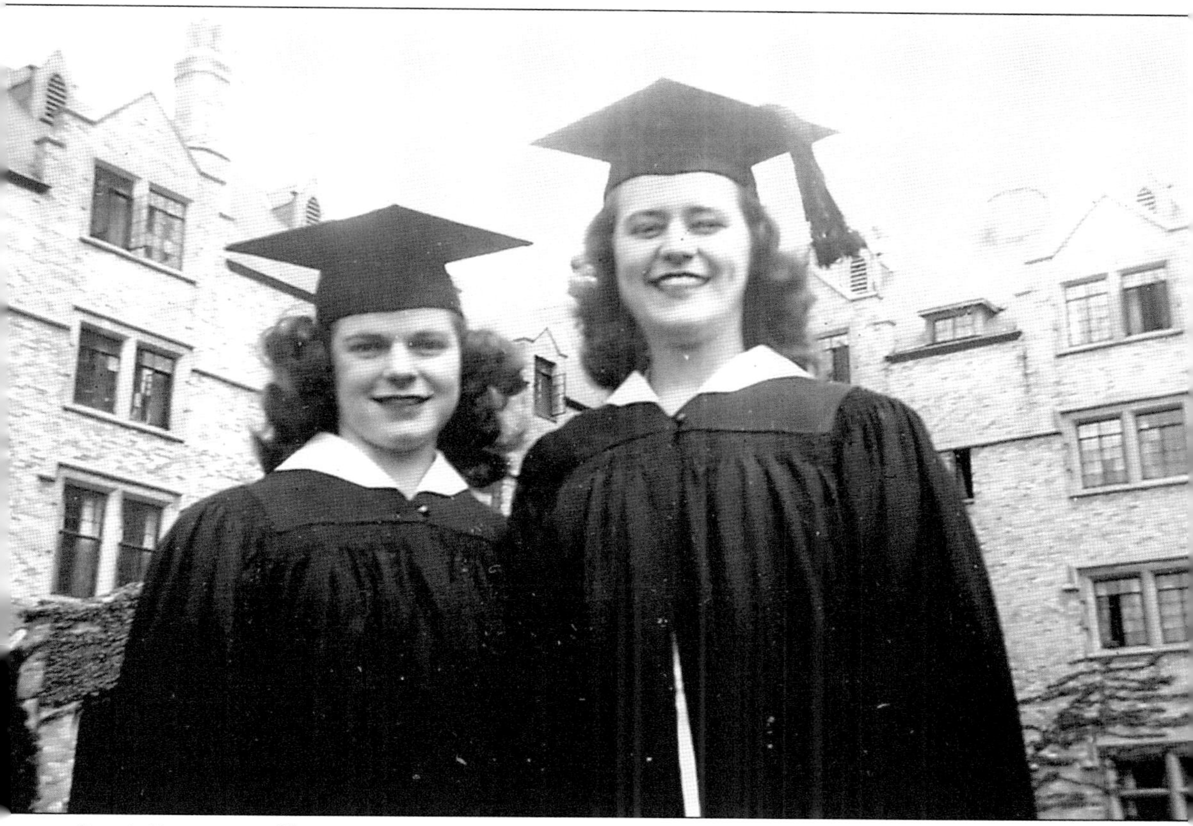

Carrie Powers and her roommate stand proud in their caps and gowns outside the front of Le Mans before honors convocation, which took place in the Social Hall on May 30, 1947. The program for the honors convocation included a processional march to Mendelssohn, announcement of officers 1947–1948, the Mother Pauline prizes, the presentation of awards, the summary of honors for graduates of 1947, valedictorian Patricia Jane O'Toole, an address by Sister Madeleva titled "A Little Less Than the Angels," followed by the recessional march to Verdi. Carrie was awarded $5 for being the recipient of the Mother Pauline award.

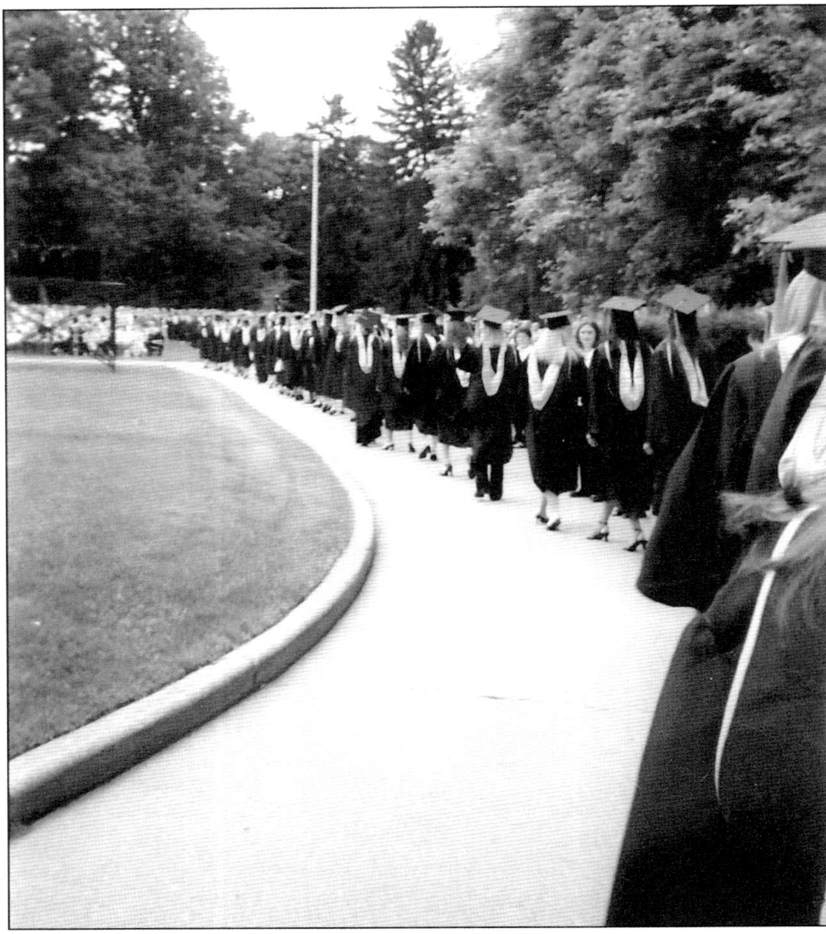

"...Barbara Baker...Anne Barnes...Patricia Bauervic..." That's you, Senior. That's you receiving your diploma from Sister Madeleva. That diploma...it means the result of three hours of psychology, that course in Victorian literature, those hours of Constitutional history, and the long biology labs. That diploma represents afternoons of tennis and softball, SMC Spring formals, bridge in the Rec, parties in the clubhouse, and oh those mixers.

That diploma represents your friendships, never to be forgotten. It will help you remember those nights you and your roommate whispered long after lights out. It won't let you forget Christmas time at Saint Mary's...the hanging of the wreath and the mad dashes for trains, but most of all the good cheer. No, it won't let you forget a thing.

Still, it means much more...daily Mass and Communion, Holy Hour on First Friday, the retreat. They're all here now, wrapped up in this diploma.

"...Anne Bittorf...Julie Bohan..."Take out that diploma often. Dust it off and look at it. See if it doesn't bring back your history of Western art, that Sophomore Cotillion, those Variety Show finales, the hot fudge sundaes in the Oriole, all the rainy class picnics, your "We Are The Senior Class of '57..."

Take good care of your diploma. It means four hard years of wonderful living that will live with you forever. It means that part of you will stay here through the long years after you've gone.

"Everlyn Werner...Helen Werner...Anne White..."

—May 24, 1957

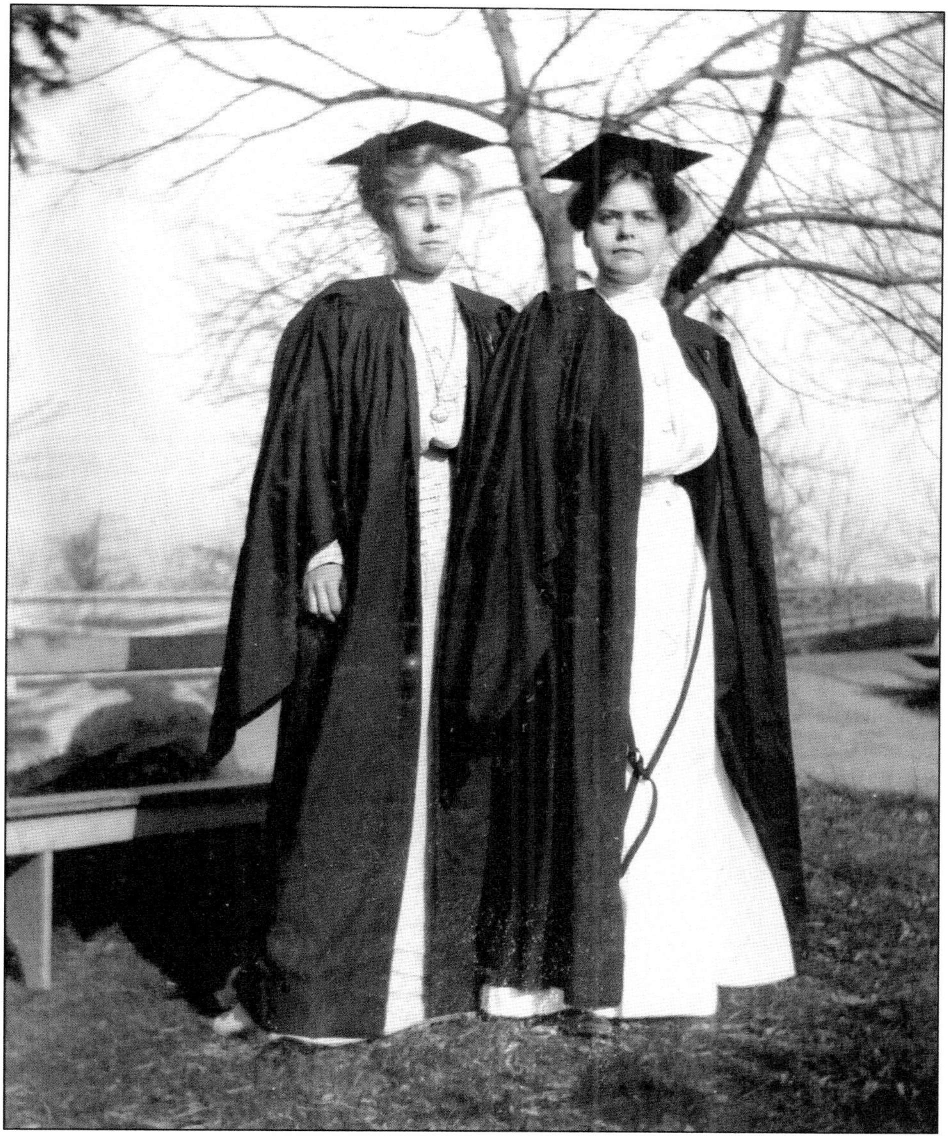

Tuesday, April 28, 1908:
Valedictorian was chosen this morning and much to my disappointment as well as that of a good many others, it was given to Amelie Lyons. As Mother Pauline said, "They always tried to give it to the girl who had been here the longest." Amelie having spent eight years of her existence in this noble institution was evidently sufficient to entitle her to the honor. Although from the standpoint of character and brilliancy, Mary Kennedy or Margaret Johnson are both far ahead of her. Queena said the applause in study hall was nothing to compare with that of previous years. Of course we expressed ourselves as pleased and proceeded to dress Amelie up in the traditional robe and haul her around on a cart, tooting horns, beating tins buckets, and ringing cow bells. In the afternoon we went into the Bend and had a little luncheon at the Oliver, after which we had our pictures taken at the penny gallery, did our shopping, and returned home.

—Excerpt from the diary of Cora Miller '08

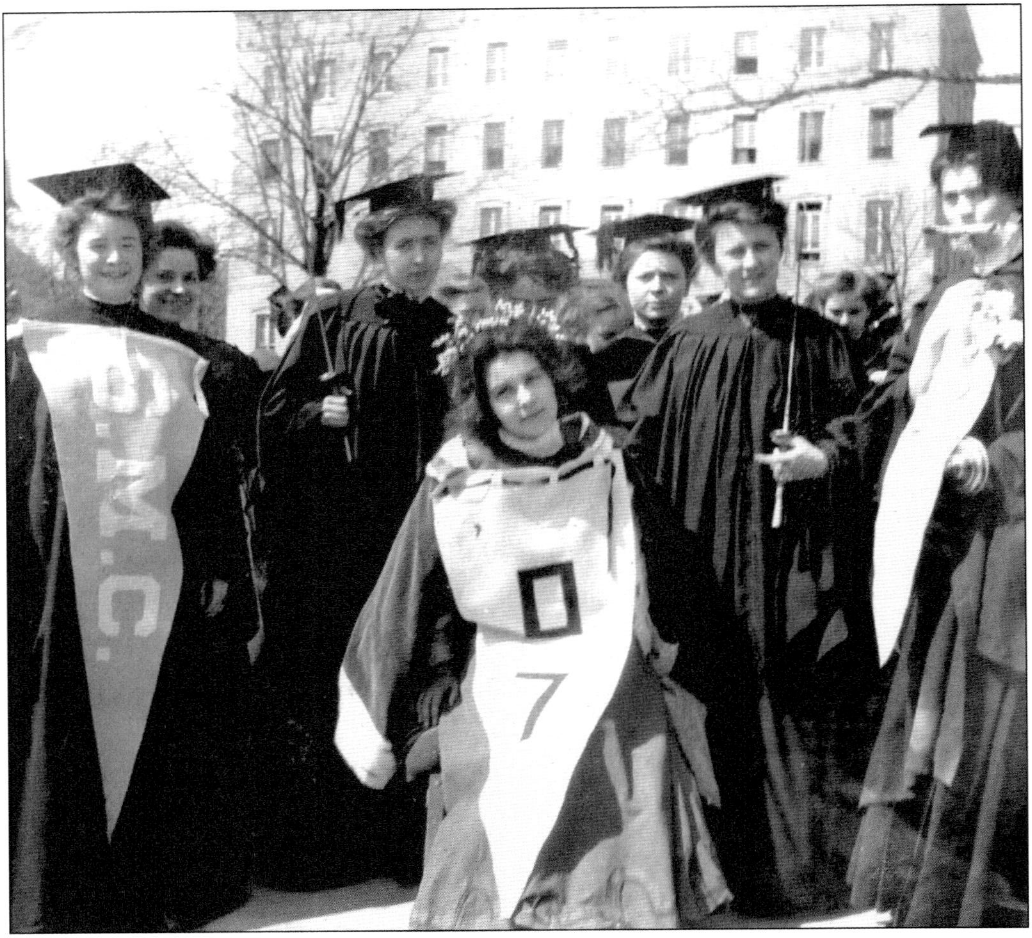

Thursday, June 18, 1908:
The all important commencement day. Went over to Assembly Hall right after breakfast and Mother Pauline gave our certificates and honor pins. Then got our money and flew. Went to my trunk and finished putting things in it. I took Genevieve O down to see mama, then dressed in my beautiful commencement dress, which has done service now for three such occasions and is little worse for wear.

At 9:20AM all of the girls in the marches were told to go down to the refectory as Sister Clarissa had a little treat for us. It was supposed to be ice cream and cake but we waited in vain for the man to bring the cream. Finally, it was so late that Mother Cereaca ordered some strawberries to be brought in with the cake. We had just enough time to gobble it down and rush over to the hall.

The bishop was already seated but we played our entrance march anyway. Then the short program prepared for this event was given and we received our medals. I received B.S. and Ph.C., the first ever given at Saint Mary's. Mary K. and Mabel B. were awarded Ph.B., Anne M. and Amelie L. received A.B. (classical), and Margaret J., Anna S. and Louise D. were bestowed a A.B. (English).

After lunch we spent the afternoon visiting. I took a walk with Sister Arsene from 6 to 6:30 then I went to benediction after supper, but Sisters Alma and Arsene with visiting in mamma's room till it was time to leave. Bade everybody goodbye tonight.

—Excerpt from the diary of Cora Miller '08

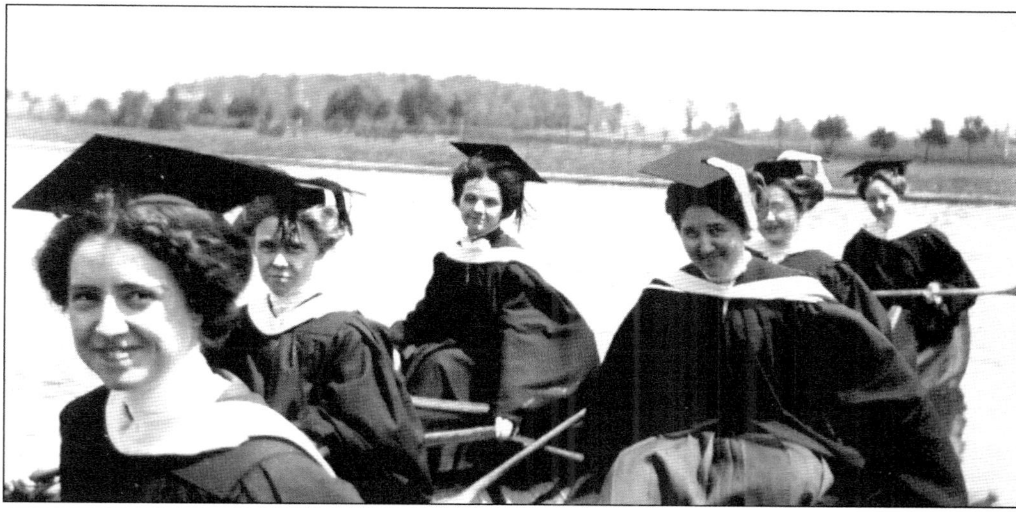

Thursday, June 18th, was one of June's most beautiful days; indeed, the weather for the whole week could not have been more delightful if made to order. All morning on Commencement Day, there was a hum of expectancy, a hurry of final packing, a mingling of glad greetings of old friends and class-mates, with good-byes, promises to write, plans for reunions, and last farewells of the Seniors. These farewells at Saint Mary's have a something in them more than the merely conventional parting, for ties formed under the soft radiance of the sanctuary light are of the heart.

—*Chimes*, June 1908

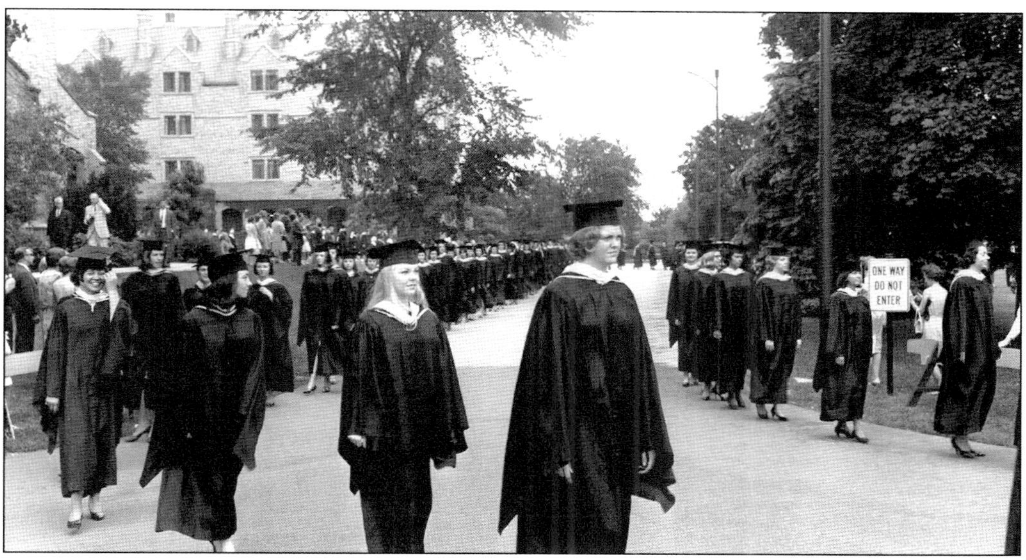

May 18th brought an end to our odyssey. We were now 21 and 22-year old women, prepared to face the world. With our friends across the road, we celebrated our graduations and said goodbye to the "campi," and to our college days. But we didn't say goodbye to each other. We still haven't. If the year ends in 4 or 9, we're there. We gather in SMC facilities that hadn't been envisioned when we graduated in '74. And we gather in beer tents at ND. We eat. We drink. We dance. We laugh. We remember. After all, we were—we are—the Class of 1974.

—Natalie Dwyer-Haller '74

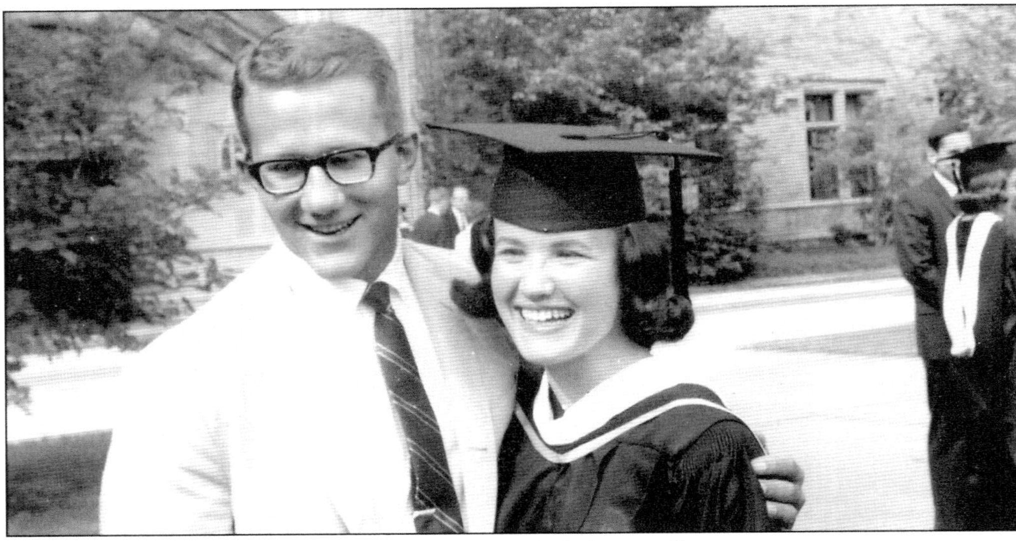

One particularly vivid memory is graduation and all the goodbyes. Having my engagement to Dave solemnized at the N.D. Log Chapel the day of graduation, with E.J. as my witness (my parents were married there). I thank my parents when I remember all that they provided for me. How fortunate we were. Every time I went to a reunion at SMC, I came home and thanked my parents again. My dad is gone now 13 years and my mom is 91. I've never missed a reunion. Now I thank my mom and send a prayer to my dad.

—Sheila Kelly Ames '65

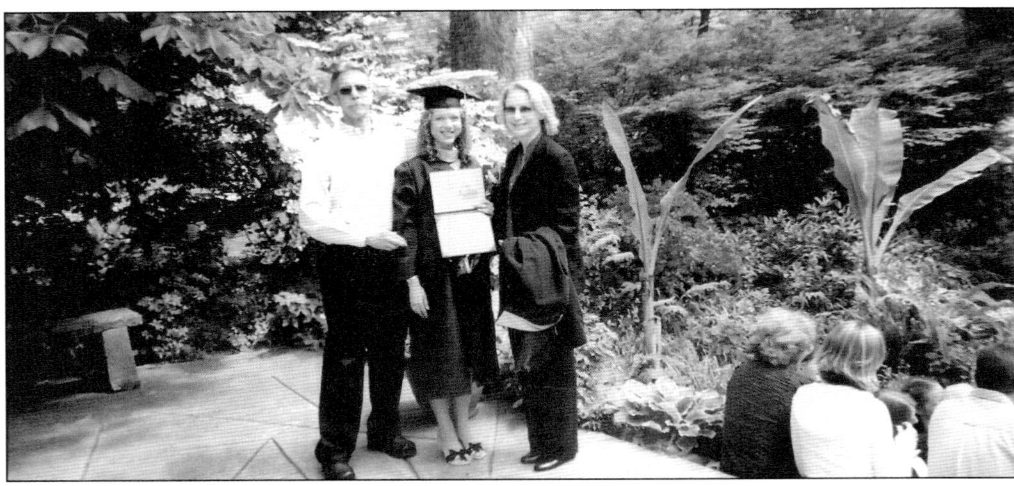

Goodbye to single sex classrooms with the occasional ND male, shower shoes, screaming down the hall at Harrison, walking around the corner to see my best friend. Goodbye to checking the Le Mans chalkboard for my name under the flower list, opening my mailbox with a key to receive handmade cards for every occasion from mom and dad, my loft. Goodbye to my window that never shut just to hear the fountain that never stopped, watching the sunrise over Lake Marion and the Basilica. Goodbye to roadtrips with the three musketeers to Grape Road or Chicago, Sophomore Parents, Junior Moms, Seniors Dads, mom and dad honking their horn as they drove down the Avenue. Goodbye to walking out the Le Mans front doors for the first time to a sea of proud parents and faculty on a Saturday morning.

—Kymberly Dunlap '04

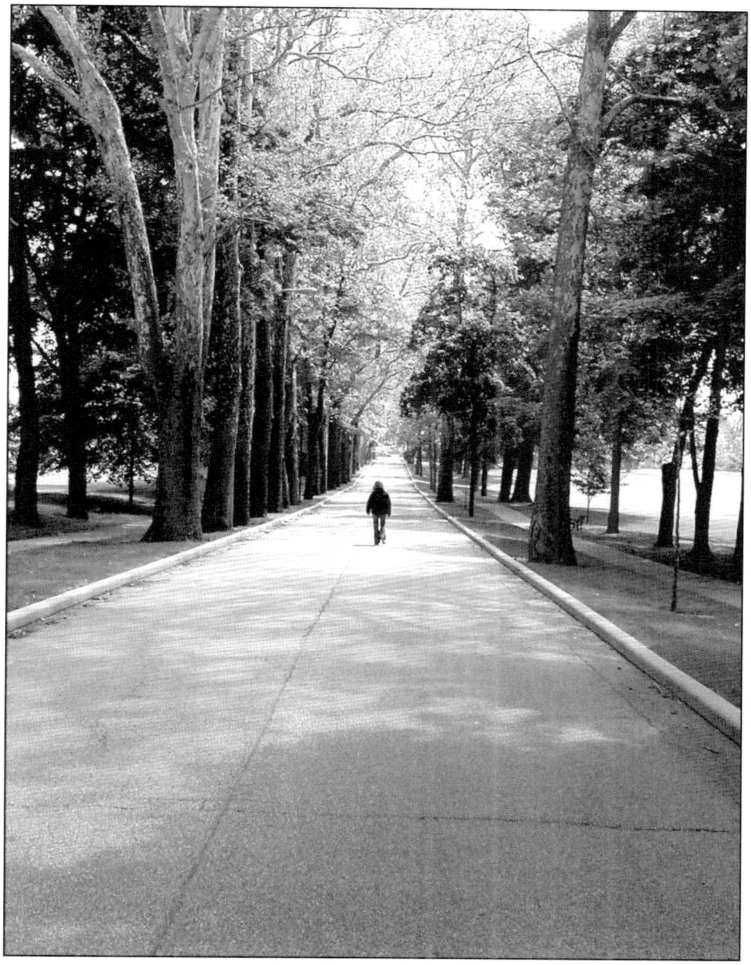

And so I say goodbye. It is Maytime, and the silver moon, speared to the sky by the tower, hangs high above the dogwood and apple blossoms, and casts an enchantment over the campus. In the shadowy stillness serene murmurs can be heard from the lake. Memories, still like gossamer fairies, comes to dance in the moonlight tonight.

So in Maytime, before we say goodbye, we look back on our four years at Saint Mary's—not at the big things, like honor grades, and officers, and awards, but the little private things we shall carry in our hearts for the rest of our lives.

How far we have come since that hot September in 1942, when we faced college, and the ordeal of "growing-up" with tears and trepidation; and how much we have learned since then! Learned things that are not in any Trivium, Trigonometry, or Epistemology book, although those, of course, have been an integral part of our education. But all of us have learned things—things like hope, and love, and how to smile through what seems to be the worst disaster. And we have learned that the answer for lonely moments is the chapel.

We hope that your years at Saint Mary's will bring you to these lessons and memories, too. We do not ask you to remember what our names were, or what we looked like, or our favorite jokes, but to remember that we went before you as Saint Mary's girls, and that as long as we shall live Saint Mary's shall live with us.

Goodbye.

—Clare Kessell '46, *St. Mary's Static*, May 1946

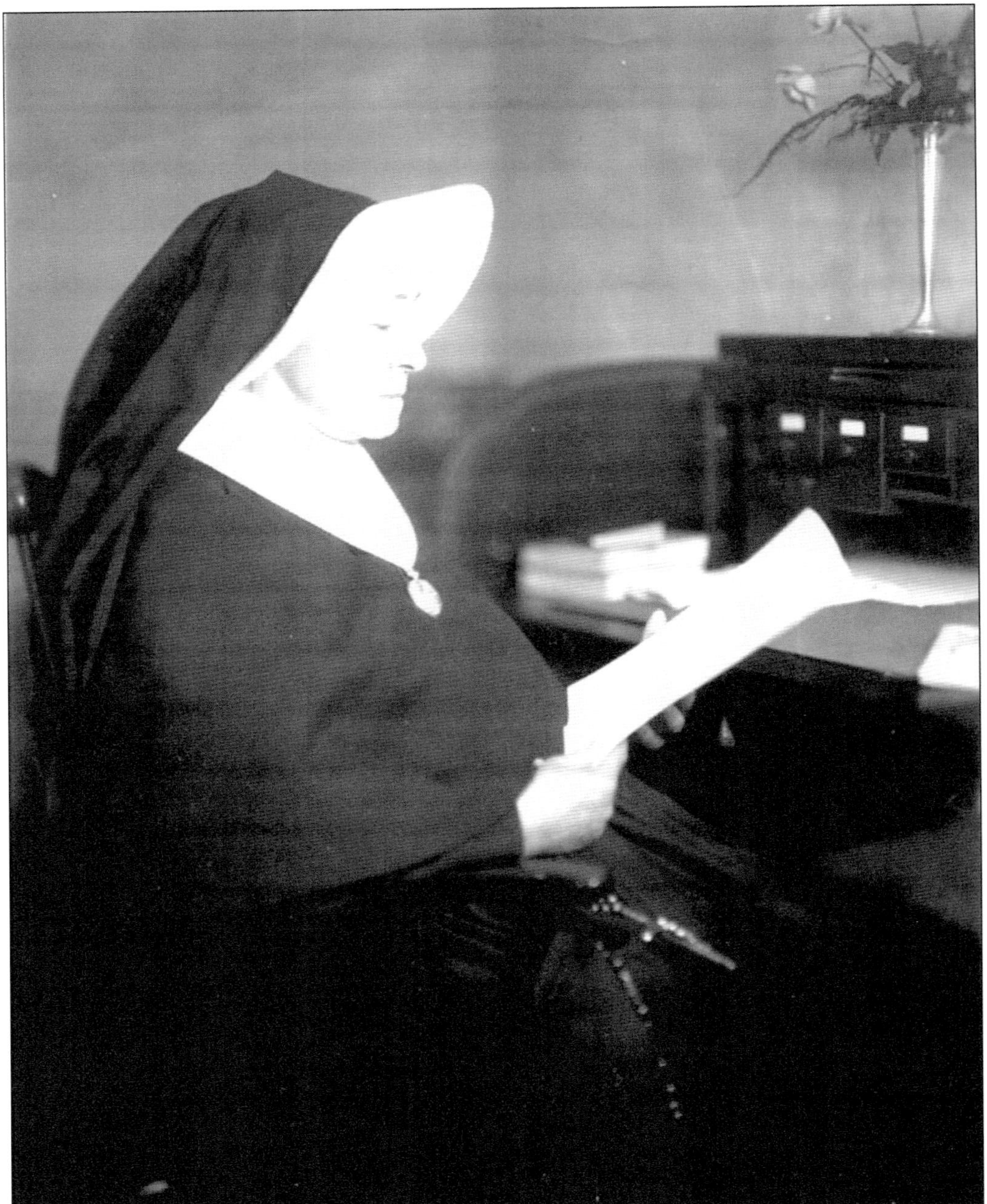

In a letter to Fr. Andrew Morrissey C.S.C., former president of Notre Dame University, dated July 10, 1910, Mother Pauline writes: "The old days are gone, but it is well to renew them from time to time, for the spirit which prompted them we cannot afford to lose."

—Sister Monica Wagner, C.S.C, *Benchmarks,* 1990.